ALLEVIATING POVERTY THROUGH PROFITABLE PARTNERSHIPS

In this book, the authors approach poverty alleviation from an atypical perspective. ____ sis is that poverty can be reduced, if not *eradicated*, both locally and globally, but this will occur only if we change our shared narratives about global free enterprise, and only if we recalibrate our mindsets regarding how poverty issues are most effectively addressed. They argue that poverty amelioration cannot be effected by the traditional means employed during the last century—foreign aid from developed nations and/or from non-profit international organizations. Rather, the authors present evidence which demonstrates that a mindset embracing initiatives developed by global corporations in response to the poverty challenge is significantly more effective. Global companies can alleviate poverty by seizing market opportunities at the Base of the Pyramid (BoP) with the implementation of three key processes: moral imagination, systems thinking and deep dialogue.

This approach to alleviating poverty offers some powerful ideas backed by the support of some of the leading Business Ethics minds in the United States. These scholars, some of whom are on the author team, have created a book that is provocative and ideal for undergraduate and graduate courses as well as any interested reader.

Patricia H. Werhane is the Peter and Adeline Ruffin Chair of Business Ethics and Senior Fellow at the Olsson Center for Applied Ethics in the Darden Graduate School of Business Administration at the University of Virginia. She also holds a joint appointment as the Wicklander Chair of Business Ethics and Director, Institute for Business and Professional Ethics, at DePaul University.

Scott P. Kelley is Assistant Vice-President for Vincentian Scholarship in the Office of Mission and Values at DePaul University. He has also served as a research fellow at the Institute for Business and Professional Ethics and as Visiting Assistant Professor in the Department of Religious Studies, teaching courses in Business Ethics.

Laura P. Hartman is a Vincent de Paul Professor of Business Ethics and Legal Studies in the Management Department at DePaul University's College of Commerce and Research Director of DePaul's Institute for Business and Professional Ethics.

Dennis J. Moberg holds the Gerald F. and Bonita A. Wilkinson Chair of Management and Ethics in the Leavey School of Business and Administration at Santa Clara University. He is also a Scholar in the Markkula Center for Applied Ethics at SCU.

ALLEVIATING POVERTY THROUGH PROFITABLE PARTNERSHIPS

Globalization, Markets and Economic Well-Being

Patricia H. Werhane, Scott P. Kelley,
Laura P. Hartman and Dennis J. Moberg

Routledge
Taylor & Francis Group

NEW YORK AND LONDON

First published 2010
by Routledge
270 Madison Ave, New York, NY 10016

Simultaneously published in the UK
by Routledge
2 Park Square, Milton Park, Abingdon, Oxon OX14 4RN

Routledge is an imprint of the Taylor & Francis Group, an informa business

© 2010 Taylor & Francis

Typeset in Baskerville by Wearset Ltd, Boldon, Tyne and Wear
Printed and bound in the United States of America on acid-free paper by
Edwards Brothers, Inc.

Library of Congress Cataloging-in-Publication Data
Alleviating poverty through profitable partnerships: globalization, markets and economic well-being/Patricia H. Werhane ... [et al.].
p. cm.
Includes bibliographical references and index.
1. Poverty–Developing countries. 2. Economic assistance–Developing countries. 3. Economic development–Developing countries. I. Werhane, Patricia Hogue.
HC59.72.P6A434 2010
362.5′57091724–dc22
2009003546

ISBN10: 0-415-80152-4 (hbk)
ISBN10: 0-415-80153-2 (pbk)
ISBN10: 0-203-87759-4 (ebk)

ISBN13: 978-0-415-80152-2 (hbk)
ISBN13: 978-0-415-80153-9 (pbk)
ISBN13: 978-0-203-87759-3 (ebk)

CONTENTS

ACKNOWLEDGMENTS

A number of people and institutions have made this book possible. The project was conceived by Laura Hartman when she gathered together the numerous faculty at DePaul University interested in poverty-reducing projects, both locally and globally. Some of the theoretical foundations were developed when we were invited by Charles Wankel of St. Johns University to contribute a chapter to his 2008 Palgrave anthology, *Alleviating Poverty through Business Strategy*.

The authors have received extensive University support from DePaul University, Santa Clara University and the University of Virginia. We would like especially to thank the Jesuit Community at Santa Clara University for funding Dennis Moberg's eye-opening immersion in El Salvador and SCU's Center for Science, Technology and Society for funding the interview that Scott P. Kelley and Dennis Moberg had with Al Hammond of the World Resources Institute. We would also like to thank the Darden Graduate School of Business Administration at the University of Virginia for the summer funding of Scott P. Kelley's research, and the Institute for Business and Professional Ethics at DePaul for continuing financial and administrative assistance.

We would not have been able to complete our work without the professional administrative and editorial support of Karen Musselman, Jenny Mead, Summer Brown, Justin Sheehan, Nathan Shepard and Jillian Wagner. Finally, the book would not be possible without the assistance of Senior Editorial Assistant Felisa Salvago-Keyes and the enthusiastic encouragement of John Szilagyi, Senior Editor at Routledge/Taylor & Francis.

INTRODUCTION

The topic of global poverty is central and of critical interest to the United Nations, the World Bank, the International Monetary Fund (IMF), and myriad other international foundations, governmental and nongovernmental organizations. Additionally, a large group of scholars including Jeffrey Sachs and C. K. Prahalad have devoted themselves to making a difference in developing countries. Poverty is a dreadful and intolerable human condition, and not merely an issue confined to regions where it is prevalent. There are enormous spillover effects from global poverty, including environmental degradation, urban slums, refugee movement and market stagnation, all effects costly to the developed as well as the developing world. Yet, as William Easterly reminds us, the industrialized world neither has been remiss in trying to address poverty nor has it been entirely unsuccessful. However, although international organizations and developed countries have contributed over US$2.13 trillion to poverty reduction since the end of World War II, significant alleviation of extreme poverty certainly remains well out of reach (Easterly, 2006a).

Our thesis is that poverty can be reduced, if not *eradicated*, both locally and globally. But this will occur only if we change our shared narratives about global free enterprise, and only if we recalibrate our mindsets regarding how poverty issues are most effectively addressed. We argue that the contention that poverty alleviation is best achieved only by aid or philanthropy is flawed. Poverty amelioration cannot be effected merely by the traditional means employed during the last century—foreign aid from developed nations and/or from nonprofit international organizations. Rather, evidence we shall present demonstrates that initiatives developed by global corporations, which represent a new mindset in response to the poverty challenge, are significantly more effective. Such poverty-reducing initiatives should not focus on social responsibility, charity or philanthropic corporate citizenship, even though these are all worthwhile ideas. Instead, companies should seek *profitable partnerships* with the poor for mutual gain. By developing new markets for their products and creating new jobs and opportunities for economic development, profitable partnerships hold the potential to create value-added for shareholders as well as for these new stakeholders. Some of these markets may be developed through public–private alliances, partnering with NGOs or interested government agencies with capabilities in a host country. But the catalyst for these initiatives should be multinational for-profit enterprises (MNEs). They are the key to effective and enduring global poverty alleviation.

If C. K. Prahalad (2005) is correct, there is a huge untapped market located at what he and Stuart Hart call the "Base of the Pyramid" (BoP). There are between two and four billion people living in extreme poverty, almost all unemployed or underemployed, and therefore without economic resources or opportunities and with little ability to buy goods and services. But the BoP is also a potential market for goods and services. If economic growth is a continuing and positive goal for the planet and for global companies (arguable, though not necessarily universally accepted), then, as we saturate markets in rich nations, these new markets provide fresh opportunities for accomplishment of this objective.

These markets are not merely new sources for product sales. In order to truly expand as *markets*, economic development needs to take place in these poor and remote areas of the world in terms of new job creation and productive capacity. This buttress will not be a defense of sweatshops—those factories that pay less than subsistence wages in the countries in which they operate. Sweatshops, by definition, do not contribute to economic development since their underpaid workers cannot afford new purchases and consequently do not contribute to market expansion. Therefore, an important proviso to our proposal is that entry into these markets includes job creation at living wages. Only then will companies be able to create new markets for their products and services. Similarly, we do not have in mind economic expansion that ignores the ecological interdependence that joins all life into a single awe-inspiring system. MNEs should never again opt for forms of economic development that degrade this system or transfer costs to future generations. Profitable partnerships only work when they are sustainable.

All of this sounds idealistic, but there is a compelling practical narrative. To entice MNEs to form profitable partnerships, it is not enough to merely report data on the enormous size of the BoP market and reiterate population and poverty statistics. Indeed, if one follows the lead articulated by Tom Friedman in his book *The World is Flat* (2006), one would redraw the pyramid as a diamond, taking into account the growing economic development of the two countries that once constituted the lion's share of the BoP—China and India (see, e.g., T. Friedman, 2006; Figure 1.1, this volume). More importantly, for an MNE to take BoP markets seriously requires reframing the corporate value proposition. In other words, profitable partnerships require changing the corporate narrative about its purpose and reconceptualizing our worn-out notions of poverty and the abilities of the poor. This includes thinking about long-term global market development in new markets with unusual challenges, framing economic value-added not merely in terms of increasing shareholder value but also increasing key stakeholder returns, and taking a systems perspective on the company and its global interactions. The latter involves decentering the corporation as the core player and imagining the company as an interactive player in a complex and multicultural global system (see Figure 1.3 for a graphic depiction of such a perspective).

Through this reconception, not only are derivative profits sustainable, thus creating economic benefits for stakeholders, but also the partnerships with the poor flourish. As a result, the notion of a "future," previously a novelty for those living in extreme poverty, becomes realized. This will certainly put to rest many fears and preconceptions about global companies, for example, that they exist to exploit rather than to develop these burgeoning new markets. Moral imagination will be required to overcome these among corporate critics. And it will also be required to reform corporate management thinking as well.

There is no doubt that the BoP offers unique challenges to even the most morally imaginative corporate entrepreneur. Markets there are renowned for their instability, corruption and absence of the rule of law. Such institutional barriers often discourage or preclude entry into these markets. Without safeguards or guarantees against corruption, organizations such as the United Nations Development Program are wary about the literal and figurative cost of entry into those countries. Jeffrey Sachs, too, is cautious in this regard, and it is important to acknowledge institutional incentives and deterrents for entering new markets (Campbell, 2007). But therein lies a dilemma. If most poor countries have weak infrastructures that create institutional disincentives, and if global corporations are wary of vulnerabilities of operations within those countries, how do we create the business case for the moral investment? Somehow corporate initiatives must be carefully tailored to both adjust to and reform such conditions. There is obviously an economic as well as moral risk in entering these markets.

Yet, we are persuaded that the presence of decently run global companies in these embryonic and often corrupt economies will actually make a positive difference in the well-being of the citizenry (see Werhane, Velamuri & Boyd, 2006). We are reminded of the successes of the Grameen Bank operating in one of the poorest, most corrupt countries in the world, while contributing to poverty reduction in dramatic ways from a for-profit point of view. Thus, there are enormous entrepreneurial opportunities if one is willing to engage in such risks; and the Grameen Model, which is but one model, could be emulated even in corrupt environments in the absence of the rule of law.

Overall, the business case for profitable partnerships is clear. With the supersaturation of markets in the developed world and the stagnant opportunities there, MNEs that remain blinded by the riches at the top of the diamond will atrophy. Strategic myopia of this kind will also allow global poverty numbers to swell and global economic conditions to wither. But there is one other important factor that drives visionary companies to create profitable partnerships. Simply put, they engage stakeholders. Poverty alleviation is uplifting. Compassion is a universal human emotion, and it is activated in people who engage in projects that promise to enrich the lives of those who are suffering. Employees develop commitment when their employers are involved in profitable partnerships. Vendors seek relationships with firms known for their poverty-fighting initiatives. And shareholders get a double bonus—an association with an organization doing something about global poverty and satisfactory economic returns.

Visionary firms that have the capacity to be morally imaginative risk takers are now beginning to enter these BoP markets. Those firms are the ones with chameleon-like responses to the markets they serve, allowing them to best understand and then innovate to meet the demands of those most in need, as well as themselves. Those pioneers will stake their claims, not only as leaders in the new economic boon from a new market of billions of new consumers, but also as leaders in contributing to a sustainable future in partnership with the world's poor.

This is a timely development. In spite of BoP market challenges and the dire global economic situation we now face, there is great financial and moral risk in *not* entering these new markets. With consumer debt piling up and demographics in the developed world moribund, MNEs must seek alternatives to stagnating markets there.

We will proceed as follows. Beginning with an exploration of various definitions of poverty, the first chapter will identify three important realities concerning global poverty in the 21st century, and we shall introduce a systems approach to deal with issues raised by these realities. The *economic pyramid* is a demographic portrait of the global community indicating where population and economic growth are or are not occurring and where the persistence of poverty in certain regions has frustrated decades of attempted solutions. Of the world's 6.6 billion people, roughly four billion live on the relative equivalent of less than US$2 per day (Prahalad, 2005). Furthermore, the bottom half of the economic pyramid represents only 1.1% of the world's total net worth (Davies, Sandström, Shorrocks & Wolff, 2008). Much of the world's future growth in population will occur in the slums of mega-cities in developing countries (Gore, 2006). The *interdependence thesis* follows from the flattening trend that Thomas Friedman identifies in *The World is Flat* (2006), a metaphor for an increased awareness of the interdependence of communities across the globe. In light of the economic pyramid and the interdependence thesis, there is a significant and persistent problem of poverty as a *global* problem, a problem that poses particular threats to the global community ranging from human rights, international security and global health to environmental sustainability. Thus global poverty is an unacceptable problem, morally and economically, and it deserves critical attention. A systems approach will be essential to this analysis.

Our assessment of poverty in the 21st century would be incomplete without a careful review of the global institutions and the approaches they have taken to the challenge of global poverty. Chapter 2 will begin with the United Nation's Millennium Development Goals (MDGs) as a relative indicator of the recent attention global poverty has received and the hope to eradicate it completely at some point in the future (Sachs, 2005a). Considering the MDG's future targets of halving poverty by 2015 and eradicating it by 2025, the chapter will examine such responses as international aid, philanthropy and corporate social responsibility. The chapter will also examine critiques of these approaches and their dubious effects on eradicating poverty (e.g., Easterly, 2006a). The chapter will conclude by arguing that the trajectory of historical efforts at poverty alleviation is insufficient to meet the noble aspirations of the MDGs and that critical questions must be addressed in order for noble aspirations to be realized.

Many of the current frameworks for alleviating global poverty are expressions of mental models that either inhibit the creative thinking necessary for innovative solutions or fail to adequately account for realities "on the ground." In Chapter 3, we introduce the problematic mental models that emerge from a number of biases that need to be reconfigured for there to be any hope of alleviating poverty. The first set of biases concerns a parochial view of for-profit ventures that clearly delineate them from "public" problems, such as global poverty, that must necessarily have "public" solutions (Hart, 2007; Kelley, Hartman & Werhane, 2008a). The second set of biases concerns the nature of poverty itself and caricatures of the poor, where common sense, conceptualism and paternalism create a top-down framework that is both morally offensive and effectively problematic (Prahalad, 2005; Easterly, 2006a). The third set of biases concerns the "research paradox," where the institutional demands for comprehensive data often impede or preclude innovative trial-and-error praxis (Murdoch, 2006). Corruption and the need for formal property rights are two examples of poverty-exacerbating conditions that must be addressed successfully if poverty-alleviation efforts are to be effective and sustainable. A fourth set of biases, a set we spell out in Chapter 4, tries to separate business activities from ethics and seeks to make sense out of corporate responsibility as a discretionary idea. Thus we see configurations of corporate social responsibilities as forms of discretionary philanthropy—gifts from the kindness of benefactors, rather than future-directed value-creating initiatives aimed at developing new markets.

Chapter 5 will identify the mental models (Werhane, 1999a) that are most likely to foster and support the new, innovative approaches to global poverty that are needed if the Millennium Development promises are to be realized, by giving new meaning to corporate ventures in less-developed countries. This chapter describes one practice that succeeds in overcoming this problem—engagement in the process of *moral imagination*. Reiterating the *gravity* of the problem, Chapter 5 will argue that an evolving, morally imaginative approach is both effective and morally responsible. Innovation will only emerge if ideas about poverty and what it means to be poor are *reconfigured*, so those in abject poverty are seen as partners in the process of economic development. Successful innovations need space to evolve and expand, thereby making a "bottom-up" approach foundational. As bottom-up approaches become more common, communities of practitioners discover new insights, which explains the evolution in thinking in the BoP approach. For-profits, including multinational corporations, we will contend, can add particular value to poverty-alleviation efforts and are able to do so in ways that are in their own strategic interests as well as in the interests of their local constituents (Kelley et al., 2008a). When the notions of poverty and profitability are reconfigured, the challenge of poverty alleviation becomes a new opportunity for sustainable growth at the bottom of the pyramid and in the for-profit sector.

As we have indicated, there are important institutional barriers to alleviating poverty in many of the poorest countries. There is often little in the way of an enforceable rule of law; property rights are often not clearly defined; and governmental and private corruption often taxes efforts to do business in those environments. In Chapter 6, we shall argue that, while these are notable impediments to market penetration, a number of companies operate in these environments simply by going around or by ignoring these difficulties or through engaging in morally imaginative solutions. Our examples will include the Grameen Bank of Bangladesh, Zimbabwe's telecommunications company, Econet, Motorola's early ventures in China, and several companies in India, all of whom have been successful despite these obstacles. We conclude that operating in these environments is morally risky, but also possible without succumbing to corrupt practices or insulting the host country.

Profitable partnerships are not meant to replace or to supersede other proven poverty-alleviation efforts (London, 2007); therefore, our starting point is where novel solutions address the unmet needs of the poor. Chapter 7 illustrates various cross-sectional (public–private) partnership models aimed at poverty alleviation in less-developed countries. While most of these initiatives involve a not-for-profit partner, none of these operates on the basis of charity or philanthropy, and each aims at creating sustainable initiatives that enable their partners to be autonomous. The chapter will conclude by highlighting some local community-based programs that illustrate many of the hidden—or ignored—

resources among the poor. All of these initiatives suggest a set of innovative partnership models, each of which might be suitable in particular settings, although, we will contend, none of them is universally applicable.

Building on the lessons from the BoP approach, our concluding chapter offers a set of rationales for involvement of the for-profit sector in less-developed economies. We begin by reconsidering contemporary interpretations of Adam Smith's idea of free markets; then we consider the notion of global citizenship and the socially embedded nature of global corporations. We acknowledge the risks entailed by engagement in such projects, but propose that, in a flat world, non-engagement entails risks as well, both moral and economic. Because many of the problems facing the global poor demand a sense of urgency, the search for sustainable solutions cannot be fettered by ideological bias or utopian social engineering that is overly and exceptionally patient for results. The focus on innovation in profitable partnerships is not a mere affinity for "newness," but a basic realization that the MDG aspirations require much more than what already exists. Simply put, the MDG aspirations require a great deal of moral imagination to get beyond the limiting mental models that we have discussed.

Studying poverty can leave one discouraged; seeing poverty can leave one hopeless. Yet, each of the chapters that follow begins with a narrative that offers both a vivid description and more than a glimmer of encouragement and hope. In these stories we will meet real people who are both the victims of the ravages of poverty and those that have found the means to do something about the challenges they face. We share these narratives both to make our message more poignant and to inspire you to join us in imagining new solutions to this wicked problem.

In Chapter 1, we will meet Mufia Khatoon, a Bangladeshi single mother forced to beg for her three children. Chapter 2 tells the story of Saroja, a married, 42-year-old mother from Chennai, India who takes in laundry and works as a housecleaner in order to help support her family. This same enterprising spirit is captured in the story in Chapter 3, again in India, about street boys like Durgesh who are clients of a bank run by other boys who, incredibly, range in age from 12 to 18. In Chapter 4, we travel to Mexico to learn about Compartamos Bank that offers small loans mostly to women to start new businesses while making itself a good profit. Chapter 5 stays in Mexico to tell the exciting story of MNE Cemex's "Patrimonio Hoy," a program through which thousands of its poor customers in Guadalajara are able to complete small-scale construction projects not possible without it. Manilla Water is the business profiled in Chapter 6. Through their initiative "Tubig Para sa Barangay," aimed at the poor, the company brought dependable, affordable water and turned a profit as well. Chapter 7 relates the inspiring story of Donald O'Neal whose design of a stove for Guatemalan cooks and alliance with an NGO resulted in an alternative to the conventional cooking system that drained productive capacity from the family. And finally in Chapter 8, we learn about how Nike was able to help alleviate poverty in Vietnam through its innovative approach to housing, micro-financing and humane factory working conditions. These are not the only case studies discussed in this volume; there are scores of others. Indeed, as we have done our research for *Alleviating Poverty through Profitable Partnerships*, we have never felt discouraged. And meeting the people through the narratives we tell has filled us with hope.

1

WORLD POVERTY IN THE 21ST CENTURY

> Mufia Khatoon is from a small village in Bangladesh. She was
> married by her father at age thirteen to a fisherman, Jamiruddin,
> and went to live with his family, as is the tradition in Bangladesh.
> While he was at sea, Mufia's mother-in-law verbally abused her and
> made sure she received little to eat. When Jamiruddin was at home,
> he often beat Mufia. Suffering from malnutrition and anemia, she
> had three miscarriages, but finally gave birth to three children. The
> beatings and semi-starvation continued until a village elder arranged
> for a divorce. Now Mufia was free, but very poor. She received no
> support from her former husband for herself or the children, and
> she was reduced to begging in order to survive (Yunus with Jolis,
> 2003, pp. 67–68).

Mufia Khatoon is extremely poor by any measure. How and whether she will be
able to improve her living situation and provide for her children remain her
highest hurdles. It is those hurdles that serve as the motivation for this book as
we consider the most effective and productive means by which to reduce global
poverty.

From a global, bird's-eye view, Mufia is one person among several billions of
others who live on less than US$2 per day, constituting what is sometimes
referred to as the base or bottom of the economic pyramid, or "BoP" (Prahalad,
2005). In this chapter, we shall describe a visual and emotional image of the
global economy that accurately depicts the paradox of profound economic
growth amid a vast majority of the human population plagued by poverty, conflict, corruption, hunger, illness and illiteracy. In so doing, we shall make the
argument that Mufia's plight is significantly interconnected with the experiences of those living toward the top of the pyramid; in other words, the global
economy is radically interdependent. Finally, this chapter will propose a broad,
cursory outline of a morally imaginative approach to this global challenge, one
that gets beyond the mistaken assumptions, half measures and failed policies of
the past.

Pyramid or Diamond?

Since images and symbols have a profound impact on how we think through
complex problems, it is fitting to start with a clear visual image of the global
economy. While no image of the global economy can capture all of the

challenges that Mufia faces on a daily basis, it is still important to reflect on the strange paradox that there is growing disparity amid profound economic growth in the aggregate.

The pyramid is a popular image of the global economy that portrays the relative size of the several billion people with incomes of less than US$2 per day. But the BoP is not a single monolithic group and instead can be further divided into subcategories: those living in "extreme poverty" who have incomes of less than US$1 per day and those living in "moderate poverty" who have incomes of between US$1 and US$2 per day. These distinctions are often used to describe when a person moves above "the poverty line." Mufia lives in extreme poverty, eking out not even 50¢ per day from her begging, barely enough to subsist, even in Bangladesh. By virtually any measurement, Mufia is extremely poor.

Though figures vary to some extent, there are approximately three billion individuals in extreme or moderate poverty (Sachs, 2005a). Above those at the BoP, there is a mid-level comprising 1.5–2 billion people who make up to US$20,000 a year, and a relatively small top tier of 75 million comprising a privileged group of consumers and the most elite decision makers (Prahalad, 2005).

The *economic pyramid*, then, is a demographic portrait of the global community indicating the distribution of population and income according to World Bank statistics.

Though interdependent, life at the BoP is drastically different from life in the middle or at the top, which brings the extent of global economic *inequality* into sharp relief: the top 1% of the world's population represents 40% of the world's total net worth, while the entire bottom half of the world only represents 1.1% of the world's total net worth (Davies, 2006). Less than 1% of the world's population participates in the financial markets as shareholders. Wealth created by MNEs accrues almost exclusively to an elite group of executives, employees and shareholders (Hart, 2007). Mufia is unlikely ever to participate as a shareholder in the great engine of the global economy, so she is likely to fall further and further behind those who are able to participate.

Amid the great wave of economic growth in the last two centuries, the gap between the top and the bottom is widening, even though there is strong

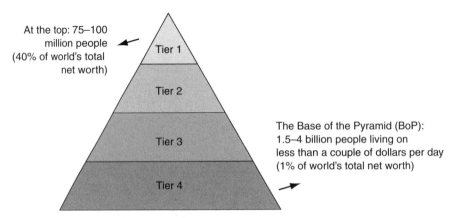

At the top: 75–100 million people (40% of world's total net worth)

Tier 1

Tier 2

Tier 3

Tier 4

The Base of the Pyramid (BoP): 1.5–4 billion people living on less than a couple of dollars per day (1% of world's total net worth)

Figure 1.1 The Economic Pyramid[a] (source: adapted from Prahalad and Hart (2002)).

Note: a *Numbers are subject to contention, though no one really contests the* relative *figures.*

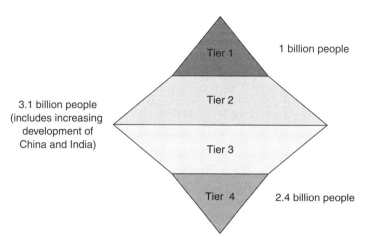

Figure 1.2 Population Growth in the Middle Tiers (source: World Bank (2006)).

evidence to suggest that population growth in developing economies may cause the pyramid to spread from its center into a diamond (Sachs, 2005a; *The Economist*, 2004; T. Friedman, 2006).

Spreading occurs in the middle tiers largely because of the recent economic growth in India and China which has created development, job opportunities and a growing middle class of educated people who now live well above the poverty level measured by those countries' standards. Growth in these two countries in particular mirrors the spread of higher living standards that were unimaginable two centuries ago (Sachs, 2005a). Despite this significant growth in the middle, however, there is also an increase in the numbers who live in abject poverty, even in India and China and certainly in most of Africa. So, although some have moved up above the poverty line, others have found themselves further away from anything approaching a comfortable life. Today's global economy, while beneficial in the aggregate, has winners and losers.

Future projections reinforce this sober portrait and underline the challenges faced by those who want to do something about global poverty. The unprecedented growth in population during the last century is projected to plateau at nine billion around 2050. Most of this growth will occur in the slums of megacities in developing countries (Gore, 2006; Hart, 2007). Thus, while the world has experienced significant economic growth *in the aggregate*, extreme poverty persists at the bottom. The diamond, therefore, has elongation in two directions: on a vertical axis, denoting the growing gap between rich and poor and on a horizontal axis, denoting greater transition toward middle income.

Although the horizontal spread of the economic diamond symbolizes a positive economic trend in many respects, at least when compared to the economic pyramid of centuries past, it is of no comfort to Mufia or many like her. Mufia's type of poverty has persisted in certain regions of the world, frustrating decades of attempted solutions. Aid, philanthropy and grand economic theory have failed to help Mufia participate in the kinds of freedoms many in the world have taken for granted. Considering the record of the past, it seems unlikely that the current wave of economic growth in neighboring India is likely to help Mufia in any meaningful time frame. The burning question that naturally emerges is what can be done to facilitate a wave of development that enables those mired in poverty like Mufia to climb out of their present situation? Whether the global economy looks more like a pyramid or a diamond from the bird's-eye view is not of great consequence to our argument. We will use BoP throughout the book to refer broadly to the four billion people who live on less than US$2 per day and only as a general point of reference. While the relative poverty in the United States and the developed world is a problem that merits attention as well, the global poverty we are referring to at the BoP does not exist in the developed world.

The primary aim of this discussion is to imagine and to encourage a sustainable response to the pressing challenges faced by people like Mufia; but, doing so requires that we highlight a few key obstacles that complicate matters tremendously. If this work were easy and there existed a simple solution, global poverty would not still be a problem. We humbly acknowledge that there will never be a single, technocratic response that will end global poverty. At the same time, however, there have been success stories and innovative solutions that can be replicated and multiplied if the limited mindsets and failed solutions of the past are examined closely and methodically.

Definition or Description?

How one defines or describes Mufia's situation has significant consequences for any potential solution. There remains strong disagreement among scholars whether daily income measured in dollars accurately depicts poverty (*The Economist*, 2008b). Since relative living standards mean that US$2 of daily income in India is not truly the same as a daily income of US$2 in the United States, the World Bank uses the "purchasing power parity [PPP] exchange rate" to standardize the poverty rate in different currencies. Typically, the PPP is based on surveys of the costs of a given group of goods, often called the market-basket approach. While this adjustment is helpful for a broad overview of the world economy, it was never designed to measure poverty per se.

For the billion or so who live in extreme poverty, it is true that a greater portion of income is spent in meeting basic needs; but, standardized income by itself does not always paint a clear portrait of the multitude of stressors that ignite a daily struggle (Deaton, 2006). In some communities, barter may be the primary means through which individuals and villages survive and even flourish. Standardized income tells us very little about why Mufia has resorted to begging or whether subsistence farming or fishing are a viable option for her, as they are in other BoP regions. The stress of poverty in Oceania is quite different from the experience in Bangladesh or in Darfur.

PPP is attractive because it draws the attention of affluent communities to those in dire need using terms and a vocabulary they can translate into their own lifestyles. Used by some international organizations and first-world non-governmental organizations (NGOs), it does help establish a common language for those institutions interested in this issue. However, PPP often reveals more about an organization's ideological commitment for or against globalization than it does about those who live in poverty. Those in favor of globalization tend to use national income averages to argue that poverty is declining, while those opposed to globalization, particularly economic expansion by multinational enterprises (MNEs), use income gaps between the richest and the poorest to argue that this gap is getting larger. How international organizations and first-world NGOs measure poverty significantly impacts their ability to secure resources (see Chapter 2). Unfortunately, statistical poverty reduction is much easier to effect than actual poverty reduction. While PPP may be useful when examining the global economy from a bird's-eye view, it is not an accurate depiction of poverty and is woefully inadequate for addressing the problem. Even though the term BoP, which we use throughout the book, is based on PPP, our aim is merely to draw attention to the billions like Mufia who have been excluded from and would benefit greatly from the ordinary goods and services that global free trade provides.

That is not to argue, however, that poverty-reduction efforts should not be subjected to measurement, definition or description. We simply argue that poverty measurements, definitions and descriptions are also *normative*; the way in which one describes the problem and frames the data shapes how one envisions the solution and allocates resources. The more generalized the definition, the more blunt the instrument. We shall explore this connection more thoroughly in Chapter 3 when we discuss the power of mental models and the use of moral imagination to expand them when exploring possible options for solutions.

Local NGOs often have a practical and field-oriented grasp of how definitions shape the allocation of resources. The Institute for Integrated Rural Development (IIRD), for example, is an NGO operating in remote villages in Bangladesh. It defines poverty in an interesting way:

- "The poorest of the poor": An individual or a family living in extreme poverty, who has *at most* one meal a day, inadequate shelter, as defined by local standards, no clean water or latrines, and the inability to send their children to school. In Bangladesh, "adequate shelter" translates into a one-room, four-sided hut with roofing adequate to protect against the rainy season and heat.
- The "very poor": Those who may have adequate shelter and eat at most twice a day, but who often cannot afford adequate nourishment, again defined locally according to customary eating habits.
- The "poor": By IIRD's standards, individuals or families who have adequate shelter, eat two or three meals a day, and usually send their small children to the local government primary schools. Note that, again, eating habits vary, so, in some communities, small meals or snacks eaten five times a day may be the norm for those not in abject poverty while, in others, two larger meals may be the norm (Institute of Integrated Rural Development, 2008).

The IIRD employs this working definition so that practitioners in the field can make quick assessments of who is eligible for their services. In this regard, it matters little whether Mufia has crossed the US$1 per day threshold of the PPP, since she will be lucky to scrape together one meal a day for herself and her children. Both the World Bank and the IIRD must have a working definition of what poverty means, but they define it for very different purposes. The PPP, therefore, is not particularly useful for effectively allocating resources to reduce poverty or for understanding the various factors that exacerbate it. We will examine the normative function of definitions and descriptions in greater detail in a later chapter. For now, we contend that global poverty is a complex phenomenon whose contributing factors are often hidden from the bird's-eye view. On the ground, there are a number of factors that make life at the BoP extraordinarily challenging, and we shall explore each in turn.

Conflict and Corruption

Poverty is often exacerbated by armed conflict or the fear of returning to armed conflict. Economist Paul Collier found that a full 73% of the bottom billion have recently been through a civil war or are still involved in one. Civil war acts as "development in reverse," because it reduces economic growth by 2.3% per year, creates mass movements of population and costs US$64 billion to a country and its neighbors. Roughly two new civil wars start each year, which have a global cost of more than US$100 billion, a sum twice as large as the entire budget of global economic aid (Collier, 2007). Although Mufia's situation in Bangladesh may not be affected by civil war directly, her counterparts in Somalia and Sudan are plagued by open hostilities.

In addition to the threat of open hostility, endemic corruption also plagues the global poor. The Transparency International Index on Corruption, published annually, demonstrates a strong correlation between poverty and corruption. Corruption diverts public goods from ever reaching the poor and further victimizes them by requiring bribes for any interaction with government officials. The spousal abuse that Mufia suffered occurred in part because the police in Bangladesh are unresponsive to crimes that promise them little economic payoff (Zakiuddin, 2008). Monies earned from oil and other natural resources in countries like Sudan, Nigeria, Chad and Cameroon flow into the political elites' Swiss bank accounts. While it may appear that a rising tide lifts all boats, even at the BoP, this is only true for those with beach-front property. Corruption chokes the economic engine so desperately needed at the BoP (see Table 1.1).

Hunger and Illness

Food security may paint a more vivid picture of extreme poverty than income-based statistical descriptions. Since the physical effects of poverty (stunted growth, malnutrition, short lifespans and health risks) are quantifiable and often visible, these can be used as biometric measures of poverty; and, since such effects can be passed on to children and grandchildren, these measures are particularly poignant and breathtaking in their ability to permeate an entire population (Kent, 2005). As such, some rely on the predictable connection between poverty and hunger to calculate the cost in the local market of buying a bundle of food containing 2,000 calories per day (Deaton, 2006). But, Mufia's plight is not simply a struggle to increase her caloric intake or that of her children. She has many other challenges to address simultaneously.

At least one out of six in the global population cannot meet the basic demands of survival—a staggering and unimaginable number, by any count (Sachs, 2005a). As a result, there are stark contrasts in lifestyles and life spans across the globe: a child born in Malawi, for example, has a life expectancy half that of a child born in Japan (United Nations Development Programme, 2006). Not surprisingly, life at the BoP is also plagued by disease, not just hunger. In

Table 1.1 Transparency International 2008 Corruption Perceptions Index

A country or territory's *CPI Score* indicates the degree of public sector corruption as perceived by business people and country analysts, and ranges between 10 (highly clean) and 0 (highly corrupt)

Country Rank	Country/Territory	CPI Score 2008
1	Denmark	9.3
1	Sweden	9.3
1	New Zealand	9.3
4	Singapore	9.2
5	Finland	9.0
5	Switzerland	9.0
7	Iceland	8.9
7	Netherlands	8.9
9	Australia	8.7
9	Canada	8.7
11	Luxembourg	8.3
12	Austria	8.1
12	Hong Kong	8.1
14	Germany	7.9
14	Norway	7.9
16	Ireland	7.7
16	United Kingdom	7.7
18	USA	7.3
18	Japan	7.3
18	Belgium	7.3
21	Saint Lucia	7.1
22	Barbados	7.0
23	France	6.9
23	Chile	6.9
23	Uruguay	6.9
26	Slovenia	6.7
27	Estonia	6.6
28	Spain	6.5
28	Qatar	6.5
28	Saint Vincent and the Grenadines	6.5
31	Cyprus	6.4
32	Portugal	6.1
33	Israel	6.0
33	Dominica	6.0
35	United Arab Emirates	5.9
36	Botswana	5.8
36	Puerto Rico	5.8
36	Malta	5.8
39	Taiwan	5.7
40	South Korea	5.6
41	Mauritius	5.5
41	Oman	5.5
43	Macao	5.4
43	Bahrain	5.4
45	Bhutan	5.2
45	Czech Republic	5.2
47	Malaysia	5.1
47	Costa Rica	5.1
47	Hungary	5.1

continued

Table 1.1 continued

Country Rank	Country/Territory	CPI Score 2008
47	Jordan	5.1
47	Cape Verde	5.1
52	Slovakia	5.0
52	Latvia	5.0
54	South Africa	4.9
55	Seychelles	4.8
55	Italy	4.8
57	Greece	4.7
58	Turkey	4.6
58	Lithuania	4.6
58	Poland	4.6
61	Namibia	4.5
62	Samoa	4.4
62	Croatia	4.4
62	Tunisia	4.4
65	Kuwait	4.3
65	Cuba	4.3
67	Ghana	3.9
67	Georgia	3.9
67	El Salvador	3.9
70	Romania	3.8
70	Colombia	3.8
72	Bulgaria	3.6
72	FYR Macedonia	3.6
72	Peru	3.6
72	Mexico	3.6
72	China	3.6
72	Suriname	3.6
72	Trinidad and Tobago	3.6
72	Swaziland	3.6
80	Burkina Faso	3.5
80	Brazil	3.5
80	Saudi Arabia	3.5
80	Thailand	3.5
80	Morocco	3.5
85	Senegal	3.4
85	Panama	3.4
85	Serbia	3.4
85	Montenegro	3.4
85	Madagascar	3.4
85	Albania	3.4
85	India	3.4
92	Algeria	3.2
92	Bosnia and Herzegovina	3.2
92	Sri Lanka	3.2
92	Lesotho	3.2
96	Gabon	3.1
96	Mali	3.1
96	Jamaica	3.1
96	Guatemala	3.1
96	Benin	3.1
96	Kiribati	3.1
102	Tanzania	3.0
102	Lebanon	3.0
102	Rwanda	3.0

Table 1.1 continued

Country Rank	Country/Territory	CPI Score 2008
102	Dominican Republic	3.0
102	Bolivia	3.0
102	Djibouti	3.0
102	Mongolia	3.0
109	Armenia	2.9
109	Belize	2.9
109	Argentina	2.9
109	Vanuatu	2.9
109	Solomon Islands	2.9
109	Moldova	2.9
115	Mauritania	2.8
115	Maldives	2.8
115	Niger	2.8
115	Malawi	2.8
115	Zambia	2.8
115	Egypt	2.8
121	Togo	2.7
121	Viet Nam	2.7
121	Nigeria	2.7
121	Sao Tome and Principe	2.7
121	Nepal	2.7
126	Indonesia	2.6
126	Honduras	2.6
126	Ethiopia	2.6
126	Uganda	2.6
126	Guyana	2.6
126	Libya	2.6
126	Eritrea	2.6
126	Mozambique	2.6
134	Nicaragua	2.5
134	Pakistan	2.5
134	Comoros	2.5
134	Ukraine	2.5
138	Paraguay	2.4
138	Liberia	2.4
138	Tonga	2.4
141	Yemen	2.3
141	Cameroon	2.3
141	Iran	2.3
141	Philippines	2.3
145	Kazakhstan	2.2
145	Timor-Leste	2.2
147	Syria	2.1
147	Bangladesh	2.1
147	Russia	2.1
147	Kenya	2.1
151	Laos	2.0
151	Ecuador	2.0
151	Papua New Guinea	2.0
151	Tajikistan	2.0
151	Central African Republic	2.0
151	Côte d'Ivoire	2.0
151	Belarus	2.0
158	Azerbaijan	1.9
158	Burundi	1.9

Table 1.1 continued

Country Rank	Country/Territory	CPI Score 2008
158	Congo, Republic	1.9
158	Sierra Leone	1.9
158	Venezuela	1.9
158	Guinea-Bissau	1.9
158	Angola	1.9
158	Gambia	1.9
166	Uzbekistan	1.8
166	Turkmenistan	1.8
166	Zimbabwe	1.8
166	Cambodia	1.8
166	Kyrgyzstan	1.8
171	Congo, Democratic Republic	1.7
171	Equatorial Guinea	1.7
173	Guinea	1.6
173	Chad	1.6
173	Sudan	1.6
176	Afghanistan	1.5
177	Haiti	1.4
178	Iraq	1.3
178	Myanmar	1.3
180	Somalia	1.0

Source: Adapted from "Transparency International 2008 Corruption Perceptions Index." Copyright 2008 Transparency International: the global coalition against corruption. Used with permission. For more information, visit www.transparency.org. Appendices with sources can be found at www.transparency.org/policy_research/surveys_indices/cpi/2008.

East and Southern Africa the HIV pandemic accounts for up to one-third of deaths. Professional and white-collar workers and mothers with small children are the primary victims, leaving a dearth of the middle class and a large, now impoverished, orphan population (World Health Organization data; WHO, n.d.). Thanks to medical advances, polio and river blindness are now in decline. However, tens of thousands of the world's poor continue to die from diseases like malaria and tuberculosis that are passé in the developed world. It is not well-known that diarrhea is the third-highest cause of death in the world in the category of infectious diseases (Prahalad, 2006). Mufia may cross the threshold of having 2,000 calories per day; but she and her children are still susceptible to various pathogens from non-potable water, close contact with fecal matter, or from malaria carried by mosquitoes that breed in the stagnant water of the muddy, unpaved streets during the rainy season.

Deprived of Capability

Nobel Prize winner Amartya Sen is perhaps the most significant and effective voice for pushing poverty metrics beyond income inadequacy or biometrics to include broader measures of human flourishing. In *Development as Freedom* (1999), Sen argues that economic earnings are an important *starting point* for studying poverty, since they are often a major cause for other deprivations such as starvation and famines; however, poverty metrics must not end there. Low

16

income also inhibits substantive freedoms to choose a life that one has reason to value (Sen, 1999). Thus, Sen describes poverty as a form of capability deprivation, which can be measured in the life that is actually achieved or in the relative freedom to function to one's potential. This understanding illuminates the strain that poverty places on the human person physically, psychologically, emotionally and existentially. Even if Mufia had 2,000 calories per day and was not ill from malaria, she still faces other challenges. She cannot fully participate in the formal economy because she is illiterate, nor can she participate in the political life of her country because she is a poor woman. In many ways, poverty is synonymous with exclusion and silence.

One tangible poverty measure that takes account of Sen's broader perspective is the Human Development Index used by the United Nations. The measure incorporates not only income and life expectancy, but literacy as well. While it is important to consider the far-reaching effects of poverty *as a condition*, it is equally important not to underestimate the ability of the poor *as people* to overcome even the most challenging life circumstances.

However Mufia's poverty is measured, defined or described, it is a *complex reality* marked, in part, by exclusion from institutions and global free enterprise. Global free enterprise, we contend, can positively serve people like Mufia, but only if we change our shared narratives about for-profit ventures and only if we recalibrate our mindsets regarding how poverty issues are most effectively addressed. While Mufia may fit many of the descriptions and definitions above, none of them portend her capacity to develop a bamboo-stool-making business through micro-loans from a rural bank. It requires a new mindset to get beyond the mental image of Mufia as a helpless, hungry, sick, dependent poor person and to see her capacity to be a customer, client and business partner. Give a woman a fish, the proverb goes, you have fed her for today. Teach a woman to fish, it continues, and you have fed her for a lifetime. Our approach is not interested in merely giving (traditional philanthropy) nor solely in teaching (forms of development), but instead in maximizing the yield of the fish pond and the distribution of the fish by truly forging partnerships with the poor. Before we develop our approach further, however, it is important to understand *why* Mufia's situation at the BoP is of consequence to those who live at the top and why working with her is a strategic and moral imperative for that constituency.

The Interdependence Thesis

Loosely defined, globalization is the realization that the nation-state is no longer a dominant sphere of attention. It is the growing understanding of the truly interdependent and interconnected nature of the global economy, a reality described in great detail by Thomas Friedman in *The World is Flat* (2006). The last decade of the 20th century included some seismic shifts in human history, including the fall of the Berlin Wall and the growth in use of the personal computer. The end of the Cold War meant that "more and more [former Soviet] economies would be governed from the ground up ... rather than from the top down, by the interests of some narrow ruling clique" (T. Friedman, 2006, p. 51). In the mid-1990s, Internet connectivity slowly began to link people across the globe; and communities of users began to collaborate in unprecedented ways, transforming the way information is disseminated. Advancements in workflow software and standardized protocols allowed companies to establish and improve global supply chains, so that outsourcing and offshoring became common practice. Tracing the production of a Dell computer from order to delivery, for example, reveals just how global some companies are.

In Thomas Friedman's words,

> this is a triple convergence—of new players, on a new playing field, developing new processes and habits for horizontal collaboration. That, I believe, is the most important force shaping global economics and politics in the 21st century.... The scale of the global community soon is going to be able to participate in all sorts of discovery and innovation the world has simply never seen before. [In other words] the world [of the 21st century] is flat (T. Friedman, 2006, p. 212).

Even ordinary goods like T-shirts are likely to traverse the globe, passing through many hands and crossing many borders along the way, before they are sold to their ultimate users. As one economist discovered, a T-shirt that she bought in Florida had been manufactured in China with cotton originally grown in Texas. Even a second-hand T-shirt discarded in the United States can end up in a vintage clothing shop in Japan, part of a billion-dollar, second-hand clothing market in Africa, or shredded for cloth car seats in an automobile factory in another country altogether (Rivoli, 2005).

Thomas Friedman's "interdependence thesis" is both a description of the complex, global network of people and companies made possible at the end of the 20th century and a prediction that the global economy will become even more interdependent. This global reality has had a positive impact in many regards. Take, for example, Stuart Hart's description of "smart mobs," the Internet-connected coalitions of NGOs and individuals that function as a democratic watchdog for large corporations, where international governance is not up to the task (Hart, 2007, p. 20). While some argue that international law has yet to catch up to the globalization that Friedman describes, technology has afforded some creative solutions, even paving the way for social reform in some cases. Positive or negative, Friedman's interdependence thesis seems to be a fair description of the world economy today. The challenge is to understand how this level of interdependence can productively be harnessed to better serve people like Mufia.

A Global Problem: Linking the Bottom to the Top

Framed within the interdependence thesis, one can see how global poverty can be a catalyzing or multiplying factor in threats faced throughout the entire global economy. Terrorism, state failure, international crime, disease pandemics and environmental degradation all pose challenges that are of global consequence (Collier, 2007). Global poverty is an unacceptable problem, morally and economically, potentially threatening every one of us.

It is commonly understood that the breed of terrorism that 9/11 revealed is not merely a local or regional phenomenon. Al-Qaeda established training camps in the conflict-ridden regions of Afghanistan and Sudan in part through the revenue generated by purchasing diamonds from Sierra Leone and Liberia

(Rice, 2006). In order to train, equip and fund its global campaign, Al-Qaeda exploited vulnerabilities in countries where the rule of law was meager or impotent, or where the inability to enforce it created a safe space for training camps.

To combat this threat, the US Central Command's "Combined Joint Task Force—Horn of Africa" (HOA) operates in Camp Lemonier, Djibouti. HOA combats terrorism by focusing on regional stability in some of the poorest parts of Africa: Djibouti, Eritrea, Ethiopia, Kenya, Seychelles, Somalia, Sudan and Yemen (on the adjacent Arabian Peninsula). Since regional instability is preferred by transnational terrorist groups, no small part of HOA's efforts are focused on developing and increasing access to clean water, functional schools, improved roadways and improved medical facilities. HOA's mission is to create "a place where education and prosperity are within each person's grasp and where terrorists, whose extremist ideology seeks to enslave nations, do not infringe upon the right to self-determination" (Combined Joint Task Force—Horn of Africa, 2007). It is clearly not too great a leap to state that the threat of terrorism in the 21st century is inextricably linked to global poverty.

Political economists have found a strong correlation between economic failure and state failure (Collier, 2007; Rice, 2006). Weak states pose numerous problems to global security because, in addition to providing safe space for terrorist networks and transnational criminal syndicates to operate, they can potentially up-end the world's nuclear nonproliferation regime. Terrorist groups employ tactical alliances with transnational criminal syndicates operating in lawless zones from the Somali coast and Central Asia to the tri-border region of South America (Rice, 2006). It is no surprise that 95% of the global production of hard drugs, for example, is from poor countries prone to conflict (Collier, 2007). In recent decades, about two new civil wars have started each year, and the consequences of this reality create ripples far beyond immediate borders, swaying stock markets on the other side of the planet (Foreign Policy, 2007).

Not all threats to global security are obvious. There are more hidden threats posed by mass migration and disease pandemics (Sachs, 2005a; Gore, 2006; Collier, 2007). Mass movements of people fleeing nation-states with collapsing public-health systems create epidemics (Collier, 2007, pp. 27–28). Even for countries that are not in the midst of civil conflict, poverty precludes the allocation of private and public resources to detect and contain lethal contagions. The World Health Organization has found that low- and middle-income countries suffer 90% of the world's disease burden but account for only 11% of its health-care spending. The global spread of communicable diseases has increased vastly as people and cargo now traverse the globe with unprecedented speed and frequency. Poverty exacerbates water-borne diseases like cholera, which often result from bad sanitation. Many communicable diseases such as antibiotic-resistant tuberculosis, for example, are mutating dangerously and spreading through immigrant populations, explaining its resurgence in the United States. More recently, concerns about the H5N1 strain of avian flu demonstrate effectively the interdependence thesis. H5N1 was discovered in northern Nigeria where poor rural people live in close proximity to animals (Rice, 2006). With unexpected and alarming rapidity, it evolved from an isolated, regional concern into a global one.

Environmental degradation is another example of the not-so-obvious threats posed by global poverty. Environmentally short-sighted use of raw materials and fossil energy has increased dramatically during the past 50 years, especially in the developing world, with dire consequences for the world environment. The 2005 Millennium Ecosystem Report reveals that approximately 60 of the systems that support life on Earth are being degraded or used unsustainably. Fresh water, marine fisheries, soils and climate are all under considerable stress. Rapid urbanization, industrialization and the increasing demand for products and services place intense pressure on ecological and social systems in the emerging economies of the developing world (Hart, 2007).

While population growth in poor regions of the world is likely to exacerbate unsustainable patterns of resource consumption, pollution is another global challenge with a strong connection to poverty. The *maquiladora* industry, for example, contributes both indirectly and directly to environmental degradation in the border region of the United States and Mexico. San Diego, Southern California's iconic image of sun and surf, is profoundly impacted by environmental practices in the border region. Assembly plants in nearby Tijuana attract migrant workers from central and southern Mexico and blight the environment through undisciplined and illegal disposal of waste material, dumping raw sewage and toxic metals into the local environment. Having grown 61% from 1980 to 1990, Tijuana illustrates the increasing tensions caused by profound economic growth, an exploding population and the spillover effect of environmental degradation (Williams, 1995). Residents of San Diego can clearly see the link between global poverty and environmental degradation.

The threats created by global poverty present a persuasive case that poverty anywhere is a threat to prosperity and peace everywhere. But, so far, we have not entertained and explored the various moral arguments that extreme poverty violates human dignity as well as human rights. Our argument to this point has been limited to a showcase of the particular challenges that extreme poverty poses to the global community in light of the interdependence thesis.

Poverty as a Moral Problem

Extreme poverty threatens the very premise of moral principles such as fundamental justice and human rights. Over 40 years ago, Martin Luther King, Jr. made the argument that "injustice anywhere is a threat to justice everywhere" (King, 1963). At that time, Dr. King was commenting on the interdependent nature of people across the United States who allegedly value but do not always practice justice. Similarly, while developed nations appear to espouse basic human rights, the global poor live without adequate nourishment, shelter and security, and thereby are deprived of fundamental human rights.

In 1968, the United Nations agreed that the *Universal Declaration of Human Rights* "constitutes an obligation for the members of the international community" to protect and preserve the rights of its citizenry (UN, 2008). As such, the 192 member nations espouse various universal rights including the right to security, to work, to own property, to participate in government and so on. These rights, however, risk becoming mere ideals unless they are operationalized. As Henry Shue has argued, people living without basic needs of nourishment, shelter and security, however defined in a particular culture, cannot exercise their basic rights to life and freedom, even if there are no other barriers to that exercise. Similarly, when these rights are not fulfilled, the nuclear essence of human dignity is seriously threatened (Shue, 1980).

20

Morally, it matters deeply to all of us that Mufia and her children are nourished, educated and have decent shelter; and it matters that she is able to become a self-sufficient, free individual who has learned to and is then permitted to make a living for herself and her family. To extend Martin Luther King's argument, the absence of rights in some communities threatens our own rights.

Toward a Solution

The three realities that bound our discussion, the elongated shape of the global economy, the prevalence of global poverty and the nature of global interdependence, challenge us to think more systemically—and with more imagination—about poverty. The possibility of a sustainable and inclusive global economy inspires us to imagine alternatives that we may have previously overlooked. Although the worst pockets of poverty are in the poorest and least-developed countries of the world, global economic growth, environmental stewardship and global health can no longer be viewed as finite, independent problems that will be solved along geographic, national or political lines.

In a 2007 address to Harvard University graduates, Bill Gates articulated a simple principle as a road map for poverty reduction. He explained that "[i]f we can find approaches that meet the needs of the poor in ways that generate profits for business and votes for politicians, we will have found a sustainable way to reduce inequity in the world" (Gates, 2007). The business community already has been incredibly inventive and adaptive; but these approaches remain difficult to discover and a general shift of mindset has not yet occurred.

The central purpose of our argument throughout the book will be to demonstrate that it is feasible to alleviate global poverty, but only if we change our narratives about global free enterprise, and only if we rethink our mental models regarding how poverty issues are most effectively addressed. Proposals surrounding poverty alleviation are greatly impacted by the ways in which we think about the poor and poverty. The relative success or failure of those proposals depends largely upon their organizing mental models, as we will examine throughout this discussion.

Systems Thinking

While others have previously envisioned a role for multinational enterprises (MNEs) in alleviating global poverty, these schemes often lack the moral imagination and systems thinking that are likely to yield sustainable solutions by creating broad-based stakeholder value. But, what do we mean by a *systems approach* and *systems thinking?*

- A system is a complex environment of interacting components, together with the networks of relationships among them, that identifies an entity or a set of processes (Laszlo & Krippner, 1991, p. 51).
- Systems thinking is the habit of mind that considers any social entity as a complex interaction of individual and institutional actors each with conflicting interests and goals and with a number of feedback loops (Wolf, 1999).

21

A systems approach presupposes that most of our thinking, experiencing, practices and institutions are interrelated and interconnected. Almost everything we can experience or think about is in a network of relationships such that each element of a particular set of relationships affects some other components of that set and the system itself. Almost no phenomenon can be studied meaningfully in isolation from other relationships with at least some other phenomena. The interdependence thesis illustrates that interconnectedness.

One example of a system approach to the alleviation of poverty is the Siongiroi Dairy in Kenya. With the help of NGOs, the Siongiroi Dairy buys 11,000 liters of milk per day from 2,000 local dairy farmers. Prior to the collective dairy, individual dairy farmers did not have the market power or presence necessary to command fair—or even subsistence—pricing for their product. It is critical to learn not only from the ultimate successes of cases such as the Siongiroi Dairy, but also to learn from the processes from which those successes originated. It is from this examination that we see the underlying system that the dairy built in order to survive.

Without a system analysis, we would not have learned that over 100 new businesses emerged throughout the dairy-related system, all reliant on each other, including transportation services, veterinary supply stores, clothing shops, new restaurants, food stalls, butcher shops, hardware stores and mechanic shops, and all as a result of the single identified need of the farmers. We would not have learned that those who lived in the Siongiroi village used to travel many miles to get to the market; however, once the dairy was created, it became a draw for other traders who now bring a market to the village. Once an *interdependent system approach* was established, involving not only the farmers but other suppliers and purchasers as well, the farmers found an assured market for their milk and received a fair price in a timely fashion.

Systems are connected in ways that may or may not enhance the fulfillment of one or more goals or purposes. They may be micro (small, self-contained with few interconnections), mezzo (within organizations), or macro (large, complex, consisting of a large number of interconnections). MNEs are mezzo-systems embedded in larger political, economic, legal and cultural systems. These are all examples of "complex adaptive systems," a term used to describe open systems able to change themselves and to effect change in their interactions with other systems. As a result, systems are sometimes unpredictable (Plsek, 2001). Any phenomenon or set of phenomena that are defined as part of a system have properties or characteristics that are altered, lost or, at best, obscured when the system is broken down into components. For example, if one focuses simply on an organizational structure in examining an MNE, or merely on its mission statement, or its employees or customers, one obscures if not distorts the interconnections and interrelationships that characterize and affect that organization internally and externally. Siongiroi Dairy is a complex network of relationships, not merely a place for farmers to sell milk.

Because a system consists of networks of relationships between individuals, groups and institutions, how any system is comprised and how it operates affects and is affected by its components. The character and operations of a particular system or set of systems affects those of us who come in contact with it whether we are individuals, the community, professionals, managers, companies, religious communities or government agencies. A change in a particular system or in relation with other systems will often produce different kinds of outcomes. Thus, part of moral responsibility is incurred by the nature and characteristics of the system in which individuals, organizations and political economies operate (Emanuel, 2000; Werhane, 2008a). On every level, the way in which individuals and corporations frame the goals, procedures and networks make a difference in what is discovered or neglected. These framing mechanisms will turn out to be important normative influences of systems and systems thinking (Werhane, 2002). The milk producers who sell milk to Siongiroi Dairy are also customers, business partners and consumers. A narrow-framed view of their activity in terms of strict production is likely to miss the ancillary relationships that participate in this network.

Adopting a systems approach requires a "Multiple Perspective" method (Mitroff & Linstone, 1993). Such a method proposes that problems emerging within the phenomenon of system should be dealt with from a variety of disparate perspectives. Each perspective involves different world views that challenge others in dynamic exchanges of questions and ideas (Mitroff & Linstone, 1993). A multiple-perspectives approach holds that each of us individually, or as groups, organizations or systems creates and frames the world through a series of mental models, each of which, by itself, is incomplete. While it is probably impossible to exhaustively account for all the networks of relationships involved in a particular system evolving over time, a multiple-perspectives approach forces us to think more broadly and to look at particular systems or problems from different points of view. This is crucial in trying to address global poverty because each perspective usually "reveals insights … that are not obtainable in principle from others" (Mitroff & Linstone, 1993, p. 98). It is also invaluable to try to understand other points of view, even if one eventually disagrees or takes another tack (Werhane, 2002). So a multiple-perspectives approach is, in part, a multiple-stakeholder approach, but with many configurations and accountability lines. It is also an attempt to shake up our traditional mindsets without at the same time ascribing too much in the way of obligation to a particular individual, an organization or a political economy. Figure 1.3 illustrates one example of the complex interconnected networks of relationships in which global companies operate.

There are a number of good reasons why a systems approach is a worthwhile approach for thinking through the problem of global poverty. First, all organizations including MNEs, NGOs, foundations, aid agencies and local governments cannot fail to take into account those who affect and are affected by their choices and actions, their internal and external stakeholders. The difference in using a systems model is the adaptation of multiple perspectives, trying to access the mindset of each group of stakeholders from their points of view. Second, viewing through a lens of rights and justice, a systems perspective brings into focus the responsibilities as well as rights of various stakeholders, not merely the poor, to the individuals and organizations who affect and who are affected by others. Third, a systems approach forces each of us and each institution to consider its multiple relationships. Because we are all affected by even remote events, this perspective serves the needs of the individual while encouraging that individual also to consider a sustainable global economy, even if it is only for the survival and well-being of companies, our mutual political economies and our offspring. A truly imaginative approach to poverty alleviation, one that embraces

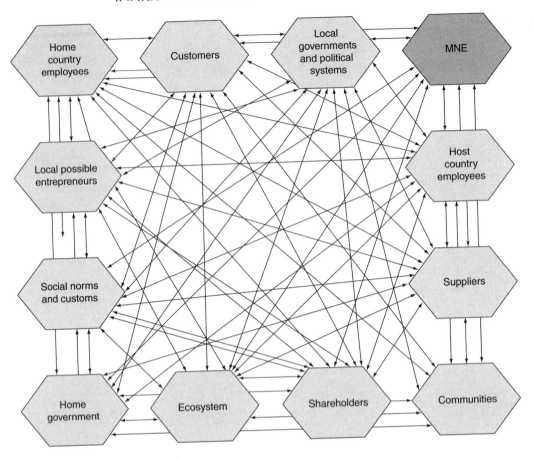

Figure 1.3 Stakeholder Networks.

systems thinking, will engage a wide range of partners with overlapping interests. One such partner, we argue, is the for-profit venture.

Profitable Partnerships

While profitable partnerships abound in mature markets, they are scarce in the BoP, in part because the *separation thesis* has been a dominant mental model for decades. The separation thesis is based on a traditional perception of business and ethics (or social responsibility) as two discrete concepts (Freeman, 2006; Agle et al., 2008). Its logic does not allow us to imagine the possibility that Mufia, while a hungry beggar, is also an excellent candidate for a bank loan. But instead of this false dichotomy, profitable partnerships encourage a new mental model, one based on a "strategic convergence" between business and social values that are aligned by incentives. The process of *mutual value creation* seeks, finds and imagines new opportunities to satisfy multiple objectives simultaneously, creating a commitment based on aligned strategic objectives.

Within organizations—especially profit-driven corporations—managers who strive for success and excellence in many cases find themselves bounded in a cognitive trap, where only a narrow, partial perspective on reality emerges as possible. Imagination is the mental tool that allows corporate decision makers to envision and operationalize new possibilities that are not merely context or organization dependent, and evaluate those possibilities. Moral imagination can be thought of as

> a necessary ingredient of responsible moral judgment [that entails] ... the ability to discover, evaluate and act upon possibilities not merely determined by a particular circumstance, or limited by a set of operating mental models, or merely framed by a set of rules or rule-governed concerns (Werhane, 1999a, p. 93).

It is through moral imagination that MNEs can reconfigure pressing social challenges into opportunities for strategic growth given the interdependent nature of the global economy and the pervasive nature of global poverty. When there is a convergence of value, firms invest capital into relationships and support long-term strategic interests, both of which enhance sustainable investment. When firms begin to realize that poverty alleviation is not tangential to their core interests, but instead core to the achievement of their mission-central objectives, they harness their most effective resources and competencies. This possibility only exists, however, for those pioneering firms who exercise the moral imagination to shake loose of the separation thesis and to envision the bleak market conditions at the BoP as strategic opportunities for growth.

Profitable partnership is not a new strategy for the business community, but merely novel as it is applied to poverty reduction. Porter and Kramer articulated a similar approach for strategic philanthropy when they said

> [w]hen a well-run business applies its vast resources, expertise, and management talent to problems that it understands and in which it has a stake, it can have a greater impact on social good than any other institution or philanthropic organization (Porter & Kramer, 2006, p. 92).

If, in the realm of their core competence, firms addressing this social issue can gain competitive benefit, their creation of shared value will lead to self-sustaining solutions that do not depend on the fickle resources of philanthropic capital or the political winds that determine government or NGO subsidies. If firms begin to apply their vast resources, expertise, core competence and talent to poverty alleviation—a challenge in which they now have a stake through profitable partnership opportunities—the contention is that they will have a far greater social impact as a long-term, stable partner than if their involvement is merely philanthropic.

The need for a change in mindsets and moral imagination in approaching poverty alleviation is not limited to MNEs. NGOs and governments often see for-profit ventures as suspicious partners in these efforts and must recalibrate their view of these stakeholders. The socially conscious are often skeptical of business interests, considering well-publicized patterns of exploitation. Furthermore, they may uncritically overlook the potential of the market and of business ventures to respond to these fundamental human needs. As Nobel

Prize winner Muhammad Yunus explains, "it is tough to bring efficiency to charity." But,

> the moment you bring in a business model, immediately you become concerned about the cost, about the revenue, the sustainability, the surplus generation, how to bring more efficiency, how to bring new technology, how to redesign, each year you review the whole thing ... charity doesn't have that package (Parker, 2008).

It was precisely this kind of innovative partnership that helped Mufia begin the slow climb out of her poverty trap. After receiving micro-loans from the Grameen Bank of Bangladesh, loans that she used to make and sell bamboo products, Mufia was able to provide two meals a day for her family, some clothing and a rain-protected shelter (Yunus with Jolis, 2003). Although the impact of micro-finance, in particular, may be mixed in some cases, we are interested in the underlying mindsets that create the possibility of sustainable solutions like micro-finance. Mutual value creation and profitable partnership cannot exist without deep stakeholder dialogue first. Mufia must be a full, vocal participant in any endeavor intended to serve her needs.

Deep Dialogue

With moral imagination, Mufia is not merely the victim of spousal abuse or national economic underdevelopment, but rather she is at the nexus of a complex set of forces and processes that shackles her to a life of privation and misery. Unlike the researchers who may observe her, she is the expert of those particular forces and processes. Her experience surviving in such adverse conditions constitutes a wealth of resources and knowledge vital to mutual value creation. But, many institutions overlook Mufia's wisdom and experience, and instead reach assumptions about her and her conditions based on limited data. Yunus did not discover the need for micro-loans until he abandoned the global, bird's-eye view of poverty and began to dialogue with the poor women in Jobra. By taking "the worm's-eye view" through deep dialogue, Yunus discovered the exclusivity of the formal banking system. Micro-lending was not born from grand economic theory, but from listening attentively to people like Mufia (Yunus, 2003).

Perhaps ironically, deep dialogue is a well-developed skill for business, since most MNEs have a great deal of marketing sophistication to take customer viewpoints seriously. However, unless and until Mufia is viewed as a potential consumer, those marketing skills are unlikely to shape the design and distribution of the products and services that she needs. So long as she is a passive recipient of aid or philanthropy, there is little hope that she will be empowered to thrive in a system that has excluded her until now.

This chapter has argued that Mufia's story represents a majority of the global population and is an important one to understand. Whether on moral or strategic grounds, moderate and extreme poverty are problems that must be addressed in today's global economy. They can no longer be seen as regional phenomena on the other side of a vast planet or social system. Most would agree with these foundational claims. However, alleviating poverty has been an aim of many institutions for decades or longer, yet global poverty still persists at an abominable level. In order to move from the sense that "something must be done" to "what must be done" or "what will we do," it is important to identify previous approaches, which is the focus of the next chapter.

2

FAILED STRATEGIES IN THE ALLEVIATION OF POVERTY

In this chapter, we move beyond definitions and descriptions to identify the strategies that are most often proposed by which to mitigate global poverty and the institutions that support these strategies. In doing so, and based on our contentions in Chapter 1 that efforts in this area have been relatively ineffective to date, we do not intend to label these efforts as disingenuous. Indeed, it is our experience that the people who work with these institutions that are working on global poverty are sincere, well-meaning individuals. As we saw in the last chapter, the unfortunate fact is that, in spite of the efforts of these good people, the number of people in the world who are living in poverty is growing. Although billions of dollars in foreign aid, philanthropy and other interventions have been invested, global poverty remains one of the most vexing problems in human experience. Before we plunge into the world of failed strategies, let us not forget that poverty is more than an abstraction. It shapes the hourly struggles of its victims in ways that few of us can truly imagine. Consider the narrative of just one victim of global poverty.

A Day in the Life of Saroja[1]

Meet Saroja. She is 42 years old and a resident of Chennai, India. She and her family rent a small room on a side street off Greenways road, a busy thoroughfare in the city. Follow her through a day in her life...

5:40 a.m.

The strident horn of the water truck rattling down the street jolts Saroja awake from a fitful sleep. She fights the urge to ignore its summons. Five additional minutes in bed, and she and her family will not have water to drink or cook with that day. Forcing herself to get up, she picks up the aluminum water pots and stumbles out of the house. There is already a queue of people waiting in front of the yellow and green truck, elbowing and jostling each other to make sure they get their share of water. She manages to fill both her pots today. Cradling one on her hip and carefully balancing the other on her head she walks slowly back home.

6:15 a.m.

Saroja makes breakfast on a small kerosene stove. She carefully ladles the watery gruel into two tin plates. Her husband sprawls in a corner, snoring loudly, fast asleep. Her daughter, Prabha, asks to borrow Saroja's sandals. Prabha's old pair are falling apart. She is afraid her employers at the garment factory will not approve if she comes to work in bare feet. Saroja's younger son Suresh comes in from outside. He is in his school uniform. He gulps down his breakfast and wipes his mouth on his shirt sleeve. On his way out he reminds his mother that it is the last day for him to buy his school books. Prabha slips into her mother's well-worn sandals and silently follows him out.

7:10 a.m.

The coals in the iron burn brightly as Saroja fans them with a piece of cardboard. When he is sober, her husband manages a small business pressing people's clothes. But he has been out drinking every night for the past three days and has not been awake enough to work. Clothes from last week's orders are still stacked in one corner. Saroja knows that she will have to press and deliver them herself today, or her customers will stop giving her work. After three hot and sweaty hours, the clothes are pressed and folded. She sorts them into bundles, ties them with newspaper and string and loads them onto the family cart. To run their clothing business, they purchased the cart and the iron last year using a loan from the local moneylender. Far bigger than Saroja, the cart is difficult to push, but she manages to maneuver it through the street. She hopes her customers will not be too upset that she is late with their orders. She will have to lie again about her husband being ill and unable to work.

12:00 noon

She is done with her clothing deliveries. It has been a good day. Most of her customers have given her more clothes to press and she has earned 400 rupees (about US$9). Saroja tries to calculate how much she will have once she has paid the rent and purchased her rice and lentils for the week. She may have money left over to buy Suresh's school books but not enough to get Prabha new sandals. She worries about Prabha, almost 20. Who would marry her if they did not have money for dowry? They would have to take out another loan. She passes by her son's school and decides to give him money for his books. She has to spend the money when she has it. She plans to go to the grocery shop to get her weekly ration of rice and lentils after she has dropped off her cart. As she turns into her street, her heart sinks. She has forgotten that it is the first of the month. Her landlord and his ruffians are standing at the far corner of the street. They are on their monthly collection spree. They see her pushing the cart and move forward threateningly. Silently she hands over the remains of what she earned that morning. It would be futile to resist. Besides, she is three months behind on her rent payments. So much for her weekly rations and her daughter's sandals. But she is glad that her son will get his school books.

2:00 p.m.

Saroja arrives at her job at Mrs. Subramaniam's house and is greeted with expletives for being late. She makes her way to the pantry where there is a mound of vessels to be washed. The family is eating lunch and the smells from the kitchen are tantalizing. She has not eaten all day. She will have to wait till they have finished eating before she can satisfy her hunger. But they are soon done and she sits down with the other maid servant to her first meal of the day. She always looks forward to Thursdays when she comes to Mrs. Subramaniam's house to assist in the housework because of this one meal. There is rice and stew and vegetables and yogurt. There will even be some left to take home to her family. She spends the afternoon scrubbing floors, washing dishes, doing the laundry and polishing the brass trinkets that dot the house. Mrs. Subramaniam is hosting a party that evening and needs Saroja to stay and help with the cooking. Saroja peels and chops onions, grates coconut, shells peas and makes the flatbread that will be served for dinner. It is almost seven o' clock by the time all the work is done. Mrs. Subramaniam pays her 200 rupees (about US$5) for helping out.

7:30 p.m.

Saroja catches the 42 bus home. The fare is 2 rupees. It is a luxury she does not usually indulge in but she is exhausted after a long day. And it is not over yet. She still needs to stop at the grocery store to pick up food, coal and kerosene and then prepare the evening meal for her family.

8:25 p.m.

Saroja and her family eat their evening meal. Suresh is memorizing math tables from his textbook while he eats. She has high hopes for her son. Perhaps one day he will get a steady job and his income could help support the family. She hopes that he won't develop his father's predilection for alcohol. She looks across toward her husband. He is moody and sullen. He truculently asks her how much money she has earned. She does not answer. She knows what is coming. He will demand the money, asserting his right as her husband to have it. They will argue. He will yell and scream. It could come to blows. She is too tired to fight today. She gives him what she has left over. He takes it and leaves.

9:35 p.m.

Saroja walks down to the community restroom. It is dark and the night is warm. She splashes water on her hands and face and wipes them with the edge of her sari. She pops some betel nut into her mouth as she makes her way back home. Her children are already asleep. She lights a mosquito coil in the vain hope that it will keep the insects away. She shakes out the straw mat and lies down on it using a bundle of clothes as a pillow. She pulls the string that turns off the single bulb that hangs from the ceiling.

Saroja falls asleep as soon as her head touches her makeshift pillow. She will sleep until the strident horn of the water truck jolts her awake at 5:40 a.m. the next day.

Aid from Multinational Organizations

Many people in the developed world would like to help individuals like Saroja to escape from their problems and to live more prosperous and peaceful lives.

Several multinational organizations are dedicated to doing just that by facilitating economic development at the BoP. The purpose of this section is to provide an analysis of the poverty-reduction strategies implemented by these multinational organizations. We will begin our analysis with the strategies of the United Nations (UN) and then explore what the World Bank (WB), International Monetary Fund (IMF), and the World Trade Organization (WTO) are doing to reduce global poverty. Later in this chapter, we examine the philanthropic approaches to the problem as mobilized by individuals, nongovernmental organizations (NGOs) and other elements of civil society. Finally, we will look at business organizations and their capability to solve the poverty problem, the genesis and central thesis of this book.

The United Nations

It is a long way from Saroja's bedroom in Chennai, India, to the New York City headquarters of the United Nations; but, of all the institutions that have taken world poverty seriously, the UN may offer her the most hope. Founded in 1945, the UN is an international organization comprising 192 member states. Its stated purpose is to facilitate cooperation in the realms of international security, law and social and economic development, but we will concentrate specifically on its poverty programs. These are coordinated through the UN's Economic and Social Council. In 2000, under the leadership of then Secretary General Kofi Annan, the UN developed eight Millennium Development Goals (MDGs) in order to address the needs of those at the BoP (see Table 2.1). The MDGs provide targets to be achieved by 2015, were agreed to by all the world's countries and were accepted by all the world's leading development institutions.

If these goals seem lofty and distant, be aware that the UN has divided each goal into several more specific and measurable objectives in a country-by-country fashion. For example, Saroja would be impacted by the UN's MDGs for India, which offer the promise of more available water, better bus transportation, lower educational expenses for her children and protection from the spousal abuse that makes her life especially demanding and, at times, devastating.

Two sets of ideas animate the UN's poverty-alleviation efforts: a credible model of the sources of poverty at the BoP, and an effective model of how to implement a system of coordinated responses to the problem. Ultimately, whether the UN can fulfill its promise to Saroja depends on the validity of these ideas. Economist Jeffrey Sachs is the current director of the UN's effort to

Table 2.1 The United Nations Millennium Development Goals (MDGs)

Goal 1: Eradicate extreme poverty and hunger
Goal 2: Achieve universal primary education
Goal 3: Promote gender equality and empower women
Goal 4: Reduce child mortality
Goal 5: Improve maternal health
Goal 6: Combat HIV/AIDS, malaria and other diseases
Goal 7: Ensure environmental sustainability
Goal 8: Develop a global partnership for development

achieve its MDGs. In his book, *The End of Poverty: Economic Possibilities for Our Time* (2005), Sachs identifies eight causes for economic privation at the BoP: physical geography, governance failures, cultural barriers, geopolitics, lack of innovation and three conditions he describes as "traps" on which he believes the UN should concentrate. Sachs uses the term "trap" intentionally to imply that "the poor do not have the ability—by themselves—to get out of the mess" (Sachs, 2005a, p. 56).

One of these traps is the *demographic trap* created when the high rates of fertility among the poor prevent impoverished families from investing adequately in their children's nutrition, health and education. While half of the world is at or near the replacement rate of fertility, our global challenges are increasing as the poorest places on earth have the highest rates of population growth. Predictably, this exacerbates poverty in these locations and dooms millions of children to a life of hunger, hard work, poor health and early mortality. In Saroja's case, one can plainly see that she and her family may have fared better *economically* if she had only one child instead of two.

Sachs' second concern is the *fiscal trap*, the cycle of economic stagnation one finds so common in the developing world in which low per capita income yields low tax revenue; corrupt governments siphon tax revenue to private goods; and international debt diverts needed funds abroad. The fiscal trap chokes economic growth and creates economies that are immune from standard policy remedies. While India's overall economic growth rate has been stellar of late, the rigid government bureaucracy left over from years of troubled times means that the poor like Saroja do not share in India's economic growth.

Both the *demographic* and *fiscal* traps intensify Sachs' third problem—the *poverty trap*. With their entire income devoted to basic survival, the poor have nothing to invest in the future. We certainly see that in Saroja's case. The best she can do is put off saving for her daughter's dowry for the sake of paying her rent and getting enough food for the table. Strapped by the survival needs of her family, she cannot even afford to buy her a pair of sandals. Together, the *demographic* trap, the *fiscal* trap and the *poverty* trap operate as a system that Sachs hopes can be put on track with targeted economic interventions.

Sachs has been criticized for misunderstanding the forces that contribute to global poverty. For example, Paul Collier (2007) has observed that Sachs' demographic, fiscal and poverty traps are secondary to four other problems that plague those at the BoP. First, Collier identifies civil war as a major cause of global poverty. Collier points out that nearly three-quarters of people at the BoP have recently been through a civil war or are still in one (Collier, 2007). Two new civil wars have started each year in recent decades, at a total cost of over US$100 billion a year, roughly double the amount that flows to the BoP in foreign aid (Collier, 2007).

Second, Collier claims that a lack of export diversity plagues the world's poorest nations. Called "Dutch disease" by economists, developing countries typically damage their economic growth prospects by relying on single exports, thus crowding out other products that might have the potential to grow rapidly (Collier, 2007, p. 39). Ineffective internal governance is a third problem that Collier claims Sachs' model overlooks. A well-functioning governmental system in the developing world translates to an economic growth rate of 10%; but bad governance erodes an economy at an even higher rate (Collier, 2007). Table 2.2

Table 2.2 Lowest Ranking Countries in Terms of Perceptions of Corruption By Businesspeople and Country Analysts (2007)[1]

Rank	Country
169	Laos
172	Afghanistan
172	Chad
172	Sudan
175	Tonga
175	Uzbekistan
177	Haiti
177	Iraq
179	Myanmar
179	Somalia

Source: Transparency International (2007).

shows a listing of the worst governments by country in terms of corruption, as ranked by Transparency International.

Finally, there is the problem of being landlocked between neighbors who may face their own internal struggles. Since landlocked countries have no access to their own ports, integrating into global markets requires a great deal of transportation. Switzerland depends on the reliable transportation infrastructure of Germany, Italy, France and Austria. Uganda, on the other hand, depends on Kenya, Sudan, Rwanda, Somalia and the Democratic Republic of Congo, each one plagued by civil strife (Collier, 2007, p. 55). While Sachs' diagnosis in the form of his three traps has validity, the importance of Collier's criticism is that it reminds us that poverty is not only an *economic-development* problem; it is also a geopolitical one that any multinational organization like the UN may not be able to affect in its entirety. This recognition is vital, for it reminds us that poverty is a highly complex problem that must be treated holistically rather than merely from an economic perspective.

In any event, Sachs' hope is that the UN will infuse *capital* into the developing world. His principal intervention focus is on foreign aid through intermediaries like the World Bank in the form of official development assistance (ODA). The theory is that ODAs help jump-start the process of capital accumulation by flowing through three primary channels: directly to households for humanitarian emergencies; through public investment; and through investment in domestic businesses (Sachs, 2005a). By his estimates, all such investments will raise the level of capital per person, effectively ending poverty by 2025. For example, to reach this target, Sachs calls on the US to contribute 0.7% of its gross domestic product in ODA. While this compares favorably with US aid in support of the Marshall Plan (2.0%), it is far below the present level of investments in ODA from the US (0.2%). Accordingly, Sachs' Big Plan may encounter resistance from the US and the rest of the developed world.

Even if this level of funding could be collected, the UN's capacity to effectively distribute such an increased amount of aid cannot be supposed. Investment allocation must emerge from what Sachs terms "clinical economics," that is, economics that addresses the particular problems of a particular region in dialogue with poor communities. Since the "plumbing" of international development assistance is "clogged or simply too narrow" to carry the sufficient flow of aid, there also needs to be corresponding plans for institutional reform that address investment, finance, donor-commitments and public management (Sachs, 2005a).

Sidestepping these institutional challenges, Sachs has proposed an interesting series of quick wins that would cost relatively little, but that could have a significant constructive effect on world poverty. These are:

- Direct assistance to local entrepreneurs to grow their businesses and to create jobs.
- Access to information on sexual and reproductive health.
- Action against domestic violence.
- Appointments of government scientific advisors in every country.
- De-worming products for school children in affected areas.
- Drugs for AIDS, tuberculosis and malaria.
- Elimination of school fees.
- Elimination of user fees for basic health-care in developing countries.
- Free school meals for schoolchildren.
- Legislation for women's rights, including rights to property.
- Planting trees.
- Provision of soil nutrients to farmers in sub-Saharan Africa.
- Provision of mosquito nets.
- Access to electricity, water and sanitation.
- Support for breast-feeding.
- Training programs for community health in rural areas.
- Upgrades to slums and provision of land for public housing.

Even though the United Nations has assumed a leadership role in achieving the 2015 goals, success ultimately depends on the commitment of its member states. In general, the actions of the UN have been plagued by high transaction costs (in coordinating among member states), pragmatic difficulties in distribution due to inadequate infrastructure and corruption in developing nations, and the problem of sustaining execution given the reality of leadership changes in the secretariat. Moreover, the role of the UN seems to have been somewhat paternalistic, in effect leaving out an active role for the poor themselves. Still, the UN is a major force for economic development on the world stage, and some of its agencies and affiliates have had a positive impact on the lives of those at the BoP. We turn now to the role of global financial institutions.

Global Financial Organizations

Saroja would probably feel quite out of place in the arcane world of international finance. Yet, decisions made at the World Bank, the International Monetary Fund and the World Trade Organization affect people like Saroja as surely as they affect capitalists in global markets. What these organizations have in common is a body of knowledge on international trade and development, and a belief that economic, trade and currency policies drive macroeconomic realities that are felt by every human being on the face of the Earth.

The World Bank

ounded in the same year as the UN to address the economic reconstruction of
estern Europe after World War II, today the World Bank (WB) provides low-
terest loans and grants to developing countries which currently have no access
international credit markets. The World Bank has formally accepted the UN's
DGs. It works cooperatively with that body in financing the building of infra-
ructure, strengthening governance, eradicating corruption and developing
ffective in-country financial and banking systems. Although loans from the WB
re significant, its major poverty-alleviation strategy is the US$25 billion in gifts
grants to 80 poor countries. This is a sum that constitutes "the core funding
at poor countries rely on" (Landler, 2007). Saroja is probably most affected by
e 2006 direct grant of US$1.7 billion from the WB to her country, plus an
dditional US$6.6 billion in loans and other investments, an amount equivalent
less than US$8 for each man, woman and child in India. At the same time, it
ould be noted that a loan from the WB financed a new highway between Saro-
's hometown of Chennai and neighboring Hyderabad, allowing a better flow
f agricultural commodities to Saroja's grocer. Presumably, that drove down the
rices that she had to pay for lentils and rice.

International Monetary Fund

he International Monetary Fund (IMF) is an international organization of 185
ember countries established to promote international monetary cooperation,
urrency stability and orderly exchange arrangements; to foster economic growth
nd high levels of employment; and to provide temporary financial assistance to
ountries to help ease balance-of-payments adjustments. The IMF monitors inter-
ational currency and trade markets, gives direct aid to countries facing balance-
f-trade difficulties and provides technical assistance to developing nations. The
MF works cooperatively with the UN and WB in poverty reduction, mainly
hrough country-by-country poverty-reduction strategies developed in conjunc-
ion with in-country stakeholders and tailored to the unique conditions on the
round (papers describing these strategies for many BoP countries are available
n the IMF website[2]). In early 2008, the IMF expressed a keen interest in whether
he poor in India have benefited from the impressive economic growth of the
ountry at large. After careful study, it concluded that the lives of the poorest of
he poor have *not* improved and that developmental assistance should be directed
t building educational infrastructure. Although there is no guarantee, Saroja's
hildren may enjoy better schools as a result (Topova, 2008).

World Trade Organization

he World Trade Organization (WTO) is the youngest of these three interna-
ional financial bodies. Founded in 1995 as a successor to GATT (General
greement on Tariffs and Trade, established in 1948), the WTO is an interna-
ional organization designed to manage and liberalize international trade. Since
ts mission is to ensure that international trade flows as smoothly, predictably
nd freely as possible, it generally stands against protectionism and tariffs and
or transparent and cooperative bilateral and multilateral trade agreements. As

an organization favoring free trade, the WTO supports the notion that trade liberalization is a significant force in long-run poverty alleviation since free trade results in economic growth (the mental model here is that a rising tide lifts all boats). Accordingly, the WTO's principal anti-poverty strategy is to do what it does—that is, liberalize trade. For example, the principal goods many developing countries export are agricultural, and they are often subjected to tariffs by developed countries attempting to protect their own agricultural sector. So, to the extent that the WTO can get Japan, for instance, to lower its tariffs on rice, it supports poor rice farmers in Vietnam and Indonesia. However, since market liberalization does not always serve the interests of those at the BoP, the poverty-fighting effects of the WTO are not uniform. For example, some developing countries enforce tariffs to insulate their own nascent industries from dumping and other forms of predatory competition from MNEs originating in wealthier nations. Such regulation may mean that Saroja pays slightly more for her sandals than if they were imported from China; but, it also means that Saroja's daughter has a better chance of being employed by a domestic sandal manufacturer.

All three of these international financial organizations have come under significant fire by critics from both the political left and right who argue that their actions have exacerbated rather than relieved global poverty. For example, some contend that the WB should make performance-based grants rather than broader loans since the latter are often subject to default (Lerrick & Meltzer, 2001). A consortium of NGOs alleges that the IMF is pro-American and undemocratic (Khor, 2006). And the WTO has been criticized for being anti-labor (Global Exchange, 2007). We do not intend to be glib about dismissing these criticisms; indeed, we will address them in Chapter 3. For the time being, however, it is more instructive for us to understand how these financial institutions purport to alleviate global poverty. To do so, it is helpful to consider their "take" on the economics of poverty at the BoP as well as their precise methods for alleviating it.

In general, the WB, IMF and WTO all support a free-market-based view of the world. As such, officials of these institutions perceive the situation at the BoP as in part a side-effect of inefficient financial and currency markets. Acknowledging that market imperfections may be enduring, these financial institutions are also prone to paternalism and elitism in determining how and where to target corrective actions. Thus, rather than trust the masses, they instead rely on experts and officials in governments, and on their own judgments, about the recipients of aid. Above all, they are pro-national economic growth. They trust that efficient markets create the conditions in which everyone will benefit.

In fairness, there is a bit of hypocrisy in the idea that the solution to global poverty lies in free markets. The developed countries of the world

> did not get to where they are now through the policies and the institutions that they recommend to developing countries today. Most of them actively used "bad" trade and industrial policies, such as infant industry protection and export subsidies—practices that these days are frowned upon, if not actively banned, by the WTO (Chang, 2002, p. 2).

So, exactly what do these institutions do to address poverty in the developing world? First and foremost, these organizations act against any impediments to free-market transactions. They oppose trade restrictions between nations and facilitate the resolution of trade conflicts. They intervene when there are market failures due to natural disasters, government upheavals and currency crises so that normal market mechanisms can be resumed quickly. And they act as a major instrument of the UN in bringing markets into alignment with its MDGs.

Second, global financial organizations provide loans and grants directly to the governments of less-developed countries so they can distribute them as needed. This method of aid increases the possibility of corruption or the misallocation of resources, but the aid comes with regulations and policing mechanisms to guard against these possibilities. For example, the WB has an active anti-corruption program.

Third, the WB, IMF and WTO "go around" national governments and make direct investments in local economies. For example, specific infrastructure projects like roads, bridges and schools are spearheaded by the WB, and the IMF may provide training and expertise to support a local bank's entry into the micro-credit market. Such targeted interventions are typically conceived by the financial institutions themselves and then enacted with the cooperation of locals.

Bilateral Foreign Aid

In the last 50 years, the developed countries of the world have given over US$2.3 trillion in economic and humanitarian aid (Easterly, 2006a). Figures 2.1a and 2.1b depict the amount of foreign aid granted in 2006 by nation. Foreign aid may be granted directly to the recipient nation or pass through intermediaries like the UN or World Bank. It may be in the form of a government-to-government contribution or in the form of specific projects in the targeted country or region. Whatever its form, foreign aid has several common features. First, bilateral foreign aid is always an instrument of diplomacy. It is not granted unless it serves the strategic and economic interests of the donor country. For example, foreign aid from France typically goes to promote and maintain the influence of French culture and language. Similarly, Japan's foreign aid is heavily skewed to East Asia to nations with which Japan has commercial ties. Second, aid is often designed to benefit powerful domestic-interest groups. For example, there are interest groups in the US favoring aid in the form of weapon systems, and there are others pushing dairy products. Some aid even comes with strings that require the recipient to buy goods or services prescribed by the donor. Thus, Saroja may find subsidized butter from Wisconsin at her local grocery that came not as an import but as a form of aid from the US domestic-interest groups.

Since bilateral foreign aid is often used as an instrument of domestic politics and international diplomacy, the level of aid and its form often have little to do with meeting the needs of poor people. For example, a donor nation may come to the view that it is best to provide the poor wheat rather than currency because that case was made convincingly by the domestic grain lobby. Similarly, aid may be delivered in the form of education if it believed that it will have a larger impact on "hearts and minds" in a politically turbulent recipient country. Given its importance to the "War on Terror," the outcome of elections in neighboring Pakistan are likely to effect how much subsidized butter Saroja may be able to buy at her local grocer.

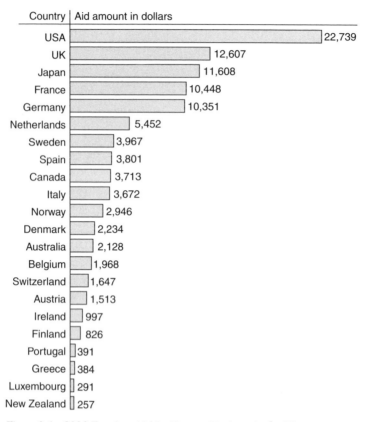

Country	Aid amount in dollars
USA	22,739
UK	12,607
Japan	11,608
France	10,448
Germany	10,351
Netherlands	5,452
Sweden	3,967
Spain	3,801
Canada	3,713
Italy	3,672
Norway	2,946
Denmark	2,234
Australia	2,128
Belgium	1,968
Switzerland	1,647
Austria	1,513
Ireland	997
Finland	826
Portugal	391
Greece	384
Luxembourg	291
New Zealand	257

Figure 2.1a 2006 Foreign Aid by Donor Nations in $millions (source: Shah (n.d.). Used with permission).

Although bilateral foreign aid to developing countries seems like it should go where it is most needed, that is, to those at the BoP, that is seldom the case. First of all, foreign aid data like those shown in Figures 2.1a and 2.1b overstate the amount that actually goes to poverty alleviation. Instead of flowing to the BoP, some foreign aid goes to debt relief; some goes to frivolous or ill-conceived projects; and some goes to training that is given to those in the middle classes of developing countries. By one estimate, almost one-half of all delivered foreign aid never reaches the poor (OneWorld.net, 2008). Moreover, aid almost always comes with strings or it favors themes that reflect the donor nation's culture rather than the needs of its recipients. For example, foreign aid from Sweden is much more likely to support programs consistent with a progressive ideology like those dealing with gender equality, permissive treatment of criminals and environmental concerns. While these are not at all irrelevant to concerns at the BoP, they are arguably ancillary to the central problems of the poor.

Personal and Organizational Philanthropy

The poignant reality of life at the BoP inspires many people in developed economies to invest their own resources in poverty alleviation. Most individuals make these investments through churches, charitable organizations or other NGOs. A

Country	2006 Foreign Aid by Donor Nations as a Percentage of National Income
Sweden	1.03
Luxembourg	0.89
Norway	0.89
Netherlands	0.81
Denmark	0.80
Ireland	0.53
UK	0.52
Belgium	0.50
Austria	0.48
France	0.47
Finland	0.39
Switzerland	0.39
Germany	0.36
Spain	0.32
Australia	0.30
Canada	0.30
New Zealand	0.27
Japan	0.25
Portugal	0.21
Italy	0.20
USA	0.17
Greece	0.16

Figure 2.1b 2006 Foreign Aid by Donor Nations as a Percentage of National Income (source: Shah (n.d.). Used with permission).

few of the NGOs that have missions directed at poverty reduction at the BoP include Oxfam, Net Impact, Catholic Relief Services and ONE. While the particular reasons behind philanthropy are too numerous to examine, some philanthropists share the view that they have a unique moral obligation by virtue of their own wealth. Although derisively termed "*noblesse oblige*," this perspective implies a moral economy wherein privilege must be balanced by duty toward those who lack such privilege or who cannot perform such duty. It is a view bolstered by Luke 12:48: "For those to whom much is given, much is required," a perspective that ability engenders a responsibility.

This idea also appears in many non-Christian traditions, and some secular ethicists advance it as well. For example, ethicist Peter Singer is well-known for the extent to which he has taken the idea that the wealthy have a special duty to help the poor. "For more than 30 years, I've been reading, writing and teaching about the ethical issue posed by the juxtaposition, on our planet, of great abundance and life-threatening poverty" (Singer, 2006). Singer contends that those who have a "wealth surplus" are obliged to give "most of it to help people suffering from poverty so dire as to be life threatening," because the money spent on a new car, cruise, home redecoration or pricey new suit could realistically save children's lives (Singer, 1999). More than three decades ago in "Famine, Affluence, and Morality," Singer argued that there can be no distinction between the

39

voluntary good of "charity" and a positive moral *duty* to relieve extreme poverty (Singer, 1972). Giving to organizations like Oxfam that bring aid to the poor cannot simply be viewed as a "generous" activity because it implies that there is not an obligation for those who choose not to give but are able to do so. In the language of philosophers and theologians, giving money in this context is not "supererogatory"; it is not a voluntary good. Rather, Singer elevates the obligation to the status of moral duty, which applies to all who live in superabundant wealth. He advocates a modest lifestyle for billionaires so that they can better fulfill their unique obligations (Singer, 2007a).

Some people act on their philanthropic impulses as the result of visiting the developing world. It begins with tourism and results in the commitment of a sustained period of service in an attempt to make the lives of the poor better. For example, the Peace Corps presently has over 8,000 volunteers working in 74 countries involved in training, education and infrastructure projects. In all, the tradition of private philanthropy is more developed in the US than it is in other parts of the developed world (Hudson Institute, 2006).

We have only articulated a few of the reasons people opt to act in philanthropic manners; of course, many others exist, and the perception of private philanthropy has evolved over time. What is common to these efforts is the shared interest in raising the consciousness of donors. However, consider the difference between funding solicitations during a presentation by a scholar at a world affairs luncheon and the sale of a T-shirt that promises a percentage of the receipts will go to support those living in poverty. The impetus behind the private contribution may be distinct between the two and it is presumptuous of us—or anyone— to assume otherwise. On the other hand, once development professionals began to view philanthropy as another arm of strategy, their approaches began to expand to embrace larger populations and this expansion, in turn, created a much more heightened awareness of the challenges faced by those living in poverty. Accordingly, the cycle has been effective and it simply represents a recalibration of strategies that have been valuable in other disciplines.

Appeals by NGOs targeted at individual philanthropic investors attempt to put a human face on global poverty. They use dramatic life stories like Saroja's that feature social injustice. In order to "keep it personal," the message generally focuses on a particular problem of some specific group of the poor that an investment could ameliorate. Agencies often use emergencies, disasters and compelling tales of suffering to express the urgency of the need. Disaster assistance (emergency medical services, infrastructure rebuilding), education, orphan services and even micro-lending are all promised if one pledges a voluntary donation. Generally, the message is conveyed that foreign aid is ineffective or insufficient. That way, the prospective philanthropist comes to believe that her or his investment will provide assistance that is not only personal and urgent but also unavailable from any other source.

By far the most significant type of individual and organizational philanthropy is giving by ex-patriots in the form of remittances. For example, El Salvadorans working in the US send millions of dollars home to support the families they have left behind. In 2004, US$47 billion in remittances flowed to the developing world compared to US$19.3 billion from individuals, foundations, universities and religious and other voluntary organizations. This sum is more than twice the amount received from foreign aid (Hudson Institute, 2006). Most remittances convert directly into consumption by those at the BoP in the form of durable goods, health-care and housing, so the economic effect of remittances is immediate and profound in lifting those at the BoP out of poverty (Airola, 2007). According to Donald Terry and Gregory Watson of the Inter-American Development Bank, "remittances constitute one of the broadest and most effective poverty alleviation programs in the world" (Terry & Watson, 2006, p. 1).

Most people paying remittances face high transaction costs. Getting funds from the developed to developing world is often fraught with practical difficulties, and migration law enforcement often results in interruptions in support (De Haas, 2005). Similar difficulties face the individual philanthropist who worries that a donation to an NGO may not get into the hands of someone at the BoP. Accordingly, NGOs and other intermediaries are now offering new promises of accountability, transparency and minimal overheads so that donor generosity will translate into benefits for the poor themselves (Thurman, 2006).

The Role of Business in Global Poverty Alleviation

Prior to globalization, business did not really view global poverty as a business issue. Certainly, individual business leaders were as moved as any citizen by the plight of the world's very poor. However, they acted on this issue as individual philanthropists, not as agents of the companies they led. By the mid 20th century, business philanthropy had become strategic. Businesses only contributed to causes important to their stakeholders or otherwise significant to their operations. When MNEs moved some of their operations into developing countries in the second half of the 20th century, they began taking poverty in those countries more seriously. At first, their efforts at poverty alleviation at the BoP took the form of capital investments; that is, they built factories which employed the poor. Yet, too many of these ended up exploiting workers in sweatshop conditions. This attracted a great deal of negative publicity, so MNEs were forced to take worker rights more seriously.

At roughly the same time, the world was rocked by the scourge of AIDS and by other diseases for which Western medicines were available but which the poor could not afford (Bennett & Tomossy, 2006). In one of the first acts of genuine business philanthropy directed at the BoP, pharmaceutical firms from the developing world decided to subsidize purchases of its life-saving drugs (Vachani & Smith, 2004).

Because of the issues of sweatshops and medicine, the poorest of the poor had become an important new stakeholder of the multinational corporation. At first, global poverty competed with other causes for business's philanthropy dollar. Starbucks' principal philanthropic commitment was to the preservation of the rainforest; and IBM supported computer literacy throughout the world. Then, in 2002, an article was published in the *Harvard Business Review* by C. K. Prahalad and Al Hammond subtitled "Serving the World's Poor, Profitably" that asserted that the poor constituted a sizable market opportunity as consumers. This publication was followed by Prahalad's influential book, *The Fortune at the Bottom of the Pyramid* (2005), that argued that markets in the developed world were headed for stagnation and that tremendous profit potential lay at the BoP. It appeared that poverty alleviation at the BoP was not only a social cause worth supporting but constituted an opportunity for MNEs to do good by doing well.

In January 2008, Bill Gates introduced a new term into the lexicon of global poverty reduction—"creative capitalism." According to Gates, creative capitalism is a system in which the incentives to make a profit drive an MNE's principles and commercial competencies to do more for the poor. Both Prahalad's original contentions and Gates' creative capitalism are based on two ideas: (1) there are huge, unexplored markets at the BoP, and (2) these markets should be explored if global economic growth is to be sustained and the lives of the poor are to be improved. As examples of creative capitalism, Gates cites the efforts of two MNEs. One is pharmaceutical manufacturer GlaxoSmithKline which is developing medicines targeted for the poor and the other is Sumitomo Chemical which used its expertise to build a bed-net factory that it donated for the prevention of malaria. What makes "creative capitalism" unique is its focus on market-based rather than aid-based incentives. In Gates' words:

> Some people might object to this kind of market-based social change, arguing that, if we combine sentiment with self-interest, we will not expand the reach of the market, but reduce it. Yet Adam Smith, the very father of capitalism and the author of "Wealth of Nations," who believed strongly in the value of self-interest for society, opened his first book with the following lines: "How selfish soever man may be supposed, there are evidently some principles in his nature, which interest him in the fortunes of others, and render their happiness necessary to him, though he derives nothing from it, except the pleasure of seeing it." Creative capitalism takes this interest in the fortunes of others and ties it to our interest in our own fortunes in ways that help advance both. This hybrid engine of self-interest and concern for others can serve a much wider circle of people than can be reached by self-interest or caring alone (Gates, 2008).

In spite of this nod to a "concern for others," Gates acknowledges that the profit motive alone may be insufficient to drive a business to serve the very poor. In such cases, he points out,

> there needs to be another incentive, and that incentive is recognition. Recognition enhances a company's reputation and appeals to customers; above all, it attracts good people to an organization. As such, recognition triggers a market-based reward for good behavior. In markets where profits are not possible, recognition is a proxy; where profits are possible, recognition is an added incentive (Gates, 2008).

In a sense, then, creative capitalism is only slightly different from philanthropy directed at the BoP. Enhanced recognition may align nicely with the strategic objectives of many multinational corporations, so the only thing "creative" about "creative capitalism" is Gates' personal insight that capitalism does not contradict caring for others.

However, two ideas remain missing from his concept. First, there is the idea that the poor themselves are hungry for a chance to participate in economic activity not just as consumers but as producers as well. Consider Saroja. She would probably love to buy a computer so her son could complete his studies more efficiently, but she obviously cannot afford one. If she received a computer as a gift from Bill Gates, she would probably be grateful. However, merely having a computer will not enable Saroja to participate in the global economy. Only if she can also leverage her ironing and housekeeping talents into a viable business will she ever pull herself out of her economic misery. In general, businesses that enable the poor to become producers kindle an economic engine that may do more for economic development at the BoP than all the philanthropic aid and creative capitalism rich benefactors can provide.

Second, there is a need to bring together all the efforts at poverty alleviation into one system that truly benefits the poor. This means that, rather than acting alone, businesses should forge new partnerships with the other governmental and nongovernmental institutions that are working on global poverty. Imagine the benefits to Saroja if a sewing machine manufacturer worked with an NGO that focused on women's issues in order to provide her micro-loans with which to enhance her productive capacity and to expand her business.

Saroja does not need one single computer; Saroja needs a system. In later chapters we will explore how those systems are conceived by recalibrating the mental models of MNEs. In the next chapter, however, it is important to first examine why these imaginative approaches to business's role in global poverty alleviation are so often overlooked.

3

MENTAL MODELS AND CONTRIBUTING BIASES ON GLOBAL POVERTY[1]

The Fatehpuri night shelter for street children near the heavily congested Old Delhi Railway Station is quite a contrast to the chaos outside. Around 20 children, aged between 12 and 16, are gleefully watching cartoons on a television set placed in the middle of a spartan hall painted bright pink.

There is a wooden table and chair for the caretaker, neatly piled bedding for the children and a wall covered with graffiti. There is also a cubicle, around three by three feet, at the far end. This red-and-yellow enclosure is the Children's Development Bank (CDB)—run by street children, exclusively for street children.

As soon as the bank opens at 6:30 p.m. (unlike regular banks, CDB operates only in the evening because street children work during the day), its young customers line up to make withdrawals or deposit their day's earnings. Thirteen-year-old Durgesh waits patiently as the cashier—who is as old as Durgesh—makes an entry in his passbook and hands him a note of Rs 50 (US$1.10). Apart from his daily expenses and an occasional movie outing, Durgesh is saving up hard to go home. "The bank is a safe place to deposit my money," he says.

There are many like him—runaways from desperately poor rural homes who join the big city's floating population of rag pickers and street vendors. "Most of them are boys; there aren't many girls on the streets," says Suman Sachdeva, development manager of Butterflies, the NGO behind the initiative.

The bank opens for an hour every day—a busy time for its manager-cum-cashier, a nominated child volunteer who runs the affairs. The job is rotated every six months, giving youngsters (usually in the 12–14 age group) a chance to learn accounting and be responsible with money.

Dressed nattily in navy blue trousers, sweater and white shirt, with hair neatly combed back, he looks every inch the typical branch manager. Studying in fifth standard at a school nearby, Ajay has been running the show for four months now.

"Daily savings range anything between Rs 150 and Rs 300," he says. Initially, CDB's young employees were trained by HSBC in the basics of banking. Children were taught how to maintain cash, ledgers and passbooks. "They were also taught how to budget their earnings and the value of saving. Earlier, they spent all their earnings on watching films," says Sachdeva.

Launched in 2000, with Rs 2 lakh (200,000 rupees) as seed money from the National Foundation for India, CDB began with a membership of 20. These street children agreed to be part of the project because no mainstream bank would give them entry. This core group also framed the rules and regulations. Any working child, for instance, can approach the bank—except those who are in the habit of stealing, begging, selling pornographic material or substance abuse.

Like any bank, CDB too has two kinds of accounts—*jama khata* (savings account) where a minimum of Rs 1 can be saved, and *chalta phirta* account, which is the current account. Members get a 3.5% interest return on their savings. The bank also sanctions advance loans linked to vocational skills. A committee of nine members (comprising NGO volunteers and children) assesses the requests during monthly meetings. "These loans have played a special role by empowering girls, who would otherwise be pushed into prostitution," says Sachdeva. A few girls with skills in embroidery and tailoring have got loans to start businesses of their own.

Over the years, this streetside story has traveled way beyond the capital. In the first year, membership grew from 20 to 800 at the Fatehpuri center alone. At present, the bank operates from three night shelters and 14 contact areas in Delhi. But its network is spread all over: parks, bus stations and pavements.

The bank, which has international training meets and online support, now boasts a membership of 8,000 across India.... [M]embership ceases when the child turns 18. The youngster has the option to either close the account or shift to a mainstream bank (Sinha, 2008).

Most people who read this story of success are inordinately overwhelmed and impressed. The visual picture it creates of poor children in developing countries serving each other as bankers is almost impossible to fathom. Yet, like many innovative approaches to poverty alleviation, this narrative does not fit the way that many of us think about the poor or conceive of what might be done to ease their suffering. The reason is that the conceptual frameworks that we use in thinking about poverty and the poor inhibit us from considering solutions like these or they fail to account adequately for realities "on the ground." Unfortunately, this is also the case with the approaches to poverty alleviation taken by the institutions that we reviewed in Chapter 2. As we shall see in this chapter, the United Nations (UN) and other multinational organizations too often harbor a paternalistic mindset that encapsulates the poor as passive recipients rather than active determinants of their own futures. This is not to say that the UN or other like institutions play no significant role in the alleviation of poverty. Instead, it is our contention that they are necessary but perhaps insufficient partners in any system that will eventually lead to an effective solution. We will explore the opportunities and roles for these and other institutions in that system in a later chapter. In this chapter, however, we seek to fracture the problematic mental models surrounding the particular role that multinational enterprises (MNEs) can play in this system and expose a number of biases that impede the consideration of fruitful solutions like the CDB.

This chapter begins with a definition of mental models. We shall then enumerate and dissect a series of biases about the poor and the nature of poverty itself that create a top-down framework that is both morally offensive and effectively problematic (Prahalad, 2005; Easterly, 2006a). The next element of our discussion will examine biases concerning the "research paradox," where the institutional demands for comprehensive data often impede or preclude innovative trial-and-error praxis (Murdoch, 2006). Finally, we will consider the arguments of theorists who suggest that MNEs offer discretionary philanthropy to challenge the bias of traditional corporation social responsibility—future-directed initiatives aimed at developing productive capabilities and new markets. This final consideration is, in fact, clearly the harbinger of profitable partnerships and will be explored at length in Chapter 4.

As mentioned in Chapter 2, one of the key ideas missing from Gates' concept of "creative capitalism" is the need to bring together all the efforts at poverty alleviation into one system that truly benefits the poor. By shattering the mental models around the role of MNEs in poverty alleviation, not only do we create an additional partner in that larger system, but that process of discarding biases also generates countless opportunities for innovation and expansion in economic development and job creation, and in value for shareholders, as well as for these new stakeholders.

Mental Models

Although it is not always clearly defined, the term "mental model" or "mindset" follows from the idea that human functioning does not merely result from passively forming mental pictures of our experiences, representations that are derived from the stimuli to which we are subject. Rather, our minds actively interact with the data of our experiences, selectively filtering and framing that data. These frameworks or mental models are socially learned schemata that set up parameters through which experiences are organized (Senge, 1990; Gentner & Whitley, 1997, pp. 210–211; Gorman, 1992; Werhane, 1999a). Thus, mental models function as selective filters for dealing with experience. All the mental models we employ are socially acquired and altered through socialization, educational upbringing, our religious commitments and other experiences. In focusing, framing, organizing and ordering what we experience, we bracket and leave out data simply because we cannot mentally process all that we experience. Sometimes, this limiting process taints or colors that which we experience. The resulting mindsets or mental models are incomplete, and sometimes distorted, narrow, and single-framed, and often turn into biased ways of perceiving, organizing and learning (Johnson, 1993; Werhane, 1999a). On the other hand, because they are not genetically fixed or totally locked in during early experiences, one can evaluate and change one's mindsets if one is committed to doing so.

The narrative with which we began this chapter about children engaged in banking up-ends one persistent mental model about poverty, particularly poverty in less-developed countries. The notion of a Children's Development Bank challenges one set of deeply imbedded learned mental models about the abilities of children to organize a bank, to save and to be responsible for their own and for others' finances. This narrative forces us to rethink our biases concerning the homeless and the poor as well—the ungrounded contention that the poor are unskilled and incapable of managing their own affairs. The fact that the CDB is staffed by homeless and poor children who are only 13 years old makes that point dramatically.

Interestingly, our ideas of what is right or wrong, good or bad and our moral notions are also forms of mental models, which frame or shape our normative choices and judgments. As Mark Johnson writes, "[m]oral reasoning is a constructive imaginative activity.... Our most fundamental moral concepts ... are defined metaphorically. The way we conceptualize a particular situation will depend on our use of systematic conceptual metaphors" (Johnson, 1993, p. 2). Thus, moral notions are not merely evaluative tools for making moral judgments but rather they actually shape our moral decisions. They do more than informing us about what is going on; they actually arrange what is going on by selecting the variables to be understood in a particular way (Hauerwas, 1974, p. 24). As such, they order the world in a way that is coherent, shaping one's vision of it (pp. 19–20).

For example, if one is convinced that children are helpless, it is hard to imagine them as bankers in India. Similarly, if we are convinced that the philanthropy and aid that was delineated in Chapter 2 are the only means to alleviate global poverty, that conclusion naturally will shape our moral judgments about supporting these ventures and will cause us to be suspicious about profitable partnerships at the base of the pyramid (BoP). Indeed, we might conclude, from this point of view, that such philanthropy and aid is "good," even when faced with information that almost one-half of all delivered foreign aid never reaches the poor (see Chapter 2), or that it fails to improve the lives of the poor in countries where it is distributed. And, we might then also conclude that other efforts, such as job creation, micro-lending by for-profit banks, or bootstrap projects such as the CDB are of little worth. At the same time, at least some of us will react to the CDB with the moral judgment that these must be "good kids." But, notice again, that conclusion is also an unfounded bias that frames our moral conclusions. We do not know these children, and it is surely possible that some of them may be rascals.

Even what appear to be purely objective accounts are also framed by the selective processes through which data are collected and sorted. Thus a sharp distinction between the descriptive and normative is often blurred (Hauerwas, 1974; Werhane, 1994). For example, the term "base of the pyramid" is both descriptive and normative. By linking poverty to income, the term focuses our attention on poverty as a *purely economic* problem that we in the West must solve in some paternalistic way, as if less-developed countries cannot. These sorts of accounts, framed by mental models together with normative moral notions, shape the global poverty dialogue, thereby shaping stakeholder judgment and consequential action. The act of describing poverty conditions is itself selective, sorting out what is thought to be the most relevant data and dismissing what seems to be the irrelevant in order to group together an otherwise unspecified group of features. Indeed, we cannot help but to have engaged in that practice in connection with this book by selectively choosing case narratives that will attract the reader's attention and illustrate our arguments.

As we noted in Chapter 1, one of the most common descriptive groupings of global poverty is the World Bank's Purchasing Power Parity (PPP) metric, which essentially lumps together a global assortment of cultures, peoples, economies and governments that would otherwise remain unrelated. This grouping is important since, under other circumstances, international attention and dialogue would not be possible. However, such an allegedly purely descriptive grouping also has embedded within it particular moral notions (that poverty is best measured in economic figures, or that the conditions of poverty are morally challenging) and a sphere of potential responses (wealth redistribution through government aid, as one example) that limit our ability to think more creatively both about poverty and about ingenious approaches to its alleviation. The challenge of global poverty dialogue is not to dismiss moral notions, but instead to evaluate them critically so that the sphere of potential responses includes innovative solutions and is not unconsciously and unnecessarily restricted by the constraint of mental models.

Take, for example, the use of "rights language" to describe health problems (e.g., malaria, malnutrition, AIDS) among the global poor. As part of the economic, social and cultural human rights catalog, the concept of a "right to health" has gained political importance and theoretical significance in "rights-based" rhetoric (Leisinger, 2005). But, any meaningful discussion of rights implies a corresponding discussion of responsibilities, of duty-bearers. The question is, whose responsibility? The rights formulated by the United Nations Universal Declaration of Human Rights envision nations as the primary duty-bearers. Some rights are well-served by this idea, where prohibitions expressed through laws curb the practices that threaten them. The rights of privacy and freedom of association, for example, are essentially constraints on government encroachment into the free space where privacy and association naturally operate on their own terms.

However, the use of rights language to depict the health problems of the global poor imbues the discussion with a legalistic tenor creating an obligation to fulfill a need. As such, the dialogue tends to automatically fall into the realm of public services, which preclude assigning duties to, or developing responses from, nongovernmental players. In poor countries, there is little financial support with which to provide public services; are citizens of richer nations simply to ignore the plight of those in need in the poorer countries? Or should they urge their governments to target their foreign aid toward eradicating diseases that are rampant at the BoP? As we will show with case studies in upcoming chapters, some of the most successful solutions to problems such as malaria focus more on the practical problems related to design, marketing, cost or efficient distribution of low-tech solutions such as bed nets, by getting *beyond* imagining that this is a problem only to be solved through government intervention.

On the other hand, rights-based language also refers to entitlements and responsibilities accruing to individuals as well as to nation-states. Here, the individualistic nature of rights places a high burden on individual responsibility (thus blaming poverty on those who are poor!) and shifts the thinking about solutions to what seem to be intractable problems. Most adults in the developing world who are poor have capabilities and can take responsibility for their lives. But, holding people like Mufia in Chapter 1 and Saroja in Chapter 2 solely responsible for their poverty is absurd, just as imagining that all homeless children can take care of themselves in the manner in which the street-bankers do. And, notice that the CDB was founded by adults, and the children are trained by a bank, HSBC. Thus, opportunity and training, not collective government programs *or* pure individual initiative helped establish the CDB. In general, rights language is helpful in framing and addressing some global poverty problems, but only when it is taken beyond the mindset that identifies rights with collective or governmental responsibilities, or alternately, the mindset that attributes all rights and responsibilities to individuals.

The Biases of Conceptualism and Common Sense

One of the most lucid voices on the subject of the biases introduced by our mental models is that of the Jesuit philosopher Bernard Lonergan. Lonergan spent much of his career examining what he termed "insight," which he contended to be the pinnacle of human understanding. Described as "active ground whence proceed conception, definition, hypothesis, theory, system" (Lonergan, 1971, p. 213), insight is the ability to examine, evaluate, challenge and even reformulate mental models. But this occurs, Lonergan contends, only when we critically investigate and question our thinking and behavior. For example, in the 19th century, many colonialists thought that they were doing the right thing by opening up "primitive" countries to civilization, just as missionaries thought it was the right thing to convert "natives" to Christianity to save their souls. It was only when critics called attention to these interventions that new thinking developed to counteract them. Following the critical and sustained attention to the relevant data, insight consists of "a grasp of intelligible unity or relation in the data" (Lonergan, 1971, p. 213). According to Lonergan, insight is often undermined by several biases that dismiss relevant data and foreclose subsequent inquiry. Two in particular are the bias of conceptualism and the bias of common sense. We see these at work as people strive for insight into solutions to the problem of global poverty.

The bias of conceptualism is evident when "a strong affirmation of concepts" and "excessive abstractness" create a skeptical disregard of other insights (Lonergan, 1958, p. 695). In other words, we sometimes discount certain solutions because they conflict with the abstract labels and conceptual frameworks used to understand the problem. We see this at work when people perceive that global poverty is so enormously complex and intractable that its solutions must be similarly multifaceted and attempted only by large international organizations. The bias of conceptualism leads us to overlook the possibility that a number of small-scale solutions woven together into a self-reinforcing system could enable the poor to pull themselves out of poverty if simply given a chance.

The bias of conceptualism undermines discussions based on the PPP (described in Chapter 1) or other poverty measurements in economic terms. Subtly, the reliance on such aggregate measures conveys the impression that global poverty is a comparable—and always relative—phenomenon, no matter where it arises. This shifts the view from the concrete problems that face particular people in particular contexts to those that require an abstract understanding of poverty. Clearly, the problems facing the urban poor in Ecuador are often quite different from those facing the rural poor of Somalia. Poor children in Somalia would have a much more difficult time establishing a bank account than poor children in India, not because they are incapable, but because there is no banking system at all in Somalia. So, the bias of conceptualism can cast attention away from the details and particularities of context on behalf of more sweeping generalities. Our inquiry may therefore unintentionally ignore otherwise evident solutions that one might glean from those details.

Similarly, since business did not view global poverty as a *business issue* prior to globalization, MNEs have only recently begun to explore the role that they might play in the system of poverty alleviation. They have been subject to a bias of conceptualism that created a regional perspective and that viewed global poverty as too large a concept for them to solve from their home countries. However, with the advent of globalization, MNE orientation shifted their mental models and allowed them to recognize the extraordinary power they had with which to create a multifaceted solution, serving the interests of multiple stakeholders, including the MNE. Therefore, it has been not only a distrustful mental model surrounding the perception of MNEs that has excluded them from a seat at the table in connection with the poverty-alleviation system, but also a historical *self-perceptive* mental model on the part of the corporations themselves.

The bias of common sense similarly plagues many of our insights about global poverty. This bias involves the refusal to get beyond the familiar world of the way things appear to us (Lonergan, 1958, p. 419). Suffering from the common-sense bias, people become unwilling to search for or to challenge underlying patterns that serve as the basis for our experiences. These patterns serve as blind spots that prevent viable solutions from being considered. For example, the idea of lending money to people who have no collateral was thought to be fiscally untenable until actual experiences in micro-lending proved this to be wrong. At first, the notion of selling cellphones on credit to mostly poor, illiterate women with no collateral in Bangladesh sounded like pure economic idiocy. Yet, to date, the Grameen Bank has lent money under these conditions to millions of village women; today, Grameen Telecom is the largest cellphone server in that country. Importantly, since extending this so-called unsecured credit, the Grameen Bank has profited from these transactions (Grameen Foundation, 2007). Together, both the bias of conceptualism and the bias of common sense point us toward incomplete, partial or limited solutions that often constitute only a small segment of the enduring responses necessary to alleviate global poverty.

The Research Paradox and Bird's-eye Perspectives

These narrow mental models often distract us from effective responses to global poverty in two other ways. First, there is the research paradox: that tendency to rely on theoretical models purporting to explain the mechanisms underlying poverty rather than on the on-the-ground data that might not fit these abstractions. Second, there is the proclivity to base one's mental models on a perspective that ignores those whose experience with poverty is most direct.

There is a paralysis created by predicating action based on abstract research rather than on experiential data. Consider the statistics from Chapter 1. Although billions of dollars in foreign aid and philanthropy have been invested based on theoretical conclusions of what might help, global poverty persists. Perhaps even more persuasive, 30 years ago this research paradox could have prevented the revolution of micro-finance from getting off the ground altogether. When Mohammed Yunus first conceived of micro-lending, the Bank of Bangladesh thought he was crazy, since lending to those without collateral was counter to all common sense about money lending; and lending to women in particular was thought to be pure folly. It was "standard economic theory" that poor people do not pay back loans; and, of course, who could imagine that women could engage in loan processes? However, Yunus decided to oppose the mindset, backed by theoretical research, that the poor are bad credit risks. He launched Grameen Bank, lending initially only to collateral-free, first-time borrowers, 97% of whom were women. It was only *after* the trial-and-error lessons of the early Grameen Bank that there was even the possibility to collect data to support Yunus's trust in the capabilities of the poor in Bangladesh.

Today, the same tendency to put one's confidence in theory rather than in on-the-ground data threatens to impede the development of another promising solution to global poverty. Jonathan Murdoch (2006) argues that micro-insurance could be the next great tool for helping the poor pull themselves out of extreme poverty. Insurance is a crucial safety net for many people across the globe, and it might well prove to abate the numerous risks experienced among the poor. Health, life and property insurance are all attractive vehicles for managing the exigencies that place the poor in peril. So, what is preventing the growth of micro-insurance? Aside from the biases discussed above, one of the most challenging obstacles is a lack of usable field data on such risks as disease, fire and mortality from poverty-stricken areas. Insurance is a data-driven enterprise, and data that might help understand what it takes to mitigate risks is simply unavailable. The data that do exist either are not completely trustworthy or are insufficiently longitudinal to have value. In its preference for theory over empirical details, the research paradox restricts data gathering to a set of questions that may not always serve the interests of the poor or may not help build support for systems that do.

One of the greatest challenges to addressing poverty is getting beyond mental models that view the poor from "a bird's-eye" or self-referential point of view. *Imagining* what life must be like on less than US$2 per day or *trying* to identify what the commonalities might be among those at the BoP is far less informative than listening to those who do it every day. This insight is why the idea of *partnerships* is such a vital component of the profitable partnerships concept. Effective solutions must necessarily require significant input from the poor. What are the needs of the poor and who determines them? Yunus discovered that the best way to approach this question was to ask the poor themselves. By doing so, he learned that the poor were systematically excluded from the formal banking sector because of their entrenched and limited understanding of collateral.

Yunus benefited from an insight he received when he visited a poor village of Jobra near his home in Bangladesh. There, he came upon a woman making bamboo chairs, earning only 2¢ per chair. She had needed to borrow money to buy the bamboo at usurious interest rates of around 200%, so that all her earnings went to pay off her loan. This one example focused Yunus's thinking on the real-life economics of poor women in his country (Yunus, 2003). After his direct experience in Jobra, he simply could not inhabit the existing bias of conceptualism with its emphasis on the necessity of collateral and an implicit cultural bias of common sense that women could not be earners. By attending to and respecting the small bamboo-stool-making ventures, Yunus began to understand that the poor women of Jobra were subject to patterns of exclusion from banks, an understanding he never would have had from the bird's-eye view (Yunus, 2003). Yunus rightly sees the research paradox as behind the significant problem of a bird's-eye perspective that so often derails the global poverty dialogue. "When you hold the world in your palm and inspect it only from a bird's-eye view," he writes in his autobiography, "you tend to become arrogant—you do not realize that things get blurred when seen from an enormous distance" (2003). Instead of the bird's-eye view, Yunus opts for "the worm's-eye view," a perspective that helped him understand the burden of economic collateral and envision its alternative: social collateral. He argues elsewhere that it is "the concepts we developed to understand the reality around us" that made us "see things wrongly." It is "our policies borne out of our reasonings and theoretical framework" which constitute a "failure at the top—rather than lack of capability at the bottom" that are the root cause of poverty (Yunus, 2003).

Another way to think about a "worm's-eye view" is to adopt what Ed Freeman and John McVea call a "names and faces" approach (Freeman & McVea, 2005). Trying to grasp the reality of a billion people living in abject poverty is difficult. But, hearing stories about particular individuals helps to reorient the problem into manageable terms. For example, approximately 45% of the 150 million people living in Bangladesh live in abject poverty (Central Intelligence Agency, 2008). Those are numbers that are impossible to grasp concretely, but the story of Mufia Khatoon we told in Chapter 1 helps us to "wrap our minds around" her dreadful reality. Her particular story helps us to fathom the poverty that characterizes life at the BoP. Out of those 150 million, there are approximately 2 million women in Bangladesh working in sweatshops. But that number is also too difficult to comprehend. But, if we focus on one worker, we get a worm's-eye view and we begin to grasp the plight of sweatshop laborers. A 14-year-old girl, working in a Bangladeshi-owned factory, attaches metal buttons onto jeans with a machine that presses the buttons onto the fabric. She is expected to do one button every seven seconds; and she works about 14–16 hours a day with only two days off a month. Unfortunately, her supervisor cannot always count correctly, and she is seldom paid fully for every hour she works. If her productivity decreases, say, to one button every 12 seconds, she will be fired and replaced by a more nimble person (National Labor Committee, 2000).

Many of the mental models that prevent us from conceiving of MNEs as appropriate partners in a system of poverty alleviation and that bias us against profitable partnerships, not only as one solution but perhaps the *preferred* solution, are evident in an interesting debate that has taken place between two University of Michigan scholars who have vastly different approaches to the problem: Professors C. K. Prahalad and Aneel Karnani. Prahalad's contention is that the BoP constitutes a significant market opportunity on which multinational enterprises (MNEs) should capitalize given limited market opportunities elsewhere in the developed world. In his now classic article with Al Hammond, "Serving the World's Poor, Profitably" (2002), Prahalad argues that money can be made by adapting marketing efforts to those at the BoP (see also Prahalad & Hart, 2002; Prahalad, 2007). In contrast, Aneel Karnani (2006) labels Prahalad's proposition "a harmless illusion" and challenges his estimation of the size of the BoP market. Further, Karnani declares Prahalad guilty of "false advertising" because, Karnani contends, the BoP market is neither as big nor potentially as profitable as Prahalad suggests.

In what to us seems evidence of a bias of conceptualism, Karnani (2006) sets the BoP market at around US$1.2 trillion (2.7 billion poor people multiplied by US$1.25 per day), a figure actually closer to the World Bank's estimate than Prahalad's estimate of US$13 trillion (2005). On that basis, Karnani concludes that the "fortune and glory at the bottom of the pyramid are a mirage" because exaggerations of *size* are also exaggerations of *opportunities* for business (2006). Here, we see the bias of common sense at work in the assertion (more relevant in the developed world, of course) that market size equals market opportunity.

The different estimates of the relative size of the BoP market are understandable, given the debates about how best to measure poverty that we discussed in Chapter 1 (see, e.g., *The Economist*, 2004, or T. Friedman, 2006). What Karnani's critique fails to recognize is that the economic data on which he relies are no more "true" than Prahalad's. The World Bank's PPP metric is an adequate tool, at best, not the razor-sharp one that he expects it to be. A consensus around poverty metrics will always lag behind the relative gravity of the situation on the ground. After all, extreme poverty is a life-and-death matter. Efforts that truly alleviate it, therefore, do not have the luxury of waiting for a conclusive data consensus and will always grope their way forward. Instead, we find the research paradox infecting the argument. Whether the magnitude of the BoP market is US$1.2 trillion or US$13 trillion is less important than the fact that there are at least one billion people living in abject poverty, *however defined* (Collier, 2007), and the fact that, from a worm's-eye view, there are at least one billion individual life narratives that are riddled with suffering and privation.

Whatever the market size, it is vital for us to find some solutions to this misery. While the distinctions between such estimates are important rhetorically, they should not be used to dissuade MNEs and their partners from innovating with profitable, sustainable solutions that might serve the poor most effectively. Our worry is that, rife with the faulty mental models we have discussed, the Prahalad–Karnani debate implicitly sanctions failed solutions, or worse, justifies doing nothing.

"One Size Fits All" and Paternalism

Still another problematic mental model that creeps into both sides of the Prahalad–Karnani debate and serves to dissuade the further exploration and generation of profitable partnerships is that there is one general solution template that underlies all successful solutions to the BoP problem. For Prahalad, it is in addressing the poor as consumers, in effect tapping into the enormous buying potential of these large populations. Mobilizing the engine of modern marketing to capitalize on the poor as brand-conscious consumers will, according to Prahalad, have a humanizing effect through the dignity of attention and the autonomy of choice. In response, Karnani argues that viewing the poor as consumers is "an intellectually and morally problematic position." This is because, whatever the extent of the population at the base of the pyramid, and it is sizable, these are very poor people who actually have no money to buy much of anything. So, while the size of this population is huge, the purchasing power is minuscule. Moreover, Karnani fears that such a view encourages some MNEs to exploit this market with goods and services that do not serve the real needs of the very poor.

Instead, Karnani argues, the poor should be viewed as "producers" rather than consumers (Karnani, 2007a). Karnani's argument here is two-fold. First, as explained above, markets at the base of the pyramid are not as large as Prahalad contends, so opportunities for MNEs in those markets are exaggerated. More importantly, Karnani claims that, in order for countries to develop economically, industrialization and jobs must be available. In the developing world, most of the poor are not producers because they have no opportunities to engage in productive enterprises at any scale. Indeed, he claims, micro-lending, while admirable, is insufficient on its own to decrease poverty to any great extent.

We shall take up the challenge of job creation later in this book. Our point here is that the distinction between producer and consumer is dubious, at best, and deceptive, at worst. That is, each distinct role, on its own, is based on a narrowly construed mental model that distracts us, distorts our thinking, and discourages innovation of imaginative solutions. To consider those in abject poverty only as consumers (and we are not alleging that this is Prahalad's argument) is to imagine an untapped market of eager buyers of products; but, of course, those alleged buyers have no funds. On the other hand, to focus primarily on the poor as producers invites what exactly has happened too many times at the BoP: the development of sweatshops and other exploitive systems of production where millions of workers are paid such low wages that they can scarcely get by, thus not increasing that customer base in the least. The outcome is cheaper goods for the developed world but little in the way of economic prosperity at the BoP. Mental models that minimally distinguish between the "poor-as-consumer" and the "poor-as-producer" are inadequate, for they lock us into "one size fits all" thinking that perpetuates further the biased ways in which we think about the poor and constrain us from all other possibilities.

A related form of bias arises from paternalism. Karnani's most virulent critique of Prahalad is that the BoP proposition is a "dangerous delusion" offered to the poor themselves. He fears that corporate involvement in the BoP might reduce the welfare of the poor, since the poor "are vulnerable by virtue of lack of education ... lack of information, and economic, cultural and social deprivations" (Karnani, 2006, p. 18). He suggests that these deficiencies make the poor susceptible to exploitation and create a need for greater legal and social protections. He claims that the poor do not often demonstrate the ability to make wise consumer choices, buying alcohol and whitening creams, for instance, instead of "useful" products. The danger of the BoP proposition, he continues, is that it "de-emphasizes the role of the state in providing basic *services* and *infrastructure*" (Karnani, 2006, p. 27; italics added).

Our biggest concern with Karnani's "dangerous delusion" critique is that it reinforces the kind of objectification and paternalism that dominated the post-World War II development era. Karnani reveals an inherent skepticism that the poor are able to decide for themselves what is best. Viewing the poor as unskilled, helpless victims or questioning their purchasing preferences are two signs of top-down thinking, where grand social-engineering projects are the primary vehicles of social progress, as opposed to viewing the poor as autonomous decision makers, capable of making effective decisions about their own futures, or accepting responsibility for their own mistakes. The path representing the former perspective is both well-worn and historically unsuccessful.

A "bird's-eye perspective" is both necessary and appropriate for policy dialogue at the international level; however, poverty alleviation is not just a matter of policy. When that is the primary operative mental model, poverty-alleviation efforts can be distorted by what William Easterly calls the "ideology of development" (2007) or worse, a "utopian nightmare" (2005b). Foreign aid in the form of the Marshall Plan transformed Europe after World War II; and US aid to Japan was equally successful. The International Monetary Fund (IMF) and the

World Bank efforts have been effective in China, Japan and Korea, and in other parts of the world. But, in Africa, parts of the subcontinent of India, Pakistan and Bangladesh, and Central America, foreign aid has done little to change those economic landscapes and has accomplished virtually nothing in terms of poverty reduction. Thus, Easterly concludes, this model of developmental economics is not universally successful and should not be thought to be so.

Easterly believes the ideology of "developmentalism" is frequently an extension of colonial mental models. As a "dark ideological specter," developmentalism promises to answer society's problems in the familiar one-size-fits-all motif, one correct answer with no need to involve local actors. It is a mental model that once pervaded institutions such as the IMF and the World Bank. Viewing poverty as primarily a technological problem to be solved if enough resources are available, developmentalism often overlooks what Easterly calls the messy social sciences—how development monies will be used in particular contexts (Easterly, 2007). He dramatizes the nightmare of developmentalism by citing three key facts. First, the distribution of 12-cent medicine and four-dollar bed nets could prevent half of all malaria deaths in sub-Saharan Africa. Second, donors have given US$568 billion over 43 years to Africa. Third, 12-cent medicines and four-dollar bed nets have yet to be distributed effectively (Easterly, 2005b).

What makes paternalism so seductive has nothing to do with the poor or poverty at all. Rather, it is a version of philanthropy-as-expiation, i.e., our "burden." The economist Paul Collier argues that philanthropic or governmental aid, when administered responsibly, does make important contributions to the alleviation of poverty. However, it has probably been overemphasized, at the expense of alternatives, because it fits "so comfortably in a moral universe organized around the principles of sin and expiation" (Collier, 2007, p. 123). When global poverty is juxtaposed against the vast wealth atop the global economic pyramid, it is reasonable to see one solution as some form of charitable or government-mandated wealth redistribution. Indeed, Jeffrey Sachs argues that, although the rich countries of the world have donated a great deal of money, in absolute terms, this turns out to be a very small percentage of their GNPs. Sachs argues that, if wealthy countries allocated just 0.7% of their GNP, this could create enough funds to provide for the basic needs of the 1.1 billion people whom he estimates are living in abject poverty (Sachs, 2005a, pp. 290–291).

Buried within some of the recent calls for increases in philanthropic aid is an effort to assuage consciences with regard to the guilt of frivolous consumption or the tortured legacy of a colonial past. While such guilt might be helpful for a sober analysis of distorted trade policies, it has little to do with finding effective solutions that best serve the poor, as we have seen in the past two chapters. Instead, it operates in its own self-referential framework.

As we pointed out in the last chapter, Peter Singer has been worrying about the concurrence of great wealth amid life-threatening poverty (Singer, 2006). Concerned with the juxtaposition of what he calls "frivolous consumption" in light of the immediate demands of life-threatening poverty, Singer argues that those in a position to do something about poverty without any significant sacrifice ought to do so. Singer's critique of frivolous consumption is an important one, but not because it creates an obligation to help the poor. The most pressing danger of frivolous consumption is that such patterns of consumption are unsustainable on the current trajectory if the developing world follows the same pattern of resource use as the developed world (Hart, 2005).

Singer argues that state aid and individual philanthropic contributions are expressions of a true belief in human equality. If one truly believes in human equality, he argues, one must donate a portion of one's income to address the challenges of global inequality:

> If we don't put in those relatively modest amounts so that we are talking not of 0.1 percent of GDP but at least 1 percent or perhaps 2 percent of GDP, still $1.00 or $2.00 in every $100.00 that we earn, then we cannot hold our heads up and say, "We do believe that human beings are equally precious or equally important no matter what country they live in," and we can't think of ourselves as contributing to the development of a global community (Singer, 2003.)

Singer even creates a metric for fulfilling the obligation. Like any progressive system of taxation, he calculates the amount of money that could go toward the alleviation of poverty, if only the wealthy would give more. He begins at the top with those who earn more than US$5 million a year and could easily give away one-third of their income (leaving them with a comfortable US$3.3 million). He then calculates what every other segment of the top 10% should give, ranging from one-fifth to just 10% of annual income. His progressive metric for calculating the relative obligation each owes to philanthropy yields a total of US$404 billion without really impacting lifestyles (Singer, 2006). Singer contends that this level of giving would surely eliminate the blight of global poverty, if redistributed correctly according to his metrics.

In addition to individual philanthropic activity, Singer also justifies foreign aid using this same logic. From a compensatory perspective, aid could be seen as the *rightful restitution* to those who have been harmed by colonialism (Singer, 2003). In various articles, Singer demonstrates a great deal of nuance in his arguments in favor of philanthropy. He recognizes the disastrous effects that corruption, unfair trade policy and inefficient aid organizations can have on achieving positive outcomes. However, he consistently maintains the logic that "if it is in our power to prevent something bad from happening, without thereby sacrificing anything of comparable moral importance, we ought, morally, to do it." Some readers might agree. But Singer goes on to suggest that "doing something" can mean lots of things, but the most effective response is to donate to organizations like the Bengal Relief Fund or Oxfam because it is the best way to "provide food, shelter, and medical care" for the needs of refugees, for example (Singer, 1972).

Singer's diagnosis of the global poverty problem is quite revealing. He argues that there is a basic threshold above which people must get in order to escape the misery of poverty. Below this threshold, people are unable to educate their children, for example, which is essential to any notion of development. The wealthy can create the conditions that put the poor over the poverty threshold, which will put them on the road to economic security, education and healthcare. Eventually, the poor can move to self-sustaining economic growth and will be independent of foreign aid (Singer, 2003).

Along the way, Singer evinces signs of the problematic mental models we have discussed. Arguing along the lines of Sachs' description of the "poverty trap" ("the poor do not have the ability—by themselves—to get out of the mess" (Sachs, 2005a, p. 56)), Singer argues that outside intervention is vital for economic development. Private philanthropy is a more direct and effective way to address the conditions of the poverty trap, although aid plays an important role. Responding to the challenges to foreign aid raised in earlier chapters, Singer concedes that, naturally, there will be instances where some aid is ineffective; but, assuming it is not counterproductive, even inefficient assistance is morally superior to the "luxury spending" of the wealthy (Singer, 2006).

Singer's argument uncritically connects the "sin" of frivolous consumption at the top of the economic pyramid, the "expiation" of philanthropy and the ordinary demands of poverty-alleviation efforts at the base of the pyramid. For Singer, the driving logic of philanthropy is a function of *giving without return*, which is a very different obligation than creating sustainable solutions that effectively address the needs of the poor. So long as poverty-alleviation efforts operate in a moral universe organized around the principles of sin and expiation, new, non-paternalistic mental models such as profitable partnerships are unlikely to take root. While frivolous consumption and global poverty may overlap in some key junctures, they are separate and distinct problems that need to be treated as such. The unfortunate consequence when philanthropic effort is organized around sin and expiation is that the interests of large aid agencies do not always include the interests of the poor whom they intend to serve. A prime example is CARE's refusal to accept food aid because it suppressed local markets (Dugger, 2007).

The greatest problem with Singer's formulation is not that his moral standards are too high, but that they are too limited. They express a constrained moral imagination. Philanthropy is not and cannot be the only basis for personal or corporate involvement that results in poverty alleviation. Sustainable solutions that concretize the Millennium Development Goals (MDGs) set by the United Nations demand much more from the moral imagination—and from those who implement them—than a graduated scale of philanthropic donations that are unlikely, probably unsustainable, marginally effective in many instances, and even counterproductive in some. That is not to argue, however, that philanthropic activity has no place in poverty alleviation, but that it is certainly not the only viable approach.

In this chapter, we have developed the notion of mental models and have shown how certain biases can misconfigure solutions to poverty in untenable ways, which preclude the participatory role of MNEs through profitable partnerships. We have discussed broad classes of problematic mental models and have shown how they have penetrated important debates about global poverty, creating caricatures of the poor rather than correctly characterizing the challenges in the ultimate questions involved. Whether responding to Lonergan's biases of conceptualism or common sense, the challenges presented by the research paradox, the perception that there is a one-size-fits-all solution or the bias of paternalism, for us to make progress toward the alleviation of global poverty, these biased mindsets must be reconfigured. Moreover, if past efforts are any indicators, foreign aid and philanthropy are not sufficient to halve, much less eradicate, extreme poverty at any point in the future. The MDGs are more likely to be achieved when both MNEs *and* their potential partners begin to see that the long-range economic-growth opportunity lies in profitable partnerships at the base of the pyramid. This requires not only a recalibrated view of poverty but, as we shall see in the chapters that follow, a recalibrated perspective on corporate social responsibility as well.

4

NARRATIVES OF MULTINATIONAL FOR-PROFIT ENTERPRISES AND CORPORATE SOCIAL RESPONSIBILITY

Founded by Carlos Danel and Carlos Labarthe, Compartamos Bank of Mexico (Translated as "Let's share") was created primarily as a non-profit microfinancing financial institution modeled after the Grameen Bank of Bangladesh. Although their interest rates are high, 25% to 45% in 2007, it had lent money to over 840,000 poor microentrepreneurs, mostly women, who had no collateral with which to secure their borrowing. In April 2007, Danel and Labarthe created an initial public offering of their Compartamos Bank stock, selling 30% of their personal holdings to the public. Compartamos has consistently achieved an ROI of over 20%, at least 5 points higher than other Mexican banks. An alleged preoccupation with investor returns, however, rather than lender development has been sharply criticized by other microlending institutions, including the Grameen Bank. The worry is that the preoccupation will be about "how well the investors and microfinance institutions are doing and not about ending poverty" (Daley-Harris in Malkin, 2008). Nevertheless, Compartamos' record of reducing poverty among poor Mexican women borrowers is outstanding, and its default rate on microloans remains the lowest in the industry (Malkin, 2008).

Just as Chapter 3 exposed caricatures of the poor, so too are there caricatures of business in general, and multinational for-profit enterprises (MNEs) in particular, that skew our thinking about their roles in poverty alleviation. Distancing the for-profit venture from such biases is, therefore, crucial to imagining new and innovative solutions. In this chapter, we will show that making a profit while simultaneously and effectively working to alleviate poverty are not contradictory. By appealing to the phenomenon of mental models, an idea we developed in Chapter 3, we will show how the *separation thesis* and some contemporary conceptions of corporate social responsibility (CSR) have conspired to render inconceivable the idea that for-profit institutions could address global poverty. Only when we overcome these biases will we be able to explore productively the concept of profitable partnerships between MNEs and communities, institutions and other local and global partners seeking similar solutions. If MNEs continue, instead, to be characterized solely as exploiters or commoditized donors, and if they internalize that characterization (Gioia & Thomas, 1996) rather than defining themselves as innovative partners invested in a shared future, long-term outcomes for those enterprises and for those in poverty will not be promising.

The Red Herring of Globalization

Dialogue about the complex reality of globalization vis-à-vis the global poor has embedded within it deeply held suspicions of corporate colonialism and the privatization of "public" goods. Although these discussions rightfully expose such exploitative practices, they also preclude us from reframing the mental models that enslave the global poor to lives of economic destitution.

Perceptions of corporate involvement by environmentalists are fittingly parallel. As an early advocate for environmental rights, Thomas Berry gives a brief history of "the corporate story" in *The Great Work: Our Way Into the Future*. He defines corporations as "the organizing centers directing the discovery and use of modern science and technology in the quest for human benefit and financial gain by exploiting the living and nonliving resources of the planet" (1999, p. 118). While a charitable reading of Berry's definition might interpret "exploiting" to mean "using efficiently," it is clear from his broader critique that he is deeply concerned over what he contends to be the inherently exploitative tendencies of corporate endeavors.

Berry begins the corporation story by examining early land corporations, such as the Virginia Company, which were the arm of the property-owning elite who employed their resources to derive great wealth at the expense of a more symbiotic view of natural habitat. The need to bring goods to market created the second phase of the corporation, the canal and railroad phase, which culminated in monopolistic behavior until the advent of the oil, petrochemical and automotive industries created the third phase. After World War II, according to Berry, the corporation entered a fourth, global phase. Berry argues that a fifth, environmentally sustainable phase is imperative because the planet can no longer absorb exploitative practices.

For Berry, three conceptions of corporate activity are to blame for much of the current devastation: "corporate libertarianism," referring to the belief that law is the only constraint on corporate activity; "corporate welfare," referring to the undue allocation of public resources to support corporate activity; and "corporate colonialism," referring to the allegedly oppressive, transnational conduct of organizations such as the World Bank and International Monetary Fund (Berry, 1999). Clearly, Berry does not have a positive view of corporate activity. He hopes that corporations will enter the fifth phase of their evolution, taking seriously the challenges of an environmentally sustainable perspective, but his view of the for-profit venture per se is certainly skeptical.

Others echo Berry's skeptical view of global free enterprise and multinational corporations. Joseph Stiglitz argues in *Globalization and Its Discontents* that there is no "world government" to oversee the process of globalization. Instead, there is a system of "global governance without global government," where the World Bank, the International Monetary Fund and the World Trade Organization dominate the scene without giving voice to those most affected by their decisions (Stiglitz, 2003, p. 22). Accordingly, Stiglitz argues that participation and transparency are necessary to overcome hidden interests and overly ideological approaches to economic challenges (2003, pp. 216–227). Without adequate global governance, MNEs are free to pursue their own exclusive interests, even leveraging influence to shape foreign policy in the process. As Stephen Kinzer argues in *Overthrow: America's Century of Regime Change from Hawaii to Iraq*, "as American companies accumulated vast sugar and fruit plantations in the Pacific, Central America, and the Caribbean, they forced countless small farmers off their land" (2006, p. 106). Employing the rhetoric of liberating oppressed peoples, military interventions were in fact the coercive arm of powerful corporations operating through foreign policy; the United Fruit Company in Guatemala and the Anglo-Iranian Oil Company in Iran, for example, convinced those MNEs' close contacts in government to conduct covert operations by which to depose local governments hostile to their interests (Kinzer, 2006). We make no excuses for this sort of behavior, but, nevertheless, these examples are dated. The United Fruit Company sold its Guatemalan operations to Del Monte in 1972. The Anglo-Iranian Oil Company was a British, not an American, company that was nationalized by the Iranian government in 1951. Still, some today see the American invasion of Iraq in 2004 as part of the same narrative: big MNEs exerting undue influence on foreign policy. While such interpretations might be dismissed as overly cynical, their popularity illustrates an interpretation of globalization that cannot be overlooked when discussing for-profit contributions to poverty alleviation.

The Biases of Mental Models

Scholarly assessments like those of Berry, Stiglitz and Kinzer strongly influence current thinking about business activities and ideas about CSR. In the last chapter, we made the case that human experience is socially constructed through various mental models. These mental models have the potential to unduly bias our experiences as individuals in ways that prevent us from thinking more broadly or in fresh ways about business's role in addressing abject poverty.[1] Similarly, entire organizations function on the basis of these same mental models. Organizations make sense of themselves through mental models and use them to interpret their past, current and future actions.

One of the ways in which some MNEs frame themselves may involve defining their mission and goals as primarily economic in intent, thus virtually bracketing out any normative ethical responsibilities from consideration. For example, when Shell Oil was drilling in the Ogoni territory in Nigeria, it refused to become involved in various political debates surrounding its drilling operations. While there may have been persuasive reasons not to become involved in Nigeria's politics, a country run by a ruthless dictator at the time, Shell nevertheless depended on the Nigerian military to defend its drilling operations. Later, when one of the most vehement Nigerian critics of this oil extraction, Ken Saro-Wiwa, and eight others were executed by the Nigerian government, Shell remained silent despite the fact that its voice (and money!) could have made a difference. Shell separated its economic interests from the political climate within which it was operating (Newburry & Gladwin, 2002), and this selective framing of itself and its responsibilities resulted in disengagement from its Nigerian context, a decision not without stakeholder consequences.[2]

A second common way that MNEs frame their corporate responsibilities is to assume accountability to the communities in which they operate as a discretionary and philanthropic matter. For example, United Airlines is a large donor to the Lyric Opera of Chicago as part of its contributions to what it sees as its corporate social responsibility to that community. This is discretionary, obviously, as it is not a "responsibility" in the legal sense of the word. But United Airlines separates its central purpose and activity, commercial air travel, from its charitable activities. The former is its operational core; and United *is* required to do that well in order to survive economically, while the latter is not mandatory. In these examples, unlike the example of Compartamos Bank of Mexico with which we began the chapter, we see corporate mental models that separate economics from CSR, and instead envision CSR as philanthropy. In other words, unlike Shell and United Airlines, Compartamos saw their economic and social missions as in essential alignment. It illuminated a path out of poverty for nearly a million Mexican entrepreneurs, not by treating its contribution as charity, nor by ignoring their plight as irrelevant, nor (alternatively) by taking the entrepreneurs' economic salvation as their *raison d'être*. On the contrary, Compartamos had the imagination and foresight to see the possibilities of a union between profitability and poverty alleviation.

In what follows, we shall challenge the model of philanthropic CSR, and we shall argue that, despite well-meaning mental models on which corporate philanthropy is based, companies can reformulate who they are to better align themselves with a more globally inclusive notion of creating economic value. This reformulation depends on a well-developed corporate moral imagination, the active and deliberate processes of reconstituting operative mental models and giving new meaning to corporate thinking and responsibility. This new framework or mental model is meant to give different meanings to some aspects of an individual's or an organization's experiences or provide fresh ways to frame thinking about organizations or even systems. Because mental models are socially constructed, for organizations this implies that companies can change their mission, direction, goal orientation and operations to fit new challenges and ventures, redirect these models and give new attention to its strategy and operations.

Compartamos Bank of Mexico, for example, began as an NGO and then reformulated itself as a public for-profit bank. It now defines itself both as a micro-lender engaged in poverty reduction and also as a vibrant economic institution. Both of these activities create economic value for both shareholders and poor Mexican families. Indeed, the fact that it makes solid profits enables the bank to continue to expend its micro-loans to very poor people.

The Separation Thesis

The Shell–Nigeria case illustrates one form of corporate responsibility that requires a sharp distinction between its operations and the political/social context in which these operations take place. In this case, Shell carefully separated its operations from the Nigerian context, and thus did not engage in what we called *systems thinking* in Chapter 1. In the case of United Airlines, the company also distinguished between its operations and its environment, but took an active stance with its environment under the aegis of philanthropy. Both of these cases illustrate a view often traced to what R. E. Freeman and others have called "the separation thesis" (2006; Agle et al., 2008). The *bête noire* of the economist Milton Friedman, the separation thesis is the notion that business and ethics are two discrete subject matters that have different modes of reasoning and practice (Freeman, 2006). This translates into the persistent mental model that the function of business is economics, and ethics has no role. The implied conclusion is that for-profit companies are in business only to achieve economic value for their owner-investors, leaving the public and nonprofit sectors to serve noncommercial needs and to provide public goods. That mindset is evident in Friedman's famous article "The Social Responsibility of Business Is to Increase Its Profits," originally published in the *New York Times Magazine* in 1970; although, as we shall explain, his view has been grossly misread. Friedman begins the argument by distinguishing between a business executive, as a person who can have individual moral responsibilities, and a corporate entity, as a legal person by analogy only, and thus an entity that cannot properly have or take on such responsibilities. Companies, then, cannot be said to act; only individuals as agents for the corporation act on their behalf. Companies are formed for and by investors; thus, the executives who run these companies have fiscal responsibilities that are also predicated on moral responsibilities to be guardians of investor monies and to create returns for shareholders. While any executive can give to the charities of her choice, individually, Friedman argues that it would be tantamount to theft if corporate executives used corporate profits to serve a social good *other than* maximizing shareholder returns.

What is most important to note for our argument is the dichotomy between serving the "private" interests of shareholders and serving the "public" good, which would be "to act in some way that is not in the interest of his/her employers" (M. Friedman, 1970, p. 33). Friedman includes some interesting examples. One is a company that voluntarily reduces the price on a product, not to increase profit but, instead, in order to curb inflation that is causing economic pain to those on fixed incomes. Another is a company that decides to take on additional expenses in order to reduce pollution beyond that which is required by law. In Friedman's view, both of these instances of "social responsibility" contradict private, shareholder interest. As long as the corporation engages in open and free competition without deception or fraud within the provisos of law, culture and tradition, Friedman contends, it cannot be said to have any additional "social responsibility."

Embedded within Friedman's discussion of corporate responsibility are two distinct conceptual frameworks. Ethicist and theologian H. Richard Niebuhr uses the phrase "man-the-citizen" to signify the responsibility that each citizen has toward civil society. He juxtaposes this against the idea of "man-the-maker" that denotes the responsibility of a person as a goal-seeker, be the goal personal, financial or social in nature (Niebuhr, 1999). Extending this formulation by analogy, we have the notions of "business-as-citizen" and "business-as-maker" which are quite helpful for interpreting Friedman's argument.

For Friedman, the phrase "social responsibility" operates predominantly in a business-as-citizen framework. By voluntarily reducing price points with the aim of curbing inflation, the business-as-citizen acts foolishly by serving the public good over and against its obligations to owner/shareholders. By going beyond what the law requires in curbing pollution, the business-as-citizen acts contrary to its own interests, acquiring an undue burden that is more properly addressed by those who govern. Paying taxes and obeying the law are primary duties of citizenship that must be embraced by any corporation; however, it is foolish to go beyond what is minimally required of citizenship because doing so often conflicts with the fiduciary responsibilities of the corporate venture.

The notion of business-as-maker fundamentally reformulates and gives new meaning to Friedman's social responsibility argument. Under this rubric, businesses as makers do not have a citizenship obligation imposed on them from the outside. Rather, they pursue various ends as part of their mission and strategy. By successfully engaging in creative activity, that is, by providing jobs, goods and services in light of limited resources and abilities, businesses *inherently* serve markets and thus serve many social needs. In this construction, there is no substantive distinction between the strategic pursuit of profit and the pursuit of social ends. The railroad monopolies of the early 20th century illustrate this notion of social responsibility well. As Friedman himself argues, it was not regulation that effectively ended the railroad monopolies, but the emergence of less expensive road and air transport (M. Friedman, 2002). Joseph Schumpeter uses the phrase "creative destruction" to describe this process, where new innovations disrupt and unseat established technology that is not effectively serving markets (Schumpeter, 1950). Whether, in the early 20th century, the upstart Ford Motor Company had "the public good" in mind or whether it was merely responding to new market opportunities as its aim when it promised "a Ford in every garage" is academic to the moral pragmatist. What Ford did with its limited resources in light of its core competencies is far more important. The pursuit of social goods, in this understanding, is a creative, dynamic process inexorably intertwined with economics, although it is economics that motivates corporate decision making. Thus, by this reading of Friedman, Compartamos is a company that is both interested in investor returns *and* in reducing poverty through micro-lending; and these should not be separated. Indeed, the founders of Compartamos argue that its approach enables the bank to generate more capital availability for more loans, thus increasing its poverty-reducing initiatives while still making money for its investors. Each objective is indeed *reliant* on the other. Recent research by Bird et al. reinforces this conclusion; "indeed, the capacity of a firm to generate sustainable wealth over time, and hence its long-term value, is determined by its relationships with critical stakeholders" (Bird, Hall, Momentè & Reggiani, 2007, p. 191).

R. E. Freeman and Brad Agle suggest a conceptual alignment here between stakeholder theory and a more traditional shareholder focus that might otherwise be seen to preclude CSR activities. As Agle explains,

> [t]he primary responsibility of an executive is to create as much value as possible for stakeholders because that is how you create as much value for shareholders. Where there is a conflict between stakeholders and shareholders, executives have to rethink the problem so that the interests go together. No stakeholder interest stands alone here. Where interests conflict, the job of the manager is to figure out how to redefine things so as to create more value for both ... without resorting to trade-offs, or fraud and deception (Agle et al., 2008, p. 166).

An example of the Freeman–Agle conception is the Sustainable Tree Crops Programs Alliance (STCP), a public–private partnership. STCP is a coalition between NGOs and three global companies that works to improve the economic stature and environmental sustainability of small cocoa farmers. Membership in STCP ranges from the US Agency for International Development (USAID) to members of the World Cocoa Foundation and includes MNEs such as Hershey, Nestlé and Kraft Foods (STCP, 2008). Since cocoa is the most important tree-based commodity in West Africa, it provides a livelihood for millions of small-scale family farmers. However, deforestation, fungal diseases and insects have destroyed a third of the annual crop in the past, and significant market inefficiencies have hampered the livelihood of small farmers. Not only has STCP improved the quality and availability of cocoa beans through shade-crop biodiversity methods, but it has also solved some of the problems that historically have dogged the industry such as crop disease, insect infestation and inadequate crop rotation. Moreover, by linking farmers to markets through producer organizations, STCP opened access to global markets and freed farmers from the price exploitation that often victimized them. Ultimately, the members of STCP realized that the future of the chocolate business is directly linked to the future of rural families growing cocoa. STCP was not a grand social plan; it was merely a collaborative partnership by multi-sector organizations who all shared a mutual objective: the desire to empower rural families.

Clearly, the corporate partners that chose to join STCP did not participate solely as an exercise of their civic duties. Rather, membership in the partnership made sense as a viable vehicle by which to satisfy their shareholders' interests. Indeed, what made the STCP partnership so attractive was that it was a sustainable mechanism whereby *all* stakeholder interests could be advanced. The NGO partners could claim a social return; the farmers benefited from technological assistance otherwise unavailable to them; and the shareholders of Hershey, Nestlé and Kraft could enjoy satisfactory returns: a *profitable partnership* for many affected stakeholders who share a vested interest in the relationship and a commitment based on aligned strategic objectives, the model we advocate in this book.

The "Great Trade-Off Illusion"

Today, even with the growing focus on CSR, however defined, the separation thesis still persists as a bias (McKinsey Report, 2006). Journalists and business critics continue to treat benevolent corporate behavior only as a deviation from the allegedly miserly, selfish actions that otherwise are deemed "normal." This thinking is evidence of what Stuart Hart calls a "great trade-off illusion" (2007). To illustrate, because the "public good" of environmental protection is commonly seen within a public policy or regulatory framework, there is a strong sense that pollution is the necessary by-product of corporate activity. This "end-of-pipe" thinking pits the for-profit venture against the public good of environmental protection. When conceived this way, the biased mental model of the separation thesis persists. The business-as-citizen is required to comply with costly legal regulations that limit its profitability.

However, beginning with the "greening revolution" of the late 1980s and early 1990s, many business executives began to see the business venture in a new light, with sustainability as *strategically* important for future economic corporate growth (Hart, 2007). Taking this concept even further is the radical "cradle-to-cradle approach" advanced by William McDonough. McDonough advocates a maxim, "waste equals food," to argue that everything produced ultimately ought to be either recycled or reused. Framing environmental sustainability in this way, McDonough raises the possibility that profitability can be aligned with an environmentally "green" approach. Quite aside from respecting the rights of future generations, McDonough points out that using fewer new raw materials can generate massive corporate profits as well (McDonough & Baungart, 2002). This is precisely the type of thinking necessary to obliterate the separation thesis.

Sadly, however, the social benefits of for-profit ventures are often viewed with incredulity and caution by both the media and the general public (*BusinessWeek* Harris Poll, 2000). Consider, for example, the presence of so-called "vulture funds," investment firms that snatch up a poor country's debt and use the courts to sue and harass debtors until the debts are repaid (Bosco, 2007). While some poverty activists see this practice as exploitative of the poor, others see it as pro-poor. The public scrutiny of courtrooms exerts top-down pressure on governments, while the economic leverage exercised by investment firms can induce political reform. Those opposed to "vulture funds" often fail to see that investment funds might be better positioned than public institutions to exert necessary pressure on corrupt governments. Furthermore, while the campaign for debt relief has honorable intentions, some economists argue that it has the perverse incentive of rewarding corrupt governments. Thus, the net effect of vulture funds may contribute significant "public good," in spite of the moniker "vulture" attached to it.

Corporate–NGO Dialectic

Klaus Leisinger, President and CEO of the Novartis Foundation, argues that many NGOs are seduced by an anti-globalization narrative that impugns for-profit ventures, especially those associated with MNEs. These narratives portray a story that MNEs are too big and too powerful to attend effectively to the needs of the poor. The narratives are reinforced by the misdeeds of a few corporate wrongdoers, which in turn reinforce the bias that MNEs are the primary agents of social and ecological ills. Without completely understanding the extraordinarily complex global networks within which MNEs must operate, NGO activists and others can include indiscriminately legitimate and potentially transformative for-profit ventures in their broad indictment. Accused of hidden market agendas, self-serving public relations and greedy motives, even well-intentioned corporate *philanthropy* is viewed with great suspicion (Leisinger, 2007b). Worse, when these criticisms are taken seriously by MNEs, their response is often simply to withdraw from those markets. For example, those companies in the pharmaceutical industry that provide HIV/AIDS drugs have been criticized for not doing enough in the way of donating their products to areas of high-density need such as the continent of Africa where HIV is a raging pandemic. Albeit, critics claim, rather belatedly (e.g., Angell, 2004), today all major HIV/AIDS drugs-producing companies are working on the ground in various parts of Africa to distribute their products at below cost or free. Yet, even those massive efforts have gone unappreciated and there is still suspicion that these companies have ulterior motives in these engagements (Werhane, 2002; Friedman, den Besten & Attaran, 2003). Had this pandemic been less virulent, these companies might never have entered or would have withdrawn from these arenas.

Let us consider an example of the reinforcement of these biases and the difficult task of transforming our mental models toward a trust in *profitable partnerships*. Some years ago Shell Oil decided to dismantle at sea and sink to the ocean floor one of its North Sea oil rigs, the Brent Spar. Greenpeace, an NGO well-known for drawing attention to corporate environmental disasters, fought mightily against this dismantling, arguing that the toxic waste in the oil rig would create environmental havoc in the North Sea. Shell countered, explaining that sinking the rig would be less toxic than towing it to shore and dismantling it there. It turned out that sinking the rig was, in fact, the "least worst" option, environmentally. The problem was that neither Greenpeace nor Shell initially did careful scientific studies of the toxic effects of sinking versus dismantling the rig on shore, so the debate was framed as "good guys" (Greenpeace) vs. "bad guys" (Shell) without sound data to back either contention (Kirby, 1998). Notice that one's mental models about how these decisions are made impacted how one framed this scenario, which created different perceptions about the proper treatment of the rig, which then affected thinking about the proper disposal of the rig, and tainted Shell's image in the short run.

We suggest that concern over corporate *intentions* is a major diversion from what truly matters: the development of jobs, products and services that alleviate poverty, whatever their source or motivation. So long as mental models based on the dichotomy between private interest and public good persist, however, profitability will continue to be viewed as antithetical to sustainable poverty alleviation (*The Economist*, 2008a). Too often, NGO activists configure poverty reduction, environmental sustainability and other social goods as achievable only through nonprofit ("good guy") entities and perceive profitable partnerships as a contradiction in terms. The examples in this section demonstrate that this is a biased point of view that often influences the mental models that we use to approach corporate poverty-alleviation initiatives.

What is Left of Corporate Social Responsibility?[3]

The separation thesis makes it tempting to conclude that companies have no social responsibilities to the communities in which they operate except through their economic activities aimed at increasing profitability. Thus, if an MNE operates in less-developed countries, they may, but need not, contribute to that community. Interestingly, however, despite Friedman's arguments to the contrary, in the last 15 years we have seen CSR as a growing priority for global executives since external pressure to be perceived as a good citizen has significant implications for the bottom line (e.g., *The Economist*, 2008a; Politeia, 2007, 2008), as well as for the mental models under which those executives are expected to perform. The result is that some CEOs attend closely to brand image and to risk management in trying to succeed in the marketplace. In this century, scandals at Enron, WorldCom and elsewhere have made branding as a socially responsible firm even more challenging. In addition, "smart mobs" of NGOs and activists regularly battle against any business they perceive as exploitative. But, what does the expression "CSR" mean, and how far should a firm go in holding to Milton Friedman's conclusion that the only social responsibility of a company is to its investors? Recall our opening example of the Compartamos Bank of Mexico. With relatively high interest rates, it has been able to reap quite a profit for its investors, but it has been subject to harsh criticism as well. Has it overstepped some invisible line relating to CSR, especially when the world's poor are involved?

CSR has many definitions, and each suggests a slightly different mental model that subsequently influences corporate thinking and behavior. Beginning in the 1970s, CSR was defined in terms of "business and society," in which businesses had a responsibility to the societies in which they operated. For instance, according to Davis and Blomstom, "[corporate] social responsibility is the obligation of decision makers to take actions which protect and improve the welfare of society as a whole, along with their own interests" (Davis & Blomstom, 1975, p. 23). Later, Archie Carroll expanded that definition as follows, "[t]he social responsibility of business encompasses the economic, legal, ethical and discretionary expectations that society has of organizations at a given point in time" (Carroll, 1979, p. 500).

There are two problems with these early definitions.[4] First, there is an almost exclusive focus on the relationship between business and society at large, neglecting the relationships between businesses and its specific stakeholders such as the employees, customers, suppliers and shareholders who directly account for, and depend on, company success or failure. Second, these definitions sometimes misidentified CSR with *discretionary investments* the company made to the communities in which companies operate, i.e., with forms of philanthropy or community welfare, rather than activities for which they may be held *responsible* (as in corporate social *responsibility*). The result was that companies who engaged in such practices aimed to be considered "socially responsible," despite what they did commercially in the marketplace. Enron, for example, was a large donor to the city of Houston and to a number of religious institutions to which its executives belonged. Using a mental model based on these CSR conceptions, companies can "do good" and are thus socially responsible as a separate matter from how they operate—a fig leaf to cover what may not be acceptable management practices.

Since 2001, new thinking has developed about CSR. However, some corporate practices cling to vestiges of the separation thesis. For example, it is noteworthy that many CSR programs are housed in corporate communications or public-relations departments, something that separates CSR from the core corporate operations. This placement creates and reinforces the idea that CSR is fundamentally a reputation, risk and/or brand management activity (*The Economist*, 2008a). Accordingly, CSR initiatives in various forms are seen as helping to reduce both real and potential damage to the brand (and the bottom line) that comes from a poor public image or crisis in the business environment. In addition, there is the impression that CSR is a defensive strategy against the increasing threat of legal action as the number and extent of regulatory bodies increases. Clearly, these practices are not in harmony with a corporation having social responsibilities.

When CSR is framed merely as a form of risk or brand management, firms tend to adopt a CSR posture that is defensive and reactive. Not only do glossy CSR reports frequently result in compliance and audit fatigue (*The Economist*, 2008a), they can also divert attention to CSR programs that stray from the organization's core competence resulting in efforts that are "too unfocused" or "too shotgun." Even worse, they can lead to efforts that result in some senior executive's pet project that is tangential at best to the business (*The Economist*,

2008a). If such a project does not emerge from or engage the corporation's *raison d'être*, it can neither maximize its effectiveness nor be said to be morally good in a substantive use of the term.

If CSR is merely risk or brand management, there are other significant problems. Simply put, which conception of social responsibility takes priority? Should a firm invest in solutions to social problems? Should it instead take a social stance that intelligently manages the risks associated with, for example, environmental disaster or terrorist attacks? Or should it mind its image as a good corporate citizen? As presently conceived, CSR does not define a coherent, global set of shared priorities. A global survey of "the things that matter" indicates that executives in Brazil, Russia, India and China (BRIC nations) do not share the same perceptions of what issues will be most important to business in the future (*The Economist*, 2008a). While concerns about the environment rates first or second in priority in the United States and BRIC countries, health-care benefits range from a first priority in the United States to eighth in Brazil. Thus, if an MNE concentrates on brand and reputation, it will emphasize health-care in the United States and the environment in Brazil. For a truly global company, therefore, CSR cannot operate under one global strategy (*The Economist*, 2008a, p. 11). Therefore, CSR as brand management does not help business determine how to allocate its limited resources. It is hard to imagine how a potluck of disjointed CSR initiatives serves the interests of either the firm or the affected communities in any substantive way other than in ephemeral matters of appearance and image.

Since our concern is with the alleviation of global poverty, these formulations of CSR will simply not do. In contrast, we argue that a more meaningful way to make sense of CSR is to frame it as follows. When the reasons for engaging in CSR are not a direct extension of a company's business model, the possibilities that they will have a positive societal benefit are artificially limited, and this is certainly the case with poverty. Early formulations of CSR as discretionary, philanthropic or image enhancing constrain the way in which for-profit ventures think about poverty. Since, from this point of view, CSR is rather transitory, investments can be pulled out of a poverty-alleviation project any time that priorities may shift. And, more importantly, because this viewpoint separates corporate operations with creating economic value from the communities in which they operate, CSR investments do not benefit from the synergies that make the corporation otherwise successful. For example, Enron's donations to religious institutions in Houston in no way leveraged Enron's special talents in its energy business nor, we would suggest, enhanced the religious dimensions of those churches and synagogues that it supported.

As long as the separation thesis continues to creep into our thinking and practices and thereby creates an artificial dichotomy between the private interest of profit and the public good of beneficence, such separation of various corporate responsibilities will continue to thwart meaningful poverty-alleviation efforts by MNEs. Unfortunately, CSR as discretionary philanthropy, or as risk or brand management, does not begin to address the innovative ways for-profit ventures can contribute to poverty alleviation. Business's most useful contribution to society—as originally articulated by Friedman—is to make profits and products. By doing so in partnership with others, it may be most effectively positioned both to alleviate poverty through its synergies and expertise and to thereby reap value for its shareholders (*The Economist*, 2008c).

More important than whether CSR is discretionary, philanthropic or simply responsive to risks and brand threats, is this net effect on global poverty alleviation. While glossy pictures of sporadic philanthropy may build pride among employees and appease critics, one of the greatest impacts a company has on poverty is by simply employing people. When Oxfam and Unilever did a joint study of the economic impact of Unilever's operations in Indonesia, the results were very impressive. Unilever employed 300,000 people full-time, created US$630 million in total value to the Indonesian economy, and paid US$130 million a year in taxes (*The Economist*, 2008a). Unilever's Indonesian operations were not a philanthropic venture. It simply expanded its operations into a new community, trusting that Indonesians would be good workers. It trained these workers and paid them decent wages, and created economic value for the workers through wages, for the community through taxes and for itself through profits.

Contemporary formulations of CSR are more consistent with a corporate role in alleviating poverty, but may create other difficulties. For example, Chandler (2001) defines CSR as "the responsibility of a company for the *totality* of its impact." In this rubric, CSR encompasses responsibilities to one's primary stakeholders: employees, customers, suppliers and shareholders, as well as to almost any other individual, institution, culture or society which a company may affect or be affected by this expansive definition of value creation, which may also include corporate obligations to the natural environment, the public sector, governments and NGOs, and its global impact, broadly construed. Here, CSR could turn into an umbrella term to cover almost every possible obligation, concern, effect, responsibility or discretion that an organization might encounter, including myriad externalities resulting from corporate behavior or omission. In our view, this more modern definition asks too much of companies and allows us to blame them for all the world's ills. Returning to the pharmaceutical industry and HIV/AIDS medications, there are approximately 30 million people in sub-Saharan Africa alone who are infected with HIV. If companies with these drugs gave them away to 30 million people without any financial assistance, these companies would be bankrupt and would have to go out of business. So, while their involvement in this disease is critical, it is unconscionable to ask them to solve this pandemic single-handedly. Instead, Porter and Kramer (2006) contend that

> corporations are not responsible for all the world's problems, nor do they have the resources to solve them all. Each company can identify the *particular set* of societal problems that it is *best equipped* to help resolve and from which it can gain the best competitive benefit (2006, p. 92; italics added).

Corporate *Moral* Responsibilities: Another Mental Model

One of the difficulties of CSR is the terminology itself—the use of the term "social" implies that CSR should focus primarily on social ventures, as if these were distinct from a firm's core mission and competencies. Sometimes we expect too much of companies, because of their economic largesse; other times we let them off the hook when we perhaps should not. These expectations, or lack thereof, are particularly true when we focus only on a corporation's external social responsibilities, or when we confuse moral obligations with more discretionary responsibilities.

A more substantive approach to CSR defines corporate social responsibility as a firm's *moral* responsibilities to those whom it directly affects or is affected by. This way of thinking about CSR "emphasizes the moral obligations of the corporation toward various stakeholders (employees, customers, suppliers, shareholders, and local community)" (D'Orazio, 2008). Since we are creating a new set of responsibilities, we have to be rather precise. Individuals and, secondarily, companies, because they are made up of and operated by individuals, are morally responsible under any one of five conditions.

- First, they are morally responsible when they make choices as opposed to being coerced.
- Second, they are morally responsible when they intend a certain result to occur (even if it does not) or cause an action to occur out of their own choices even sometimes when the result was involuntary.
- Third, they are morally responsible when, within their abilities and capacities, they could have prevented harm or, sometimes, improved a situation.
- Fourth, moral responsibility arises when a firm has adequate information and more than one alternative and thus could have made another choice.
- And finally, companies, like individuals, are morally responsible for outcomes of their actions.[5]

Corporate *moral* responsibility (CMR), then, refers to obligations a firm has as a result of its existence, its reasons for existence, its scope and nature of operations, and its various interactions or relationships. These obligations are formulated as obligations a company *should* have to those whom it affects and to those who constitute the company itself. This includes its most affected stakeholders, one of which, of course, is its shareholders, as well as its employees and managers, customers and suppliers, and its obligations to communities in which it operates. Note that these are normative obligations—they spell out what a company *should* do, how it should respect its various stakeholders and create value, how it should create benefits and not further damage communities or the environment, and how and in what ways it should be or is obliged to promote further social, economic and environmental well-being within the scope of its operations and capabilities. This formulation connects corporate expertise with a broad sense of responsibility *without diminishing its abilities to be profitable*, without contending that companies are responsible for all global disasters, and without claiming that companies should be endlessly philanthropic.

Let us proceed with caution, however. We are not claiming that being philanthropic is a bad idea. Rather, we are making two other claims. First, a claim surrounding a capacity issue and reminiscent of the Porter and Kramer position, above: no company can solve all problems, even those within its scope of expertise, such as the pharmaceutical industry and responsibility in connection with the HIV/AIDS pandemic. Second, we claim that every company does have a set of capabilities. If those capabilities are funneled into what it does best, most companies will accomplish their need to be profitable and their responsibilities to the communities in which they operate. For example, while no pharmaceutical company, by itself, can handle the entire HIV pandemic, by working with

71

other pharmaceutical companies, with NGOs, with communities and foundations, the pandemic can be addressed; and, in fact, this model is one that many companies, including Merck in partnership with the Gates Foundation, have already established in Botswana. By focusing attention on what it does best, developing drugs, Merck is able to channel its efforts widely, within the scope of its capabilities, capacity and expertise.

Firms should be wary, however, of extending their sense of corporate responsibilities too broadly and allowing it to encompass anything which the firm might even peripherally be involved in or affect. In engaging in such an extension, firms may also be extending their power base and influence far beyond the reasons for which they were created and chartered in the first place. One will recall that the British East India Company, chartered in 1600 by Queen Elizabeth I, was allowed almost unlimited privileges. Eventually, this led to the British colonization of most of what today is India, Pakistan and Bangladesh, not without negative consequences to a diverse set of cultures and customs in those areas. The deleterious effects the Company created for the Asian subcontinent are still evident today (Robins, 2006). That was a mistake worth not repeating.

Still, one of the criticisms of reconfiguring CSR to CMR is that the new formulation is too narrow and preoccupied with primary stakeholder relationships as opposed to sustaining a robust understanding of the complex networks of relationships that unavoidably exist between a company and its communities (Painter-Morland, 2007). A better term might be merely "corporate responsibility," a term that embraces all those to whom a company is accountable without asking too much or too little. This term works well with the systems approach that we introduced in Chapter 1. As we explored there at length, there are a number of effective reasons why a systems approach is a worthwhile approach for thinking through MNE responsibilities and the problem of global poverty. First, all organizations including MNEs, NGOs, foundations, aid agencies and local governments operate in a global system of various complex networks and relationships. It is to their peril that organizations should fail to take into account those who affect and are affected by their choices and actions, i.e., their internal and external stakeholders. In considering its future, Shell has demonstrated an evident preference for an alternative approach to its business practices, one that now takes into account the national politics, drilling locations and perception by both local and global stakeholders, a preference that might have impacted the outcome of its experience in Nigeria(Newburry & Gladwin, 1997/2002; Guyon, 1997). Systems thinking involves adapting to multiple perspectives and trying to understand the mindset of each group of stakeholders from their particular points of view. Second, a systems perspective brings into focus the responsibilities as well as rights of various stakeholders, not merely the poor, but all the individuals and organizations who affect and who are affected by others. Third, a systems approach forces each of us and each institution to consider its multiple relationships. Because we are all affected by even remote events, this perspective encourages companies to think about the future of a sustainable global economy, even if it is only for the survival and well-being of companies, our mutual political economies and our offspring. Thus, MNEs can reframe themselves as global players with a networked range of moral and social responsibilities; and, indeed, they must impact positively these mental models to dissipate the biases in order to be viable partners in many areas of the world where they operate.

We suggest further that, only when CSR is equated with corporate *moral* responsibility and linked operationally to what a company does most effectively and efficiently, taking into account the networks and systems in which a company operates, can the collaborative partnerships and innovative solutions to global poverty become part of the global strategic landscape. In the last chapter of this volume, we will argue that the *only* way in which the executive of this century will survive is to ensure that her firm is viewed as a viable partner in the innovative, imaginative opportunities that are and will become available in tomorrow's expanding global markets. By creating profitable partnerships, the MNE is serving a variety of disparate but key stakeholders, striving toward the creation of a transformative mental model and earning trust. But this requires framing the corporate mission and direction in an intentional effort to take into account this sort of partnership.

Conclusion

While Compartamos is a significantly profitable bank, it is also extremely successful in lending money to poor people, which helps them out of poverty. It does not have low-interest-rate loans, but it provides cheaper money than other credit sources in Mexico; and it lends to those who otherwise have no access to capital. Compartamos sees its responsibilities as creating economic value for *both* its poor Mexican customers and its shareholders. It is an example of what we would call a *morally risky venture.* It is engaging in good through its loans, and the bank has a very low default rate. But, by charging high interest rates, it is more profitable than most other Mexican banks. In an ideal world, we might want this bank to provide lower-interest loans to the very poor, but, in such a world there might not be any lenders. So, the existence of firms such as Compartamos presents us with a compromise—a moral compromise—and we can make sense of its projects in that way. But, to condemn it outright is not a viable or productive position. That, too, is a biased mental model that is unacceptable morally, as well.

5

GLOBAL POVERTY AND MORAL IMAGINATION

Cemex is a global manufacturer of cement and other building materials with headquarters in Mexico. Cemex leadership had the idea to attempt to distribute cement products to about 2.5 million impoverished residents of Guadalajara, Mexico, who live in extremely crowded and unfinished housing in and around the city. Without the support of any real civic, societal or economic infrastructure, it would require a typical homebuilder over a year to construct a single room and *over 13 years* to finish a modest, four-room dwelling.

Inspired by that idea, Cemex created "Patrimonio Hoy,"[1] a program through which Cemex offered financing to very low-income families (households with incomes of less than US$5 per day) with which to build or to expand their homes. In order to qualify for the financing, customers were required to participate in savings groups, each comprising three "partners," and each with well-established rules to aid the partners throughout the borrowing process. In return, participants in the program were offered technical assistance, educational programs, guaranteed quality materials and delivery, guaranteed prices and free storage of materials.

On Cemex's part, it has earned a foothold in a market previously unexplored by them, and in a market that will become increasingly critical as the markets at the top of the pyramid experience saturation. Low-income homebuilders' use of cement has tripled, from an average of 2,300 pounds consumed once every four years, to the same amount being consumed in 15 months, increasing the demand for programs like Patrimonio Hoy (Herbst, 2002). Originally, Cemex had searched for opportunities to respond to those at the BoP in a socially responsible way, but also in a way that allowed them to survive, to flourish and to enhance their long-term financial performance. Because of Patrimonio Hoy, Cemex reported a profit of US$1.5 million by the end of 2005 and anticipated expansion into Colombia, Venezuela, Egypt and the Philippines (Johnson & Nhon, 2005). Notwithstanding a relatively low profit margin, Cemex continued to thrive, demonstrated by the 2007 year-end price target set by Morgan Stanley of US$80, or 55% above its 2005 level (Wall, 2006).

Up to this point, our argument has focused on those limited mental models that are not conducive to profitable partnerships but which nevertheless strive to alleviate poverty and to achieve the United Nations Millennium Development Goals (MDGs). This chapter describes one practice that succeeds in overcoming this problem—engagement in the process of *moral imagination*. Profitable partnerships are not meant to replace or to supersede other proven poverty-alleviation efforts (London, 2007); therefore, our starting point is where new solutions address the unmet needs of the poor. Because many of the problems facing the global poor demand a sense of urgency, the search for sustainable solutions cannot be fettered by ideological bias or utopian social engineering that is overly and exceptionally patient for results. The focus on innovation in profitable partnerships is not a mere affinity for "newness," but a basic realization that the MDG aspirations require much more than what already exists. Simply put, the MDG aspirations require a great deal of moral imagination to get beyond the limiting mental models that we have discussed.

Moral Imagination

Moral imagination can be defined as

> a necessary ingredient of responsible moral judgment [that entails] ... the ability to discover, evaluate and act upon possibilities not merely determined by a particular circumstance, or limited by a set of operating mental models, or merely framed by a set of rules or rule-governed concerns (Werhane, 1999a, p. 93).

Moral imagination entails the ability to escape from defective mental models that dominate a particular situation, to envision new possibilities that are not so contextually dependent, and to evaluate and act on those possibilities. The importance of moral imagination resides in the following idea: within organizations—especially profit-driven corporations—managers who strive for success and excellence in many cases find themselves in a cognitive trap, where only a narrow, partial perspective seems possible. In such cases, managers' interpretation of reality can become distorted and their ability to exercise moral judgment is impeded. As a result, managers make decisions that are far less ethical than others expect of them and that, on reflection, they would expect of themselves. In the worst of such scenarios this may degenerate into something clinical psychologists call the *neurotic* "search of glory" (Horney, 1950) where managers tend to confuse reality with a self-created world of fiction characterized by collective *folie á deux* processes, such as forms of illusion of grandeur or depressive delusion of persecution (Kets De Vries, 1980). As a result, managerial decision making becomes biased by unreasonable optimism about the future, inconsistency in risk taking and excessive confidence in personal skills (Kahneman & Lovallo, 1993; Camerer & Lovallo, 1999).

In the now-famous case of Enron, this kind of managerial delusion was evident in the assumption that business is a game, one to be played aggressively, despite its effects on the well-being of its customers or the communities in which it operated. The result was a narrowly focused agenda on trading futures, capturing markets and on beating the competition. Even profit making played a secondary role to the lust for power and to the control of these markets. Enron managers never seemed to ask the question: who are we and what are we doing to ourselves and to others (McLean & Elkind, 2004)?

Commitments Necessary to Activate Moral Imagination

Moral imagination is a fundamental, indispensable and strategic asset in countering these delusional tendencies. Its exercise leads to an environment where ethical decision making does not require the exercise of exceptional moral talents nor does it constitute something tapped only after everything else because the circumstances are so extraordinary. Instead, moral imagination creates a secure, stable reliability similar to an "Intel Inside®" component in decision-making processes. Activating moral imagination requires at least three commitments.

1. Disengagement from the Context

First, one must try to disengage from the particular issue and its context in order to search for what mindsets are at play. Ethical failures are often the result not of weak moral development or a lack of understanding of what is right or wrong, but rather of a poor awareness of the moral implications and social consequences of "business decisions"[2] (Moberg & Seabright, 2000; Forge, 2004). This means asking questions such as:

- What is motivating the decision makers in this context?
- How do the corporate culture and its traditions play a role in this context?
- What conflicts are at stake?
- Is anyone who is involved in the decision-making process over-confident or deluded by a distorted or biased perspective?

Throughout this process, decision makers need to be guided by their imagination to appreciate the complex circumstances of reality that they are facing. By disengaging from the context of the issue they are facing they will be less inclined to underestimate salient aspects—for example, the ethical implications—involved in the decision they face.

2. Delving into Possibilities

The second commitment required to practice moral imagination involves exploring a diversity of possible alternatives while maintaining ethical norms in the forefront of one's thinking. Relevant questions here include:

- What are some new alternatives in approaching this issue?
- What societal, corporate and personal values are at stake?
- How do moral standards and norms apply here?

At this juncture, moral imagination can be seen as activating the thought process required to intelligently apply ethical standards. By going back and forth between the specific case at hand and more general principles, between the details of the issue and the organization's mission and values, between the local culture, social norms and traditions and more abstract personal values and moral principles, managers think through the issues they are facing in the context of relevant ethical standards. This does not mean that managers engaging in this process will have to deny practical demands and parochial interests. On the contrary, they will start from there but will put these contextual elements under moral scrutiny, aiming to align their "considered judgments" duly pruned and adjusted to relevant ethical standards (Collier, 2006).

3. Focus on Consequences

The third set of commitments required of moral imagination concerns practical issues. Here, each alternative is subjected to questions such as:

- Can the consequences be described in concrete, operational terms?
- What are the consequences, negative and positive, for all the stakeholders involved?
- Do the relevant stakeholders have relationships between them that should be taken into account?
- What sort of precedent is this decision setting? Would we expect all our managers to emulate this action or behavior? Would we expect other companies to engage in this activity?

Developing practical consequential sensitivity of this kind is crucial to behaving ethically. Too often in modern corporations, managers find themselves trapped in narrow decision-making frameworks, biased by short-term pressures that burden their roles and responsibilities. Accordingly, they drift into thinking that objectifies others and fails to integrate an adequate appreciation of social norms and ethical principles that govern how they should be treated (Moberg, 2006). Moral imagination allows managers to connect more broadly with the globalized world, to "feel a concern for the welfare of others"—or to take into consideration the impacts of corporate action on both the internal and external organization's stakeholders (Werhane, 1999a).

To see a demonstration of moral imagination at work, let us look more closely at Cemex. Obviously, decision makers at Cemex did not fall prey to a mental model focused merely on penetrating the cement market by offering building products at a price that would have resulted in a handsome profit. Had that been the case, the impoverished population of Guadalajara would have remained to Cemex an anonymous, faceless market segment eager to participate in clearing the market at Cemex's price. Moral imagination at Cemex supplanted this mental model with one that:

- questioned the mindset that the poor are poor financial risks;
- expanded the range of viable possibilities and customer base;
- defined the target market in human and identifiable terms;
- considered corporate social responsibility (CSR) and financial performance mutually compatible; and
- challenged the inflexibility of institutional structure at the base of the pyramid (BoP).

On this final point, rather than accepting their customer base as a set of independent actors acting in isolation, Cemex organized them into something like cooperatives with more purchasing power, but also with more capacity for mutual support. This is an excellent example of how moral imagination transforms institutional structure in the developing world to be seen not only as a work in progress, but also as one that may be subject to the process of rudimentary institution building. If the institutional field has gaps, new institutions can be created and, if corrupt institutions dominate the field, investments can be made in grass-roots campaigns that provide viable alternatives. In the case of Cemex, very poor residents faced the prodigious task of creating inhabitable structures with no institutional support whatsoever. Even if they could afford to purchase materials, they could rarely do so in quantities that allowed them to make any meaningful progress on their structures; and, the lack of storage meant that any unused materials were subject to wear, deterioration and theft. Without knowledge of building codes and basic design parameters, residents found themselves caught between corrupt building inspectors, on the one hand, and unsafe domiciles on the other. By making partnerships a condition of sale, Cemex helped to create the institutional infrastructure that mitigated these possibilities.

Moral Imagination and Mental Models

Engaging in moral imagination can help decision makers to disengage and to critically evaluate the kinds of narrow mental models that we discussed in Chapter 3: those that bias our views about the poor toward helpless, uneducated victims. Moral imagination can help us to evaluate what we mean by CSR and to disengage decision makers from imagining that public policy and philanthropy alone can achieve the MDGs, as we outlined in Chapter 4. One of the ways to overcome these mental models is to think of each stakeholder as an individual person or a group of individuals, ensuring that stakeholders do not become anonymous.

By considering each stakeholder as an individual with a compelling life story, morally imaginative decision makers take the moral status of each very seriously rather than disengaging from their plights as faceless strangers. This strategy stands in stark contrast to the tendency to treat stakeholders as members of a collective whose identity is defined only by the formal role they play. Instead of being catalogued and stereotyped as "employees," "customers," "suppliers," "shareholders" or "community," they are instead perceived as unique persons with names and faces, in effect humanizing relationships and transactions (McVea & Freeman, 2005). This process not only makes the life narratives of stakeholders both vivid and undeniable, but it also helps to create a sense of the other person, even a stranger, as a self (Benhabib, 1992). The mental model of stakeholders as instruments and objects to be exploited then becomes literally inconceivable. Action grammar is based on the first person plural, "we." Cemex treated its customers as individual, named partners who were personally capable of working within a system of rules and acting as a trustworthy partner.

Moral imagination also challenges mental models based on what Freeman calls the *separation thesis*. It renders artificial the classic debate between financial performance, on the one hand, and CSR on the other. Instead, it aims for the satisfaction of all of the firm's relevant stakeholders, whether they are owners of stock, employees, customers, suppliers or members of the broader social community. Moreover, as we shall argue at length below, moral imagination can be useful in developing a systems perspective, a view discussed in Chapter 1, and a perspective that is critical on a shrinking planet with expanding globalization. Rather than justifying this position with hackneyed arguments about the long run, moral imagination seeks pragmatic solutions to stakeholder calculus (Freeman, 2002). Cemex did not offer charity to the citizens of Guadalajara; instead, it created a system of business transactions that employed its expertise in construction and integrated competitive advantage with what it considered to be its strategic CSR (Porter & Kramer, 2006).

Moral imagination is especially effective in dealing with the problems of the global poor. It enables individuals, organizations and public policy makers to get beyond the set of biases that plague both those working in economic development and those pursuing for-profit ventures at the BoP. Robert Chambers (1989) argues that non-locals frequently have harshly distorted views of the global poor. Outsiders usually have little or no personal contact with the poor, so they rely on assumptions based on limited data from surveys and area experts. Even when they take the time to engage in dialogues with the poor, these interactions tend to be brief and under-representative, so conclusions reached often reflect culture, gender, age and myriad other stereotypes. So-called objective information about the poor is severely limited. Those who willingly respond to surveys do not always speak for the silent ones who are unable or unwilling to speak to a stranger in public. Interview data are only slightly more reliable. The poor often respond to interviews with caution, since some of the most pressing problems are neither immediately visible nor acceptable to discuss in public. Even with substantive dialogue, the lack of critical examination of one's own preconceptions gives favorable responses greater attention than unfavorable ones (Chambers, 1989). Furthermore, area research is often subject to sample bias offering more attention to urban centers than remote areas since the latter are often inaccessible, especially during bad weather seasons such as monsoons, floods or droughts.

Moral imagination is also helpful in getting beyond the bias of conceptualism that we introduced in Chapter 3. Recall that those suffering from this bias prefer to focus on social problems in the aggregate (e.g., lack of family-planning education), rather than the particular, localized problems that may be unique. The bias of conceptualism also reflects deeply embedded ideological commitments that may not fit the situation at hand. Morally imaginative decision makers are not distracted by these preconceptions. Instead, they are prone to experiments that are driven more by the demands of the situation at hand than by any general ideas about the global poor or their preferences about how the world should work.

Moral Imagination and Systems Thinking

Moral imagination drives the realization of moral vision in many circumstances, but what is sometimes missing in morally imaginative decision making is the recognition that entities and forces in the decision environment are exceedingly complex. It is not just that mental models introduce bias in the way that stakeholders are perceived; it is also that stakeholders interact with one another to create challenges of their own. Thus, Cemex not only had to imaginatively overcome the bias that its poor customers lacked the foresight to plan their construction projects, but they also had to actively manage how its poor custom-ers dealt *with one another.* As we suggested in Chapter 1, "at its broadest level, systems thinking encompasses a large and fairly amorphous body of methods, tools, and principles, all oriented to looking at the interrelatedness of forces, and seeing them as part of a common process" (Senge, Kleiner, Roberts, Ross & Smith, 1994, p. 63). So, when decision makers engage in systems thinking, they seek a view of the situation that attempts to account for the interrelatedness of forces in their environment. Here, the object is not to discern how the situation ought to be seen with alternative mental models, but rather how to put these views together systematically to enable the decision maker to identify creative options (Werhane, 2002).

Systems thinking is not simply another cognitive schema that might be con-sidered by a morally imaginative person. Instead, it is a creative mode of inquiry that pulls together different views and abstract ideas into a unified whole. In so doing, systems thinking results in "(1) an understanding of the relativistic, non-absolute nature of knowledge; (2) an acceptance of contradiction as part of reality; and (3) an integrative approach to thinking" (Kramer, 1983, pp. 91–92; cf. Rakfeldt, Rybash & Roodin, 1996). Systems thinking refocuses consideration from stakeholders who are perceived one at a time to combinations of those individual, personalized stakeholders, mentioned in the previous section. Such a thinker would also prefer improvisation and in-process adjustments to grand plans that are boldly implemented (Moberg, 2001). By encouraging and facili-tating the formation of buyers' cooperatives, political-action networks or com-munity self-help associations, Cemex essentially created new stakeholders through which to negotiate and conduct commercial activities.

Some consider that the key to ethical decision making lies in a corporation carrying out separate engagement with each of their stakeholders. For example, Campbell (2007, p. 955) proposes that "[c]orporations will be more likely to act in socially responsible ways if ... the process by which ... regulations and enforcement capacities were developed was based on negotiation and consensus building among corporations, government, and other relevant stakeholders." Co-development of regulatory structures may make sense, but what if govern-ment stakeholders are corrupt? Cemex and the Grameen Bank are among the numerous companies operating in countries that suffer from rampant corrup-tion. On Transparency International's Corruption Index (2007) of 179 nations, Cemex operates in a nation (Mexico) that is ranked no. 72 and Grameen func-tions in a nation (Bangladesh) that occupies no. 162! Yet, both Cemex and Grameen are successful, not by negotiating consensus with corrupt officials, but by building local institutional structures that *bypass* corruption. These organiza-tions spend less time negotiating with governments and more of their energies working with groups of stakeholders in developing viable business ventures. Clever moral visionaries can effectively take advantage of this principle by forging ongoing cooperative relationships with systems of local stakeholders in place of far less sustainable, one-shot stakeholder relationships. This objective generally involves the firm not just in a one-to-one relationship, but in a system of interactions with customers and local communities (Werhane, 2008b).

Systems thinking requires conceiving of stakeholders not as targets for domi-nance, but as a set of interrelated and interconnected practices and forces that can be creatively synthesized on behalf of a moral vision. Systems components can be integrated to enhance the fulfillment of any number of goals that make up a moral vision (Mitroff & Linstone, 1993). An alteration of a particular system or corporate operations within a system (or, globally, across systems) will often produce different kinds of outcomes. At the same time, because a system consists of networks of relationships between individuals, groups and institutions, how any system and its institutional structures is construed affects and is affected by individuals. Companies, political, social and economic institutions, and systems are created by, and function because of, individual human input or collections of inputs (Mitroff & Linstone, 1993; Werhane, 2002, 2008a).

SELCO of India is a prime example of the benefits of the interplay between moral imagination and systems thinking. Through its 25 regional centers, SELCO has brought reliable, affordable and environmentally sustainable electricity to 45,000 small businesses since 1995. The technical innovation supporting SELCO is a small, solar electrical generating apparatus capable of simultaneously powering a home's lights, a black-and-white television, a radio or cassette player and a small fan. By linking its prospective customers with micro-finance partners, SELCO enables small-business owners to finance purchases of their units from a share of their future earnings. In its lease-to-own program, the consumer pays one-quarter of the system cost up front and the rest through a loan secured on future earnings through partners such as Malaprabha Grameen Bank. Each SELCO branch includes technicians who service the product and collection agents who work with the bank (Winrock International India, n.d.).

It was SELCO's readiness to escape the traditional mental model that thinks of non-urban Indian customers as the collective rural poor, and think of them instead as individual participants in a vast system comprising a multitude of different stakeholders. SELCO realized that solar energy for Indian entrepreneurs was not sustainable without micro-financing and, further, that trust and confidence could only develop if the company economically benefited others within the customer's local milieu. The institutional components of SELCO's system formula were (1) regional sales/service centers staffed by locals whose compensation is based on customer satisfaction, and (2) alliances with Grameen Bank, an institution renowned for its outreach to the poor. Clearly, moral imagination and systems thinking of this sort are decisive. If the micro-financing component of the SELCO system is eliminated, the entire system loses its effectiveness—*for all stakeholders*. Without local people committed to customer satisfaction and cognizant of local customs governing the servicing of the solar generators, the results of SELCO's systems thinking would collapse.

Deep Dialogue with Stakeholders

Deep dialogue with stakeholders emanates from an attitude of identification and sense of solidarity that only comes from prolonged contact with local stakeholders (e.g., potential employees and customers). As a result, companies choose strategies for engaging with these stakeholders that are not just respectful of stakeholder customs, but also that represent the perhaps unspoken wishes, habits and practices of these groups. This approach is not some tool of market research or issue management. Rather, deep dialogue constitutes the kind of merging of commitments common to the morally imaginative (Moberg & Seabright, 2000).

In the Cemex case, the management declared ignorance about their customers and the consumers of their products. This was an honest admission that many of its consumers were "invisible" to them, an admission that inspired managers to live in shantytowns of makeshift housing for six months (Hart, 2007). This direct encounter eventually yielded data that had previously been unknown and, arguably, that no cursory survey could possibly have attained. Similarly, IBM has created the corporate version of the Peace Corps where young managers receive one-month assignments in the developing world so that they will become strategic thinkers (IBM, 2008). When managers are more attuned to social trends and sensitivities, they are better able to identify risks and opportunities they might not have known otherwise (*The Economist*, 2008a). PricewaterhouseCoopers (PwC) established its Project Ulysses, a global firm-wide citizenship- and leadership-development program, based on a similar mission: to develop the next generation of global and responsible leaders within the firm and to foster business in civil-society partnerships by strengthening the personal involvement of PwC in local communities and by building effective global networks with external stakeholders (Pless & Maak, in press). To qualify as deep dialogue, this kind of experience cannot be part of some single-minded strategy to enhance brand image through CSR. Instead, deep dialogue in the Cemex case was part of a sincere attempt to establish solidarity with poor Mexican communities in order to enhance strategic, morally imaginative thinking.

While deep stakeholder dialogue may be a newer development in the for-profit community, it closely resembles the "new professionalism" that Robert Chambers proposed for those involved in international economic development in the 1980s. The new professionals, as he described them, choose to work among and allocate their limited resources to focus on those who operate outside the sphere of existing services, rather than those who are more easily accessed through quick research expeditions. Regarding mental models, the new professionals frequently cross the established boundaries of particular disciplines, seeking new opportunities to test policy and action by critically evaluating who gains and who loses. They borrow freely from the cultures of academia and practice, and move back and forth between them to discover what fits local circumstances best (Chambers, 1989). By doing so, the new professionals prefer to work for and with those who are not well-served by existing structures more than their own professional colleagues.

Deep dialogue is practiced today by several nongovernmental organizations (NGOs) committed to poverty alleviation at the BoP. For example, the Institute of Integrated Rural Development (IIRD) in Bangladesh serves the "hardcore poor," measured by the amount of food available each day. Besides providing food, water and housing for their clients, they work with them to provide economic opportunities that fit local circumstances. Here, the operative phrase is "work with them," for IIRD's "new professionals" maintain daily contact with families in order to know and precisely understand their needs. Moreover, any economic opportunity opened up by IIRD (from fishing to silk production) must be planned and implemented jointly with the poor themselves (Institute of Integrated Rural Development, n.d.). Clearly, the successful practices and lessons learned through deep dialogue, in the Cemex case, and/or through partnerships with NGOs like the IIRD, allow moral imagination in the for-profit and development community to get beyond the gravitational biases of common sense and conceptualism.

MNEs and Moral Imagination

The globalization of free enterprise involves the operations of large MNEs that may or may not take on the challenges of operating in corrupt markets with large but impoverished customer bases. The costs seem too large, the margins too low and the opportunity for loss of shareholder value and reputation seem too great. But, taking a systems approach combined with moral imagination and a concern for poverty alleviation, MNE involvement in BoP markets can result in sustainable returns for the stakeholders involved.

Let us consider BHP Billiton. With 39,000 employees in over 25 countries, BHP Billiton is the largest diversified resources company in the world, and does business in the fields of aluminum, coal, copper, manganese, iron ore, uranium, nickel, silver and titanium minerals, with additional interests in oil, gas, lique-fied natural gas and diamonds. In 2001, BHPB sought to expand a small- and medium-enterprise loan program that it had established outside Maputo, Mozambique, where it runs the Mozal aluminum smelter. During its original Mozal project, which began in 1998, BHPB's use of contractors from the local community was not successful. BHPB's initial approach was to think of these contractors as suppliers and customers without taking into account the local cul-tural context in Mozambique. However, as with Cemex and IIRD, BHPB found that the most effective way to increase local participation was to engage in deep dialogue with local stakeholders. As a result, new partnerships were formed that created an infrastructure that supported BHPB's business objectives as well as the interests and needs of the surrounding community.

To facilitate these partnerships, BHPB developed the Small and Medium Enterprise Empowerment and Linkages Program (SMEELP). The program was designed to provide contractors with the skills necessary with which to compete for BHPB contracts, ultimately benefiting themselves, their communities and BHPB. SMEELP seeks to balance sustainable benefits to the local community with the ultimate BHPB Mozal project mission and objectives. For instance, BHPB maximizes its use of local labor (setting a goal of greater than 65% Mozambican), provides construction skills training for almost 4,000 workers and allocates selected work packages solely to local enterprises. While the Mozal operation previously sourced sweeper supplies from South Africa, SMEELP identified a source that reduced costs and directed support to the local com-munity. To date, more than 27 contracts, representing over US$5 million, have been tendered to more than 200 Mozambican suppliers. SMEELP was forged through the establishment of a collaborative joint venture between BHPB, the International Finance Corporation (IFC) and the Mozambique government.

Employing moral imagination, BHP Billiton was able to disengage itself from its standard mining practice of using local contractors solely as customers with capabilities to run smelters. It had to rethink its traditional models for smelting in order to take into account the local context and the skill sets of those local contractors and workers. BHPB was then able to create partnerships and joint ventures with local workers and communities that turned out to benefit both BHPB and those communities.

Engaging in systems thinking, one of the lessons from BHPB is the immediate applicability of this project to other ventures. Even during the midst of the program, at a time when the successes of SMEELP were apparent, BHPB was able to transfer it successfully to other sites in Mozambique and to an operations location in South Africa. The IFC and the World Bank have also replicated the model. Needless to say, the Mozal operation is successful on several levels. Mozal has had a significant impact on Mozambique's economy, contributing 55% of the country's exports and 20% of its imports in 2001 (Mead, Hartman & Werhane, 2008).

Core Competence and MNE Contribution

As we argued in Chapter 4, if MNE involvement is limited to CSR activities that are not a part of core business strategy, the assumption may well be correct that donor-centric philanthropic activity makes a dubious and unreliable contribution to long-term poverty alleviation and is, therefore, a suspicious, if not unstable, partner. In contrast, we argue that, when MNEs identify points of mutual value creation aligned with their core business strategy and leverage their core competencies to establish partnerships, they do much more for sustainable poverty alleviation than through any other activity. Task-oriented, poverty-reducing initiatives must be directly connected to core competencies, which is a substantive departure from the common understanding of CSR. As Prahalad and Brugmann (2007, p. 85) explain, "most CSR initiatives, such as Exxon Mobil's involvement in the distribution of mosquito nets in Tanzania or General Motors' management of children's education programs in the United States, are unrelated to the companies' core business activities." It is not that these are not worthwhile programs; it is that these companies have skills and core competencies unrelated to mosquito nets or childhood education.

In the alternative, by taking a systems approach, MNEs can create partnerships with NGOs and governments by which to create poverty-reducing initiatives that *link their core competencies to poverty-reducing ventures*. These sorts of partnerships require a great deal of moral imagination since they are actually antithetical to the ways in which Western MNEs have traditionally operated, seeing themselves as independent of, and sometimes in conflict with, NGOs or a government. The worry is the following: If the corporation enters into a superficial relationship in these philanthropic ventures, sometimes with an NGO, for mere brand-management purposes, the partnership is likely to be short-lived, doing little to develop new products and services for low-income markets. However, when the two partners discover genuine points of convergence, MNEs are shown paths to new markets and NGOs realize that business models can unleash powerful forces that alleviate poverty (Prahalad & Brugmann, 2007). In these cases, both sides realize that they each possess core competencies, infrastructure and knowledge that the other needs in order to operate effectively in and to serve low-income markets. A number of MNEs, including Danone, Nestlé and Microsoft, have developed such partnerships for designing and selling products in this new market space. Ranging from nutrition to education, the sectors being served by these points of convergence between MNEs and NGOs not only restore the corporation's social legitimacy but, more importantly, accelerate the eradication of poverty (Prahalad & Brugmann, 2007). We shall delineate these options thoroughly in Chapter 7.

Conclusion

While much still remains to be learned about successfully entering BoP markets, several tentative conclusions can be drawn. First, since moral vision is animated and catalyzed by moral imagination, MNEs need to develop and to encourage this capacity. Proactive engagement at the BoP requires mental models that both individualize and particularize stakeholders and break through those mental models that condemn millions to the vicious cycle of poverty. The individual etiology of moral imagination is fairly well-known (Moberg & Seabright, 2000), and MNEs should create internal organizational cultures that nurture moral imagination (Caldwell & Moberg, 2007). Second, leaders in MNEs need the tools of institutional analysis. This implies an understanding of the kinds of institutional forms that encourage proactive engagement (e.g., Campbell, 2007; Vogel, 2006; Jeurissen, 2004), and an understanding of how to transform institutions from one state to another (e.g., Hargrave & Van de Ven, 2004; Scott, 2001). For example, leaders must be mindful that some of the institutional conditions at the BoP are hostile to sustainable engagement, particularly by foreign MNEs, and therefore require intervention at that level. We shall discuss these difficulties in the next chapter.

Third, leaders must be systems thinkers. In addition to considering stakeholders (institutional or individual) one at a time, they must consider existing and potential interactions and interrelationships between those particularized stakeholders in order to most effectively recognize and analyze the impact of the system involved. Whenever possible, market entry ought to allow for or develop such interactions. We saw that demonstrated by the case of BHP Billiton; and it was most certainly a critical factor in Cemex's strategy. Of course, systems thinking at the BoP presupposes an understanding of the entire cultural milieu at the BoP, which brings us to our fourth point. There is no substitute for immersing oneself in the experience of those stakeholders with whom one intends or needs to partner. One can certainly interact from a distance, but genuine engagement requires an intimate knowledge of a partner's experience; and this is not possible without deep dialogue. Both Cemex and BHP Billiton were careful to take this approach. Moreover, intentional immersion of this kind enables leaders to understand what role stakeholders genuinely are prepared to take in a systems solution. In some cases, that might mean the need to partner with existing institutions with the local cachet (e.g., the Grameen Bank) to support the effort (SELCO). In others, it might mean that various, previously ignored stakeholders themselves have the capacity to perform in new ways.

6

INSTITUTIONAL BARRIERS, MORAL RISK AND TRANSFORMATIVE BUSINESS VENTURES

In 2008, the Philippines was listed on the Corruption Perceptions Index as number 141 in a list of 180 countries based on the perceptions of business people and country analysts (Transparency International, 2008). The Philippines is also considered one of the poorer countries in the world. Fully 30% of its population of 92 million people live below the poverty level, measured by Philippine standards (Central Intelligence Agency, 2008). Thus, doing business in the Philippines is challenging, at best.

Manila Water is a privately held for-profit company that was created when the municipal water system in Manila, the Philippine capital, was privatized in 1997. At that time, the poorest residents had virtually no access to municipal clean water. When they did, it was undependable and costly, consuming up to half of their average monthly income. Immediately after its formation, Manila Water began to fix leaks in the dilapidated system and later extended service to a broader Manila community. In time, it established a program called "Tubig Para sa Barangay" (Water for the Poor). Under this program, Manila Water set up collective billing through which poor customers had the option of participating in household group-meter cooperatives. As a participant of a cooperative, each household's water use is measured separately, but billed collectively, with the entire billing group accepting financial responsibility for the metered amount (Rangan, Wheeler & Comeault, 2007).

Through this process of rudimentary institution building, Manila Water has been able to reduce water use fees by as much as 60% while collecting a reported *100%* of the money owed in communities where collective billing has been used (Beshouri, 2006). With its outreach now extending to over one million of Manila's poor, Manila Water's financial and operational performance has not suffered (Manila Water Company, 2007). While in 1997, its system provided 24-hour water to only 26% of the people in its service area, today that number is 98% (of its over 5 million customers) (Manila Water Company, 2007). The company's other stakeholders have also fared well. Manila Water is owned partially by its employees and, in 2007, the consistently profitable private company is expected to pay close to one billion pesos in corporate taxes to the Philippines (Manila Water Co., 2007).

The promise of making a profit while simultaneously enabling the world's poor to pull themselves out of their economic problems would be more credible if the markets accessible by the poor were conducive to business activity. Sadly, many are not. Countries with sizable populations at the base of the pyramid (BoP) are perceived as particularly risky to market entry, creating significant obstacles if not absolute barriers to economic performance. In this chapter, we delineate some of these institutional barriers that local businesses and multinational enterprises (MNEs) face as they contemplate the creation of a business presence at the BoP. More importantly, we indicate some of the strategies that those firms can implement in order to overcome these barriers while mitigating the concurrent risks.

Consider the case of the West African nation, Cameroon. In November 2006, then US Ambassador to Cameroon, Niels Marquardt, addressed a group of businesspeople about the prospects of doing business there. He asked his audience, "If you had a million dollars to invest, and you could invest it anywhere around the world, in any country, in any sector, would you invest it in Cameroon today?" (Marquardt, 2006). Clearly, he knew the answer. In spite of Cameroon's wealth of natural and human resources that would certainly justify doing business there, an average business in Cameroon spends 426 days complying with license and permits requirements, almost twice the average for an African nation (World Bank Group, 2008). In fact, Cameroon ranks 160 out of 178 countries on the World Bank's "Starting a Business" index. These figures do not even tell the whole story. Roads and bridges have received scant maintenance over the last 20 years; and corruption in Cameroon is everywhere. Police routinely stop taxis and extort passengers if they do not have papers that they are *not* legally required to carry with them. Newly constructed public buildings are uninhabitable during the seasonal rains (Harford, 2006). Health-care institutions are so rife with corruption that AIDS victims go without medicines unless they bribe the authorities (Cuffe, 2006). Overall, the situation is so dire that Transparency International ranked Cameroon as one of the most corrupt among the African nations that it surveyed in 2008, ranking it along with the Philippines as number 141 out of 180 countries it surveyed (Transparency International, 2008).

Obviously, those at the BoP in Cameroon are not prime candidates for partnerships with MNEs, through no fault of their own but instead because of the risks inherent in establishing and sustaining those partnerships. By paying government employees so poorly and by tolerating corruption at every level for decades, the top government officials of this nation have made it unlikely that their poorest citizens will soon enjoy the relief promised by profitable partnerships. Yet, MNEs should not be totally deterred from entering countries with flawed business climates, crumbling infrastructures and governance systems riddled with corruption. Developing economies rarely offer perfect settings. In order to do business there, MNEs need imaginative strategies to counter the institutional and political deficiencies that they will confront. These strategies may not be potent enough to neutralize all the challenges of doing business in present-day Cameroon, but they do offer the promise that, one day, business will take the former ambassador's challenge and invest there.

Before we discuss what businesses can do to overcome the institutional barriers that plague the BoP in these types of economic and social environments and to modify the mental models that have helped to create them, it is important once again to ground the discussion in the experience of the poor. Poor people all over the world, particularly in countries that have endemic corruption, are victimized by the same institutional conditions that create impediments to entry for MNEs. Cameroon's primitive roads impede travel between markets which would otherwise allow the poor to comparison shop. When anyone participates in Cameroon's markets as producers, they must pay bribes, make grease payments and cope with nepotism, all of which increase the costs of production. Removing the institutional barriers to entry for MNEs would improve these circumstances for the poor. Anything that an MNE does to improve the corrupt system or to reduce needless government paperwork will also help to empower local people who also suffer from these barriers.

Five Institutional Barriers

In 2000, the World Bank completed a wide-ranging survey of 80 countries in order to assess how conducive they are to economic activity (Batra, Kaufmann & Stone, 2002a). The results clearly demonstrated that, in the developing world, the most significant obstacles to business development and efficient market transactions are corruption, high inflation, financing limitations, public policy instability and infrastructure. While these problems are more common in the developing world than in the developed world, each is a significant institutional barrier to forming and maintaining business partnerships anywhere in the world.

Corruption

According to Webster's *New World Dictionary*, corruption is "evil or wicked behavior; bribery or similar dishonest dealings; decay,... rottenness" (Neufeldt, 1997). In economic terms, corruption is "the sale by government officials of government property for personal gain" (Shleifer & Vishney, 1993, p. 599). From a political standpoint, it involves "violations of specific non-discrimination norms governing the access to the political process and the allocation of rights and resources" (Kurer, 2005, p. 222). Corruption includes the use of position for personal gain in the form of embezzlement, nepotism and fraud; but it is more recognizable when it involves the use of official power over others in the form of bribery, kickbacks and extortion perpetrated by governmental officials.

"A bribe is a payment of money (or something of value) to another person in exchange for his [or her] giving one special consideration that is incompatible with the duties of his [or her] office, position, or role" (Carson, 1985, p. 67). In the World Bank survey mentioned above, businesspeople complained about having "to pay some irregular 'additional payments' to get things done." In the developing countries in East Asia, for example, 62% of businesspeople objected to having to pay bribes, and a similar number pointed out that multiple bribes were often required for the same "request" (Batra et al., 2002b).

Extortion occurs when a person, an agency or a government official demands a payment or favor in exchange for services that he or she was obliged to perform without the payment or favor. Typically, such demands are accompanied by an explicit or implicit threat that some harm will come to the party if the payment is not received. This might include psychological, economic or, in its most dramatic form, physical harm.

Kickbacks are another form of corruption. These occur when "royalties" are charged for contracts or services. Such extra payments are typically exacted before the goods or services are delivered. For example, a customs official may expect a kickback in order to release a shipment from quarantine. Closely related is the "grease payment." These are payments in order to expedite the processing of a transaction or to speed up required paperwork. Since bureaucratic procedures are rarely standardized in the developing world, the opportunities for public officials to charge kickbacks and grease payments are rife.

For poor consumers, corruption adds to the economic and psychological burdens they must endure. Lacking the resources and connections necessary to make certain transactions, they are deprived of the benefits those transactions promise. Even if they themselves do not pay bribes, it influences their welfare. As Kendall D'Andrade has observed,

> [b]ribery has previously been viewed as a two-party transaction between the bribe-offeror and the bribe-taker. But, there is a third party: the person that has a prior claim on the bribe-taker's loyalty. Breaking that contract in response to the offer of a bribe is alienation of agency ... [This] is the additional immorality of bribery beyond any immorality of the act solicited by the bribe (D'Andrade, 1985, p. 239).

For those at the BoP who are striving to start or to build businesses, or MNEs entering these markets, corruption can undermine their efforts. Since corruption skews competition, it favors those who can afford to absorb a price premium on their goods and services and, in the aggregate, this preference creates inefficiencies in the functioning of the market. On the micro level, when equivalent participation in the market demands that a poor businessperson spend money on graft, it depletes the funds available that would otherwise go into building her or his enterprises.

Clearly, corruption is a scourge on developing countries and on the poor who inhabit them. As long as corruption persists in a country, MNEs will be prone to pass it by, choosing either to work through third-party representatives in that country or to invest their capital in other nations. Consequently, corruption plagues the poor by locking them out of the very markets that might otherwise give them opportunities.

High Inflation

Inflation is an unfortunate side effect of developing economies and constitutes the second institutional barrier to business development and efficient market transactions in those environments. While moderate inflation seems to stimulate economic growth, high rates of inflation strangle it (Bruno & Easterly, 1998). When inflation is high, businesspeople cannot obtain long-term loans, except at exorbitant (double- or even triple-digit) rates. Even if they do find capital, they end up paying a larger fraction of principal in the early years of the life of the loan. Just as important, in periods of hyper-inflation, prices move up unevenly, and this complicates planning. Of course, there are businesses and national economies that benefit from inflation, particularly if rising prices are in the commodities that they produce. For example, the oil price run-up in 2007–2008 positively affected oil-producing nations like Cameroon.

Regrettably, while MNEs can absorb many of the financial difficulties posed by inflation through prudent financial management, the poor cannot. Indeed, high inflation hits the poor especially hard (Easterly & Fischer, 2000). Questionnaire data from over 30,000 households in 38 countries indicate that the poor complain about inflation more than the non-poor; but, beyond those results, econometric research indicates that their *relative* wealth declines with inflation. Importantly, high inflation closes them out of the credit market. Unable to finance capital accumulation, they are stymied from any attempt to enhance their productive capacity. They cannot add employees, invest in capital equipment, nor develop new goods or services.

Financing Limitations

For businesses to germinate and to grow, they require financing. If an economy has an underdeveloped financial system or one that wrongfully discriminates against worthy enterprises, business development faces a third institutional obstacle. In developed economies, most people have access to savings accounts, mortgages, consumer credit, insurance and money transfers; and businesses can obtain working capital and long-term financing. Those seeking to create businesses in the developing world do not enjoy these financing opportunities or, alternatively, often must pay high interest rates in order to do so (Batra et al., 2002a).

Financing limitations such as these are especially felt by those at the BoP. They cannot safely store their possessions, access their funds, or transfer their money. In addition, they are impeded from leveraging their assets, obtaining insurance or funding expansion. In other words, they cannot fully participate in markets for goods and services that demand credit. This has forced many at the BoP to use informal sources of financing, largely through moneylenders, credit unions and networks of family and friends. More recently, micro-finance and micro-insurance institutions have developed to assist the poor. Led by such organizations as Opportunity International, Accion in Latin America, and BRAC and the Grameen in Bangladesh, those at the BoP have new ways to build their assets, increase their incomes and reduce their vulnerability to life's uncertainties. At the same time, it should be recognized that the lion's share of the world's poor have no access to these embryonic financial institutions.

Public Policy Instability

Unexpected or abrupt changes in governmental regulations concerning taxes, trade and ownership add significantly to the costs of compliance and undermine the trust between government and business, comprising the fourth institutional barrier to business development in developing economies. In developing economies in East Asia, for example, 70% of businesspeople in the World Bank survey reported that public policy instability was a major constraint on their operations. Particularly troublesome were changes in rules, laws and regulations, and the lack of notification in advance about policies that affect them (Batra et al., 2002a). Public policy instability is one of the key risk factors in determining whether an MNE will enter an international market (Hartman, Arnold & Wokutch, 2003). Unpredictable changes in "the rules of the game" can often deter an MNE from doing business in a country. Indeed, it is an important factor in a nation's risk index.

Policy instability also affects the poor. Because they lack access to power over policy makers, the poor are rarely the intended beneficiaries of these policies. Accordingly, when they form businesses, those at the BoP often face poorly conceived and ineffective state regulations (Campbell, 2007). So, when the situation changes, it adds an element of uncertainty to an already dismal situation.

Infrastructure

The final factor mentioned by businesspeople in the World Bank survey as an institutional barrier to efficient market transactions was infrastructure. First-time visitors to the developing world are often stunned by the transportation, communications, education and health-care problems that they observe. Although people who are native to that region may lack the same comparison standards, they commonly complain about infrastructure, particularly how it affects them as consumers and producers. Infrastructure may be thought of as having two parts: the physical infrastructure and the human capital infrastructure. In considering issues surrounding the physical infrastructure, bad roads and rail-lines raise the cost of transport and introduce unnecessary delays. Telephone, Internet access, electric power availability, irrigation and postal services are also important. Their availability and cost are both determinants of economic activity. Failed or nonexistent education and training infrastructure cripples a developing economy. It strangles economic opportunities for those who are educated and leads directly to migration, which exacerbates human capital problems. Health-care infrastructure difficulties have a similar effect on a country's human capital. Clearly, the developing world needs significant improvements in both physical and human capital infrastructure if it is to develop economically.

Together, corruption, high inflation, financing limitations, public policy instability and infrastructure create a hostile environment for both MNEs and for the poor. For the potential of profitable partnerships to be realized, and in order to enter these economies, MNEs must develop imaginative strategies that mitigate these institutional impediments. If they do enter, they must subsequently create ventures systematically involving the poor as consumers and producers who confront and, in some cases, turn them into, business opportunities.

MNE Market Entry—Balancing Moral Risks

For the transformative effects of profitable partnerships to be realized, an MNE will have to answer the question Ambassador Marquardt raised about Cameroon at the beginning of this chapter. It will have to be willing to invest in the national or local economy of this developing country. Given the stakes, this decision is not merely a financial one; it involves moral risks as well.

"Moral risk is the likelihood of doing *moral* injury to oneself or to others where there is also the possibility of eliminating some moral evil and/or creating some positive outcomes" (Werhane, Velamuri & Boyd, 2006, p. 246). Engaging in morally risky ventures entails decisions where the outcomes are unpredictable; indeed, they might not create positive outcomes. In such ventures, what might be perceived as necessary to achieve a positive outcome or a moral gain, such as the reduction of human rights violations, will probably entail interaction with morally questionable people or institutions and, thus, engagement in activities that themselves are questionable. Accordingly, the resulting set of investments may even exacerbate corruption or the conditions of poverty (Werhane et al., 2006).

The most common way of framing moral risk is according to the economic, political and moral costs of entering a market like Cameroon's on the basis of the potential for a positive impact there. As one might expect, the corruption, hyper-inflation, financing problems, infrastructure and public policy uncertainties all contribute to the moral risks involved, and no MNE is ever sure that its investments will be protected or that the taxes they pay will not go into the pockets of questionable government officials. However, the decision *not* to invest in the BoP is also risky from a moral standpoint. Here, the human and economic costs of extreme poverty make the moral risks significant. When an MNE decides not to invest in a certain country, it incurs a moral risk that is as weighty as the potential good it might do there. These may be new and profitable markets; the company may be able to mitigate some of the institutional barriers; it may become a model for efficiency; and it may improve living standards as well. Finally, to the extent that MNEs are guided by moral imagination, such moral risks will be difficult to discount and impossible to ignore.[1]

Ultimately, the decision of whether to invest in a particular economy hinges upon a comparison of the moral risk of entering and the moral risk of not entering that environment. Some of the important risk factors of entering are specified above, but the factors that constitute the risk of not entering are more difficult to specify with precision. Systems thinking is vital to this process. One can consider, for example, not just the primary beneficiaries such as immediate return on investment, the poor and their communities, but also the secondary beneficiaries like enterprises that would grow and flourish as a result of economic advancement at the BoP. Also worth consideration are the human rights abuses that might be ameliorated as a result of profitable partnerships, and the opportunities to introduce environmentally sustainable, affordable goods and services (Ilesanmi, 2004). But, let us not forget the benefits to the firm itself from market entry. Profitable partnerships mandate returns; so, the expected profits (and similar enterprise benefits, like establishing a foothold in a promising young economy) must also go into the risk calculus.

Setting aside the moral risks of *not* investing in a particular economy, let us now concentrate on the risks of entering a BoP market and what an MNE can do to manage these risks. Unlike other businesses, MNEs are less likely to be discouraged by a country's high inflation and financing limitations by virtue of their larger risk portfolio.[2] However, corruption, public policy instability and infrastructure problems are likely to be major issues. Accordingly, our focus will be on these three problem areas.

Managing the Entry Risks Due to Corruption

Recall that we defined corruption as the sale by officials of government property for personal gain, and identified bribery, kickbacks and extortion as common forms of corruption. Since most countries that have a sizable population at the BoP are also countries where corruption flourishes (Chetwynd, Chetwynd & Spector,

2003), MNEs have no alternative but to confront the risks created by the corruption in the economies they enter. In doing so, MNEs may opt to take one of four general approaches: rent seeking, acquiescence, defection and engagement.

Rent Seeking

Though not a model of which we support replication, one approach, of course, is to proactively seek to take advantages of the benefits that may accrue to the MNE from the corrupt environment. Known as rent seekers, these MNEs embrace corruption as a means of gaining that advantage and making a profit. For example, by paying fees extorted by a customs official, rent-seeking MNEs may expect that their shipments may be expedited over goods from other producers, enabling them to enjoy a profitable price premium. To justify rent seeking, officials of such corporations heavily discount the harm corruption causes to others. Additionally, they come to believe that they can evade any punishment associated with corruption.

Acquiescence

In subtle contrast to rent seeking, some MNEs merely succumb to the corrupt demands of government officials via acquiescence, distinct from rent seeking in its passive approach compared to the rent seekers' more active pursuit of advantage. While the former perceives the environment as a cost, the latter sees this same environment as an opportunity.

In one study, it was shown, for example, that exporters from the developed world regularly pay bribes as a means of gaining entry for their products ("First Enquiry," 1997). While it is not known how many MNEs intending to do business in a corrupt community actually comply with corrupt officials, some acquiescent MNEs most likely see petty corruption as a necessary aspect of doing business there. This consequence creates what some ethicists term "the dirty hands" problem, i.e., a sense of guilt derived when the action one takes, ostensibly for the net benefit of others, hurts some people (Walzer, 1973). Whether petty or large-scale, acquiescence runs counter to most MNEs' ethics declarations and codes of conduct and, in some cases, is illegal according to the US Foreign Corrupt Practices Act.[3]

> While being opposed to the practice of corruption, [acquiescence] does not demonstrate the courage or the conviction to fight against systemic corruption. It rationalizes its behavior by reasoning that it is impossible for an individual economic agent to tackle corruption when corruption is pervasive in the system. It draws comfort from the fact that many positive consequences follow from its involvement in business, such as new products and services valued by customers, new jobs, taxes, contributions and so on. The implication is that the net consequence of its business contribution is positive, even though it has had to practice corruption (Werhane et al., 2006, p. 247).

Those who acquiesce sometimes use third parties to separate themselves from the officials "on the take." Such third parties might be known as consultants, local agents or intermediaries; and they have the appearance of creating "arm's-length" distance between the business and the corrupt official.

Defection

Another option for MNEs in responding to the risks presented by corruption in host economies is to refuse completely to pay bribes or to cooperate in any way with corrupt officials. When faced with a demand for a bribe, these organizations are likely either to retreat from the situation, to pursue other more ethical alternatives or simply to refuse to engage in corrupt behavior, even when that is the standard practice. If there appears no alternative but to engage in a corrupt practice, the defector may forgo that particular economic environment entirely. Alternatively, as in the case of InfoSys, the multibillion Indian information technology company, a company may simply refuse to pay bribes or to engage in any other corrupt behavior. By steadfastly refusing to engage in corrupt behavior, despite the widespread practice of corruption in India, InfoSys has not only been highly successful operating in a corrupt environment, it also has become a model of how companies can be world leaders in their expertise and be profitable, while remaining ethical at the same time.

Constructive Engagement

The most promising approach to countering corruption involves actively resisting it when entering markets infected with corruption. A notable example of a company that used constructive engagement is Econet, a telecommunications company in Zimbabwe. Econet's founder and CEO, Strive Masiyiwa, took a firm stand against corruption from the very beginning of his firm's existence and, in spite of resultant delays, grew his firm to a dominant position in this developing-world country. Econet and Masiyiwa are critical models since critics often point to the tenacity of much larger firms in standing firm against corruption, but claim that smaller organizations would not have the leverage to do so. Masiyiwa's courage apparently grew from his religious convictions:

> I'm a born-again Christian, and that was a decision I took. I've been brought up in a family, Catholics and Methodists and so forth, but at a certain point I took a decision that I wanted to go out and practice my convictions, and every day I must persuade myself that I am practicing my conviction. And, as a businessman in that environment, there was nothing more obvious that to succeed, to do anything, it was all about patronage and corruption. You know, to get a contract, anything. So perhaps more so there was revulsion in me that that was the area I had to make a stand in, that I didn't see that we would have a future in African business as long as it was totally associated with corruption. If you go to the average man in the street and you ask them what they think of business people, they talk of kickbacks, corruption; we didn't have an image to present to the next generation. And so I decided that I wanted to make that stand (Werhane et al., 2006, p. 236).

For Masiyiwa, constructive engagement took the form of determination and persistence. In negotiating with government officials, he made it clear that he was willing to do many things, but nothing that involved corruption. For others, constructive engagement involves working with government officials to create a program of treating corruption as a systemic issue. For example, companies can predicate market entry on increased wages for public officials so they are not as motivated to demand bribes (Bose, 2004). They can also work with governments in their efforts to remove patronage from public service appointments or to "open up" government positions only to those with demonstrated competencies. Recognizing that corruption is a problem often follows the format of "the tragedy of the commons"; some constructive engagers work with other corporations in establishing "an island of integrity," or a corruption-free zone, in which all parties will refuse demands for bribes and the like. Transparency International actively recruits businesses willing to establish and enforce islands of integrity and offers tools that support such collective efforts.

One official of a nongovernmental organization (NGO)[4] whom we interviewed told us of a case where the NGO was able to obtain approvals which would have normally required a bribe simply by publicizing the NGO's program in such a way that made the official look good. Evidence of moral imagination is demonstrated by another tactic he calls "cooptation," i.e., bringing potentially corrupt officials into the planning process of the BoP intervention in order to secure their support. Similarly, corrupt officials can be played off against one another in an effort to break up the social bonds that maintain the corrupt system.

Managing the Entry Risks Due to Public Policy Instability

Economic growth is stymied when market participants are uncertain about the public policy that affects the economy (Ali, 2001). For an MNE that is considering entry into a developing economy, regulations concerning taxes, property rights and remittances (in this case, the profits that have to be reinvested in the country) are important "rules of the economic game." When these rules change, it is costly. One way that MNEs can manage this risk is by maintaining open channels of communication with local policy-making bodies. Indeed, when there is an ongoing system of dialogue with governmental stakeholders, a business is more likely to exercise ethical action (Campbell, 2007). Potentially useful dialogue of this sort might take place at a national (ministerial) or local (community) level and would provide the MNE with a means for influencing public policy and its enforcement.

Managing Entry Risks Due to Weak Infrastructures

As discussed above, a weak or nonexistent infrastructure slows down the pace of any economic activity, especially in a developing economy. However, MNEs often consider this arena outside their purview; after all, in most cases, infrastructure is a public responsibility. Sometimes, MNEs can secure a commitment by a host government to improve some element of infrastructure in return for their entering the market. While that is certainly an effective leveraging mechanism, a more promising and sustainable option, where appropriate, is to build infrastructure improvement into the BoP venture itself. Projet Radio of Madagascar is one example (Goheer, 2007). Located on a large island off the southeastern coast of Africa, Madagascar is a nation plagued by an undeveloped mass-communication and electric-power distribution infrastructure, or at least it was until Projet Radio was established in 1999. Previously, the rural population's access to information and education was severely limited, but Projet brought with it a flood of broadcasted information and instruction that has empowered the poor of this nation (Goheer, 2007).

Begun as an NGO and now functioning as a revenue-producing enterprise, Projet Radio comprises three elements. One is a system of 3,370 Village Listening Groups (VLG) in rural communities each with 10–15 members who listen regularly to broadcasts, identify informational needs, assist with program production and provide feedback during evaluations. In exchange for their support and evaluation, VLGs receive solar-powered/hand-crank radios. A second element in their system is the 48 local "Partners for Communication and Information for Development" (PCID), comprising NGOs, radio service providers and government agencies. The PCIDs identify the informational needs of the rural populations, produce educational radio broadcasts and distribute the solar-powered and hand-crank radios to the VLGs. Finally, there are the 22 FM radio stations that provide airtime for the project's educational broadcasts in exchange for equipment enabling them to increase broadcast range and technical training.

To date, Projet Radio's educational and informational services reach approximately 700,000 listeners at a cost of less than one dollar per day, rendering it cost effective and highly advantageous, economically. Not only has Projet Radio supplemented Madagascar's power and communication infrastructure, but it has also enhanced its human capital. Listeners are more prone to incorporate modern health practices in their homes, to attend literacy classes and to use safer cooking methods.

A Second Look at Cameroon

How do these ideas relate to the situation in Cameroon? Although we do not claim to be experts in the economic and market situation there, we can offer some general thoughts on the prospects of profitable partnerships in this country. First, since corruption is such a widespread problem, a strategy (rent seeking, acquiescence, defection or engagement) will have to be selected. If our preferred strategy (constructive engagement) is chosen, perhaps the MNE can predicate its investment in the country's economy on measures reflecting Cameroon's Poverty Reduction Strategies accepted by the World Bank and the International Monetary Fund in 2003 (Eberlie, Führmann & Falk, 2004). These include:

- reduction in the excessive centralization of budget administration;
- adequate punishment for those who embezzle public funds;
- better access of citizens to information on government affairs and public-sector management; and
- additional resources to strengthen anti-corruption units in government ministries.

Working with Cameroon's anti-corruption commission that was established in 2006 may also help to identify other opportunities for constructive engagement.

Public policy instability may be a critical problem for any MNE considering a BoP venture in Cameroon. Although the government of President Paul Biya has been in power for over a quarter of a century, decisions affecting the private sector have created considerable instability. Unfortunately, the country's national government has a poor track record of establishing or maintaining an open dialogue with businesses or NGOs that are committed to poverty alleviation (Eberlie et al., 2004). According to the OECD, Cameroon did attempt to improve relations with the private sector in 2006, although the results of this attempt are expected to take time (OECD, 2007). Presently, the economy in Cameroon is highly managed by the central government. Prices for fuel and subsistence goods are pegged by the government, creating significant uncertainties every time they are recalibrated. In March 2008, for example, a change in fuel prices set off a violent general strike that created widespread civil disorder. The risks associated with this governmental market meddling may stymie all but the most inventive attempt at morally imaginative capitalism in this country.

Cameroon is rich in natural resources; it is an oil-producing country, and it exports minerals and agricultural goods. However, its physical infrastructure is spotty and unreliable. Electricity, water and sanitation continue to be problem areas, although improvements have been noted of late. Still, over half of the urban population and 80% of those living in the countryside are without electricity. Some 40% of its population subsist below the poverty line, although Cameroon enjoys a relatively high literacy rate of 68%. As for health, the country does slightly better than most sub-Saharan countries, although there are significant challenges. Life expectancy is 46.2 years, and malaria and AIDS are two significant causes of death. Presently, only 20% of the rural population has mosquito nets (OECD, 2007). Business opportunities may lurk within this profile of Cameroon's current infrastructure situation; however, significant moral risks are evident for any MNE entering the economic system. Although any decision to enter Cameroon requires a more careful examination of the specifics, this brief survey offers a sense of some of the factors that must be considered for imaginative capitalism to take root there.

Designing Profitable Partnerships that Transform the Poor

Wherever they are located, ordinarily, poor people without economic clout must contend with one fundamental market reality—they lack power. As consumers, they are short of influence because, individually, their purchasing power is paltry. Without the mobility and opportunity to shop around, the poor pay more for their basic necessities (Attanasio & Frayne, 2005.). But that is only half of the picture.

The poor also lack power as producers. Whether they are workers toiling under sweatshop-like conditions, other employees, service providers or proprietors, they generally lack the ability proactively to differentiate their products or services. Accordingly, they remain or become unessential, replaceable and expendable. The trick is to perform services or offer goods that will be valued for their differentiated, if not unique, qualities.

Consider the example modeled by a small group that simply needed to figure out a way to live in a cleaner local environment. Garbage had become an increasingly claustrophobic challenge in Lima, Peru. It lined the streets, filled vacant lots and clogged rivers, creating a significantly threatening health menace. Albina Ruiz began to organize her local community and to create a positive alternative: she encouraged area micro-entrepreneurs, small business and individuals from the Lima community to collect and to process the garbage through what she calls *Ciudad Saludable*, thus simultaneously cleaning up the city and creating jobs. Ciudad Saludable charges a small fee for the garbage collection, and the garbage is either recycled into organic fertilizer by other micro-entrepreneurs or put in a garbage dump where it hopefully is processed. She now operates in 20 cities in Peru and serves over three million residents (Davis, 2005).

The story of Ruiz and Ciudad Saludable illustrates two important, additional shifts in mental models surrounding poverty alleviation: (1) successful, profoundly imaginative solutions can come from the poor themselves, and (2) government is not always the best institution to serve as a key leader or partner in every system designed to address public goods like garbage disposal. The key is perhaps instead market empowerment. As Paul Collier has observed,

> [f]or the bottom billion to reach income self-sufficiency, "empowerment" is the right word. In all these societies, there are brave people struggling for change and it is incumbent on the rest of us, who are so much more fortunate, to do whatever we can to strengthen their chances of success. For that, we need to get serious (Murali & Padmanaban, 2008).

"Getting serious," in this sense, means designing partnerships, ventures and systems that empower the poor as true and full partners and that enable them to more fully participate in free markets despite the institutional barriers we catalogued above. In the next section, we shall consider first the process by which to empower the poor as *customers* and, in a later section, we shall explore how to empower them in their role as *producers*.

Empowering the Poor as Consumers

Because the poor lack market power, they pay prices that represent a "BoP price penalty," the difference in the price that they pay compared to the price paid by the affluent. What makes the BoP price penalty possible is that the poor are typically served by local, unregulated and/or corrupt monopolies, whether it is for food, water, transportation or other basic goods and services. For example, most people at the BoP do not have a publicly provided water service. As a result, they pay a poverty penalty because water vendors charge prices at a rate 8–16 times higher than that charged by public or municipal utilities in other regions (Hammond, Kramer, Tran, Katz & Walker, 2007). Below, we suggest six different strategies by which to empower the poor as consumers at the BoP. We acknowledge that these are all morally and economically risky ventures. In addition, while the examples are by and large local ventures, they serve as models for MNE entry. They entail empowering people, many of whom are illiterate and who have never had any opportunities to help themselves; and they may fail, thus inviting negative publicity and reputational damage. Still, the extraordinary, undeniable success of these ventures invites other, larger companies to engage in such risks, because the outcomes are so promising, the upsides are so very high.

Strategy 1: Eliminate the BoP Price Penalty

High prices and monopolistic conditions go hand in hand, but they signal that there is an opportunity for a lower-priced offering. Manila Water did just that with their "Water for the Poor" program, to which we referred at the beginning of this chapter. As a private company, Manila Water is better able to serve its customers, avoid governmental corrupt activities, and be profitable as well.

Strategy 2: Offer Alternatives to Infrastructure Problems

Much of the high cost of living for those at the BoP is due to infrastructure problems. Transportation is especially troublesome for the poor. Unable to travel inexpensively, they cannot escape regions dominated by monopolistic suppliers. One business allowing those at the BoP to transcend travel burdens so common in Mexico is Mi Farmacita, a for-profit pharmacy franchise based in Tijuana. By opening 57 local outlets, Mi Farmacita allows customers in rural areas an alternative to traveling to distant cities for their medical needs. Each site offers relatively inexpensive doctor consultations and low-cost generic medicines (Coronado, Krettecos & Lu, 2007).

On the supply side, Mi Farmacita opts to engage in this practice in order to open new distribution lines and to gain new customer bases to which it would not otherwise have access. Firms who instead sell only within urban or otherwise easily accessible markets find that those markets may already be saturated. Indeed, consumers may be overwhelmed by choice. Those such as Mi Farmacita who venture to the consumer in need find that the efforts are well-rewarded. Mi Farmacita has been able to double the number of its franchise outlets in every year since its inception (Coronado et al., 2007).

Strategy 3: Encourage Customer-Buying Cooperatives

A time-proven method of rudimentary institution building is to use systems thinking to build customer power through buying cooperatives. By coming together and pooling their bargaining power, buyers enjoy lower prices and other communal benefits, as we saw with Manila Water, as well as with Cemex and SELCO in Chapter 5. Indeed, sellers are able to have more predictable sales, lower transaction costs, smaller packaging needs and lower transport requirements. The economies of scale are evident. Cooperatives have long been used in agriculture, and are especially useful when prices for equipment, products or services are outside an affordable range for each cooperative member.

A similar problem experienced by buyers is met by the pooling of risk. Those at the BoP face significant risks of death and disease. Imagine the loss to a family if the principal bread-winner becomes ill or dies. Micro-insurance is a way that buyers can manage this risk. German insurance MNE Allianz uses buyer cooperatives to offer micro-insurance in rural India. Working collaboratively with NGO CARE, Allianz helps villagers set up a community fund known as a "mutual" into which they pay their monthly insurance premiums. The cooperative retains 65% of that revenue and sends the rest to Allianz. In case of an illness, a doctor approved by Allianz and CARE treats the villagers and, if necessary, sends them to partner hospitals in the region. Most medical treatment is covered by the mutual fund up to a ceiling, agreed to in advance by the community itself. Allianz covers any costs above that amount. The cooperative collects and keeps track of the premiums themselves, the average annual cost of which is about US$10 for a family of four (Allianz Knowledge Partnersite, 2008).

Strategy 4: Provide Access to Market Information

Lack of information about available goods and services often keeps those living in rural areas, in particular, from fully participating in markets. Businesses that promote their offerings in conjunction with consumer education both empower their customers and ensure that products and services will be used to their greatest effect. One especially imaginative approach was used by KB (*Krishak Bandhu*, Hindi for "the farmers' friend") irrigation. By promoting their brand through demonstration plots and a "Bollywood-style" television production (IDE India, 2008), KB offered a great deal of information to prospective customers, some of whom had assumed that such devices were prohibitively expensive and who were unsure how to install them (Hall, Clark & Naik, 2007).

Another example is evidenced by the impact of ITC's e-Choupal on rural farmers in India. Since these farmers originally had no access to technology, they had no option but to go to a single *mandi* (a government-mandated marketplace) where commission agents were able to take full advantage of the farmers' lack of knowledge about prices in surrounding *mandis*. Since it was not possible to travel on each day of sale to all of the *mandis* to identify the best sale price, the commission agents had the upper hand in the negotiation process. However, by placing a computer with an Internet connection in a *choupal*, a traditional village gathering place, ITC offered farmers access to many different *mandis* and, thereby, to the market prices from which they could then determine their efficient sales prices, creating a more true and balanced free-market exchange. With greater parity in access to information, social standing and choice, rural farmers now can level the playing field (Prahalad, 2005, pp. 319–357).

Strategy 5: Extend Buying Power by Offering Micro-Financing

Those at the BoP often lack the resources to purchase goods and services without credit. Additionally, they may lack the ability to store their property safely. As discussed in detail in Chapter 5, through "Patrimonio Hoy," Cemex offers very low-income families (households with incomes of less than US$5 per day) financing with which to build or to expand their homes. In order to qualify, customers are required to participate in savings groups, each of which has three "partners" and well-established rules to aid the partners throughout the borrowing process. These savings groups—new stakeholders in the microfinancing *system* of interrelationships—created a new seat of power among the poor, who could not possibly have wielded that power alone. In return, participants in the program are offered technical assistance, educational programs, guaranteed quality materials and delivery, guaranteed prices and free storage of materials.

Strategy 6: Dialogue with the Poor to Discern Institutional Context and Patterns of Consumption

The poor are unaccustomed to being heard. Theirs is a situation that existing businesses at the BoP take for granted. Most MNEs have the marketing sophistication to take customer viewpoints seriously. However, the BoP context poses significant challenges to MNEs who seek to understand what the poor really want in their role as customers and how MNEs can deliver it within an institutional system that remains "foreign" to them. In their book, *The Base of the Pyramid Protocol: Toward Next Generation Strategy*, Erik Simanis and Stuart Hart argue that

> [i]f the enterprise-based approach to poverty alleviation is to flourish in the future, it is imperative that we now move rapidly to ... an embedded process of co-invention and business co-creation that brings corporations into close, personal business partnership with BoP communities. It moves corporations beyond mere deep *listening* and into deep *dialogue* with the poor, resulting in a shared commitment born out of mutual sharing and mutual learning (Simanis & Hart, 2008, p. 2).

Through deep dialogue, cultural differences are made more comprehensible and institutional distance better understood (Hofstede, 1980; Phillips, Karra & Tracey, 2007). This sort of dialoging was exemplified in the BHP Billiton case that we discussed in Chapter 5. BHPB's Mozambique project was only successful after it engaged in local partnerships with the communities where their smelters were located and imagined not a traditional MNE–vendor relationship but instead viewed their role as partners within the larger system.

Empowering the Poor as Producers

Strategy 1: Enable Poor Producers to Differentiate their Offerings

One reason that the poor lack market power is that what they produce are commodities, products that are not differentiated from those of other producers. They produce crops and T-shirts that are no different from those of other farmers or weavers. Without skill development, workers are interchangeable with other employees, and they offer goods and services that are no different than the competition.

The same could be said for many coffee growers in Latin America, but thanks to the "free trade" movement, these growers' beans sell at a premium. This practice began shortly after World War II when US churches began selling handicrafts made by European refugees (Oxfam America, 2008). Today, wholesalers, retailers and producers promote and protect the "fair trade" label through the Fair Trade Federation. Of course, branding a product "fair trade" is only one way of differentiating the products, services and efforts of the poor, but this is among the most notable and enduring practices by which to empower them in the marketplace.

Strategy 2: Create Market Discipline

The transit problems of large cities, such as Mexico City, result from the disparate roles of government, concession owners and drivers culminating in chaos, congestion and reckless driving. The traditional transport operation in Mexico is a loose collection of poorly regulated, independently operated buses that has no fixed schedule or stops and is not financially self-sustaining. Because a driver's earnings depend on the number of passengers he picks up, he has no incentive to respect designated bus stops when that negatively impacts his earnings. The result of this incentive structure is "the penny wars," where buses jockey and compete for every single passenger. As a whole, the transit system is characterized by operational inefficiencies; either the system is subsidized or service providers cut costs on maintenance, resulting in the deterioration of the system's primary capital asset, the buses. Any improvement of the existing transit system demands a new economic model that aligns and coordinates the relationships and interests of the system of primary actors.

By incorporating bus operators as partners into Mexico City's Bus Rapid Transit (BRT) system, the entire operation is more efficient and profitable with value-added from training, maintenance and capital reinvestment. This required profound changes in the current business, which incurred resistance from transport operators afraid of losing the status quo. However, by creating the space for a public–private partnership through open channels of communication, through the clear and open presentation of an alternative model, and with assistance from the bank and insurance industry, BRT has successfully both recalibrated the mental model and incorporated the interests of all system participants (Embarq, 2006).

The results of Mexico City's new BRT system are remarkable and noteworthy. Transport concession holders have evolved their practices into an official business model, resulting in a better organized, more competitive and, consequently, more profitable business. Drivers now enjoy better financial and legal protections, job security, higher working conditions and a greater standard of living. The bus corridors are safer and more efficient because of clearly protected lanes and special traffic controls. Not only are travel times shorter, but the entire process required a minimal investment from the government and has the capacity to easily incorporate new vehicle technologies as they become available (Embarq, 2006, p. 47). What may have appeared to be an intractable problem of market chaos and corruption has proven to be another illustration of the socially transformative power of ethical business ventures that emerge from public–private partnerships.

Strategy 3: Encourage Producer Marketing Cooperatives

For almost 40 years, over 12 million dairy farmers in India have been organized into a cooperative that collects, processes and markets milk products. Known as Amul, the cooperative adds tremendous value to each farmer. The numbers are impressive: the farmers are organized into over a million village-level dairy societies that are aggregated into 338 districts and 22 state-level federations produc-ing almost a billion rupees (US$21.5 million) in revenue. Besides milk, Amul produces and markets butter, cheese, ice cream and milk powder. Amul pro-vides market access where previously none existed. The guarantee of a market for their milk and a fair and timely price permits not only financial security but also emotional security that those not living in the BoP may otherwise take for granted.

Strategy 4: Provide Access to Market Information

The transportation infrastructure of many developing countries comprises inad-equate, unpaved roads that fail to traverse miles of mountains, jungles and rivers. Because the cost of building roads is prohibitively expensive, geographi-cal isolation appears to be an insurmountable barrier. However, today, informa-tion technology can eliminate many of those geographical barriers by creating a vital communications network. With cellphone technology, a dairy farmer in Bangladesh can consult with an agricultural expert in Chicago in order to learn new techniques for improving the health and productivity of his cattle (Yunus, 2007, p. 190). With 80% of the world's population now living within the range of a cellular network, "even the smallest improvements in efficiency, amplified across those additional three billion people, could reshape the global economy in ways that we are just beginning to understand" (Corbett, 2008, p. 35). The mere opportunity for enormous numbers of the world's poor to now have a call-back number opens doors to realities that those throughout the developed world commonly have taken as given, such as notices of job acceptances and credit approvals.

In one study that originally sought to explore the digital divide, Harvard economist Robert Jensen set out to determine how improvements in informa-tion impacted market performance and welfare (Jensen, 2007). Knowing that access to information is vital to effective market functioning, Jensen explored whether fishing profits would increase if Indian fisherman could have access to broader information. Indeed, his research was monumental. Since cellphone towers in the fishing town of Kerala, India, were positioned close enough to the shore so that the fishermen could retain service as far as 25 km out to sea (where most fishing is done), most of the fishermen found it highly profitable to invest in cellphones and to locate and identify possible purchasers long before turning toward shore. The profits of these fishermen increased by an average of 8% while consumer prices in that region decreased by 4%. Perhaps even more signi-ficant for the Keralan poor, Jensen found that waste, which previously consti-tuted 5–8% of each day's catch, was *completely* eliminated.

Strategy 5: Extend Market Power by Offering Micro-Financing

In Chapter 3, we learned about the Children's Development Bank that allows homeless children to bank and to protect their small earnings. One promising new form of micro-financing is mobile banking. MNEs, such as Safaricom, Ltd. in Kenya or Globe Telecom in the Philippines, offer mobile banking to those at the BoP that enables producers to reduce the likelihood of exploitation and theft. Mobile banking allows an individual to transfer money from a cellphone to a bank account and to withdraw it at a later time. Mobile banking provides an alternative that is far safer than carrying cash. For those living at the BoP, the protection of their small amounts of capital becomes paramount. Mobile-banking facilities can mean the difference in the protection of a family's entire life savings or complete financial disaster; the choice is that which permits the family the flexibility not previously available.

Strategy 6: Enhance Human Capital

Business at the BoP traditionally has taken two fundamental forms: self-employment and small business; and these have different human-capital implications (Spencer & Gomez, 2004). Research has shown that self-employment thrives when a society celebrates and admires entrepreneurs (Busenitz, Gomez & Spencer, 2000). Thus, governmental or NGO-sponsored programs that identify success narratives and associate them with positive personal outcomes (wealth, happiness, etc.) encourage self-employment.[5] The human-capital requirements for small businesses are different. Running a small enterprise requires knowledge and commercial skills. Small-business owners need to know how to legally protect their businesses, how to manage risk and how to find and to develop market information (Gnyawali & Fogel, 1994).

Community Cleaning Service (CCS) of Nairobi, Kenya is the result of a partnership between the US MNE, SC Johnson and a group of unemployed Nairobi youths. Working in the vast slums of Nairobi, CCS trains young people to be able to offer a suite of services ranging from garbage collection, indoor cleaning, insect control, window screening, to wall repair and patching (Simanis & Hart, 2008). As CCS has evolved, employees have received extensive training in the materials and technology involved in these services and the business skills necessary to make CCS a going concern. As CCS grows, its employees will also market SC Johnson cleaning products, thus a win–win, *profitable* partnership for the company and for these young people alike.

Institutional Distance and Profitable Partnerships

Some 25 years ago, in a seminal article, DiMaggio and Powell defined an organizational field as "those organizations that, in the aggregate, constitute a recognized area of institutional life: key suppliers, resource and product consumers, regulatory agencies and other organizations that produce similar services or products" (DiMaggio & Powell, 1983, p. 148). The BoP is an unfamiliar organizational field for most MNEs. Even if they have business operations in many countries, most are accustomed to global trading partners who do their best to accommodate them. If differences occur, the MNE is in a superior power position; so, the MNE is rarely put in a position of having to adapt to its host country's economic situation. Indeed, one lesson that some MNEs learn is that, when there is a large difference between the organizational field in the MNE's host country and that of the subsidiary country, it should acquire ownership in the subsidiary (Gaur & Lu, 2007). This may be due to the fact that deviations from the expected organizational field are costly; so, MNEs will naturally attempt to have as much control over them as possible. Consequently, if an MNE is unaccustomed to civil authorities exacting bribes, interventions at the BoP where that is common practice represent a challenging context. Similarly, if an MNE typically deals with stable and structured supply chains, it will find more spontaneous relationships like those at the BoP unusual and taxing.

One way to overcome institutional distance is through entrepreneurship. This involves deliberately manipulating and building institutional structures into those more conducive to the new venture. Accordingly, "where the host institutional context is highly unstructured, MNEs can play a role in developing new institutional arrangements that can form the basis of a new organizational field in the host country" (Phillips, 2007, p. 5). This represents a systems approach—thinking of new markets in their institutional, as well as cultural, context and then working through those contexts in order to create an innovative outcome.

In this chapter, we have shown that the organizational fields at the BoP create challenges, as well as opportunities, for profitable partnerships. MNEs must assess whether a particular host economy is worth investing in and, then, if the extant organizational field can be molded into one that promises a worthwhile payoff in exchange for the moral risks involved.

7

PUBLIC–PRIVATE PARTNERSHIPS AND OTHER HYBRID MODELS FOR POVERTY ALLEVIATION

Retired and doing volunteer work in Guatemala, Donald O'Neal noticed that poor women cook over dangerous three-rock, open fires inside their homes. The fires cause respiratory illness and severe burns, and they contribute significantly to air pollution. Moreover, they consume fuel inefficiently and require hours of back-breaking labor to gather the tremendous amounts of wood needed for daily cooking. As someone with an engineering background, O'Neal decided to try to design a better method of cooking.

His approach began with something we shall call a form of "deep dialogue"—he lived among the prospective users and studied the cultural as well technological issues associated with cooking in Guatemala. Two years later, he had come up with a design solution made principally of cement and called the ONIL stove. Measuring approximately 4'×2'×3', the stove can be assembled from readily-available concrete blocks. Molds for additional pieces allow construction at the site. Independent laboratories have confirmed that the stove reduces smoke emission inside the dwelling by 99%, increases the cooking surface height making for a safer system, and creates 60% savings in fuel consumption.

Lacking the funding to bring the stoves to market at a price that would be affordable, O'Neal turned to HELPS, an NGO that works primarily in Central and South America, for assistance. They worked out a subsidy arrangement that allowed him to sell over 11,000 ONIL stoves (Volvo Cars of North America, 2007; Onil Stoves, 2007). Additionally, O'Neal provides the design of the stove to other NGOs interested in distributing them. Today, O'Neal serves on the board of HELPS.

In the preceding chapters, we have been rather adamant that foreign aid or corporate or individual philanthropy by themselves have not always been successful in alleviating poverty, particularly in the poorest sectors of the globe. However, although our primary intent is to argue that for-profit initiatives can serve the economic interests of blighted communities as well as the interests of the multinational enterprise (MNE) involved, alternative examples exist of hybrid models involving partnerships between public institutions, nongovernmental organizations (NGOs) and private enterprises. This chapter will focus on these and other initiatives that create economic value-added in poor communities. These enterprises are not merely philanthropic in intent; most require capital gifts or loans, and all involve public–private partnerships, NGO involvement and/or community-based enterprises. Most are social entrepreneurial

106

ventures with an aim to improve the well-being of various communities. We shall conclude that these hybrid models are most successful when they enable individuals or communities to engage in economic development, when they enable people to become self-supporting, and when they provide actual results in the form of poverty reduction.

As Kasturi Rangan of the Harvard Business School has observed,

> [t]he private sector brings a performance-driven culture when addressing any market. The poor are no different. Once management has figured out the business model, bringing the operation to scale is a necessity for their own bottom line…. At the same time it would be a wild dream to believe that private sector investment [alone] is going to save the world. Unless the appropriate government [or NGO] actively participates as investor, regulator, or guarantor, there will not be the rush of private entrepreneurs to participate in this market. We believe that much of private sector efforts will come through an enlightened approach involving partnerships (Silverthorne, 2007).

The arrangement that Donald O'Neal forged with an NGO to finance and distribute his stove is one aspect of profitable partnerships that we have not yet discussed—cross-sector partnerships (CSPs) (Austin, 2000; Selsky & Parker, 2005). For all their potential to create value for the poor, MNEs often lack the knowledge, access, relationships and other resources necessary to be effective without noncommercial partners (London & Hart, 2004). In many cases, MNEs are late arrivals at the BoP. Many public organizations and NGOs have been fighting poverty there for decades and, while they have not always been successful on a large scale, they certainly have the potential to assist and to support meaningful ventures targeted at the base of the pyramid (BoP) (Hartman, Werhane & Moberg, 2008). In many cases, NGOs have a history of deep dialogue with communities in less-developed countries that would take MNEs years to duplicate. In other cases, public organizations have control of institutional structures that must be leveraged or accommodated for an MNE to access the BoP market.

Yet, developing such CSPs is a challenging process, especially for MNEs involved with the poor (Gray, 1989). In Chapter 2, we identified some of the different organizations and institutions that have historically led attempts to alleviate global poverty. Among these are nation-states, international organizations like the United Nations, and NGOs. MNEs traditionally view these organizations as elements of their regulatory environment. For example, MNEs with manufacturing operations in the developing world are often subject to the enforcement of international environmental standards, as well as to criticism by NGOs concerned about employee rights. When an MNE's objectives include the alleviation of poverty, however, such organizations can become potential allies. The problem is that mental models, conditioned by regulated relationships, may impede the development of CSPs. NGOs and nation-states often remain skeptical of the motives of MNEs; in return, MNEs tend to grow impatient with the inefficiencies and lack of urgency that they attribute to organizations in the public sector. In this chapter, we will examine the mental models that encumber the development of hybrid CSPs and explore the various forms that such alliances can take when they are guided instead by moral imagination.

Impeding Mental Models

As we argued in Chapter 3, individual and organizational mental models frame our perceptions and thus our attitudes and behavior. Some of these become biases that deter clear new thinking, particularly in the areas of poverty and its alleviation. In the United States at least, public and nonprofit organizations and commercial organizations have developed rather independently and with different mindsets, until the late 20th century when many public organizations began to implement administrative practices that appeared first in commercial organizations. Strategic management, total quality management and re-engineering are among those techniques originally developed in business organizations that are now replicated in public organizations. In spite of this convergence, significant cultural differences exist between public and private organizations that undermine the emergence of CSPs.

Principal Objectives

One obvious difference between public and commercial organizations concerns their objectives. Public organizations typically strive to deliver a product or service with the resources available to them, for the most part on a break-even proposition, while commercial organizations expect a profitable return on the resources committed (Milne, Iyer & Gooding-Williams, 1996; Iyer, 2003; Weisbrod, 1997). This essential difference frames mental models that frequently persuade officials in public organizations that commercial organizations are interested in customer welfare only as an instrument through which to earn a return. Under that rubric, public nonprofit organizations are assumed to hold a more pure interest in social benefits, and are thus allegedly morally "purer" (Faranak, 2004). In return, individuals from commercial organizations often criticize public agencies for their lack of urgency and efficiency attributable to their monopoly power. At the extreme, these mental models grow into well-worn and cooperation-destructive stereotypes of greedy businesspeople and lazy public officials. As one corporate manager observed:

> [w]e just move much faster. It's readjusting our employees' time clocks. And negotiations are different, and accountability is different. Everything is different. Once you understand how they work, think, and operate, you can get a lot of great things accomplished. If companies can take the time to really develop a relationship, that's what they need to do (quoted in Austin, 2000, p. 86).

One way this difference in perspective may play out occurs when an MNE approaches an NGO to become partners in a poverty-alleviation project. Plagued by mental models about MNEs, the NGO may suspect that the poor may be treated as mere profit-generating instruments in the project and not really cared for. For example, on July 28, 2008, in the midst of the subprime financial meltdown in the United States, Muhammad Yunus, the Nobel Laureate pioneer of micro-credit whose bank, the Grameen Bank, is a for-profit development bank,[1] cautioned commercial banks to stay out of micro-finance in the developing world. His worry was that, if their primary objective is profitability, commercial banks will become more interested in the return on investment than in the well-being of its micro-financed customers (Burgis, 2008). Obviously, mental models like the one on which Yunus' caution was based diminish the likelihood that CSPs will form (Das & Teng, 2001).

Scalability

In part because private organizations strive for a return on investment, they are much more attuned to economies of scale than public organizations often are. This makes commercial organizations more prone to grow ventures to the point where net economies of scale can be realized and a return can be secured. Diseconomies of scale are also a concern among private organizations like MNEs. Large projects may require more administrative expenses than their returns justify. For public organizations, scale is a concern not driven by the resource efficiencies enjoyed but by the number served, the access by special categories of citizens, and the individual success narratives developed. For example, small-scale projects that lift a handful from poverty may create compelling stories with which to secure additional funding, even though each poor person helped by such projects may cost a large sum. Many commercial organizations might not fund the ONIL stove because of the inability of potential customers to pay the full cost for their stoves. Poverty-alleviation programs may be targeted at particular groups (e.g., farmers, women) because resources are available to assist these communities. A "small is beautiful" mindset may grow from the roots of NGOs' comparative advantage in the quality of the relationships they can create, not in the scale of their programs or the size of resources they command (Fowler, 1990). As one staff member of a poverty-fighting NGO in Gambia stated:

> [t]hose of us in the field that are concerned with quality are now being expected to turn out higher numbers, which is not why we entered this work in the first place ... We're a small organization with the ability to build strong relationships with communities. We're very focused on the grassroots—that's why we are here. And if we go for larger chunks of money, bigger projects, bigger programs, I think that, we think we're in danger of losing what made us special in the first place (Fyvie and Ager, 1999, p. 1390).

Indeed, the Compartamos Bank of Mexico that we highlighted in Chapter 4 started out as an NGO, but changed into a for-profit enterprise in order to raise more capital-investment monies. This example illustrates another constricting mindset—the idea that NGOs are not as worthy of capital investment as are for-profit organizations.

On the other hand, there are signs that certain NGOs are beginning to embrace the importance of scalability. In India, for instance, the Pratham Resource Centre does not plan to establish just one or two schools to answer to the widespread literacy challenge; instead, Pratham develops reading and mathematics kits that are being used to teach basic concepts to great numbers of illiterate children. As Usha Rane, the Director of Curriculum at Pratham comments, "It is necessary to create a mass movement" (India Knowledge@Wharton, 2006).

Nearly 1.6 million children have benefited from the kits since 2005. Clearly, this is the type of mental model around scalability that makes NGOs like Pratham more accepting of CSPs.

Transparency and Accountability

In a comparison of International Non-Governmental Organizations (INGOs), intergovernmental organizations and MNEs, One World Trust found no significant differences in transparency between sectors (One World Trust, 2006b). Leading the way as the most accountable and trustworthy MNEs were Pfizer (a multinational pharmaceutical) and Anglo American (a natural-resource company). Among NGOs, ActionAid International and World Vision International received high marks. In considering intergovernmental organizations, the World Bank and the Organization for Economic Cooperation and Development (OECD) were singled out as laudably transparent and accountable.

Ordinarily, however, when specific MNEs and public organizations are looking for prospective partners, they do not rely on lists like these. Instead, they make judgments about the trustworthiness of possible partners and proceed from those impressions. Again, impeding mental models intervene to throw off the accuracy of such assessments. Psychological research has shown that people have a strong propensity to judge themselves as ethically superior to others (Pfeffer & Fong, 2005); this is particularly true when self and others are members of different groups (Polzer, Kramer & Neale, 1997). Thus, when organizations make judgments about the transparency and accountability of organizations much different than their own, they are likely to underestimate the moral worthiness of their counterpart. Exacerbating this effect is the fact that private and public organizations may have entirely different notions about the meaning of the terms "accountability" and "transparency." Conditioned by regulations such as Sarbanes Oxley in the United States, MNEs become preoccupied with accountability to and transparency with *shareholders* (rather than all their primary stakeholders). In addition, some MNEs concentrate more on the *financial* dimensions of transparency and accountability than on dimensions like the environment or employee rights. In contrast, NGOs and governmental organizations tend to associate transparency and accountability with *stakeholder* engagement and response to all types of societal criticism, whether it concerns the financial dimension or others. In short, when a public agency or NGO thinks about developing a partnership with a commercial enterprise, they often struggle to accept whether their prospective partner is morally trustworthy. As Selsky and Parker have observed, "trust in business traditionally is based on constrained contractual exchanges, whereas trust in the nonprofit sector is traditionally based on solidarity with the mission or on shared values" (2005, p. 56).

Deep Dialogue as a Process that Breaks Down Impeding Mental Models

Donald O'Neal, the inventor of the ONIL stove, was successful because he engaged in deep dialogue with the poor in Guatemala, and this dialogue led him to a design solution that reflected all the essential technical, social and cultural elements of food preparation in that environment. Importantly, the ONIL stove was not just a method of cooking food, but his design also enhanced the *productive capacity* of its users (Letelier, Flores & Spinosa, 2003). As we have seen, that is a critical ingredient of product partnerships that is often missing from other commercial approaches to poverty alleviation. If one merely sells shampoo in small sachets to the poor, it does little to build their productive capacity. Viewing the poor only as customers rather than as potential systems of production does little to help them break the chains of their privation (Karnani, 2007a).

What we mean by "deep dialogue" is similar to what some sociologists term "solidarity." Divorcing that term from its religious and political connotations, "solidarity" or "social solidarity" refers to various forms of communication and exchange where each actor or set of actors benefits, albeit differently, from the communication or exchange in ways that are at least perceived to be fair to each party and where the exchange or communication strengthens the understanding, trust and respect between each party. This benefit could be either in the form of direct communication and engagement or indirect exchange; but either can produce reciprocal value, as O'Neal's stove represents (Molm, Collett & Schaefer, 2007). But, to develop deep dialogue that creates social solidarity is a time-consuming, focused engagement that requires learning and understanding the community in which one is situated and discerning what will work in that particular context.

Often MNEs do not believe that they have the time or resources to engage in this form of dialogue. Recall the case of Shell and its disastrous experience in the Ogoni territory of Nigeria. Had they engaged in deep dialogue with the Ogoni leaders and with the dissidents who protested against Shell, Shell might have acquired a better understanding of the plight of the Ogoni and perhaps, through dialogue, developed some more viable outcomes.

What O'Neal learned by living in Guatemala was that a three-rock stove necessitates that someone in the family unit spend much more time gathering fuel than with the ONIL stove. The three-rock stove increases the possibility that the family unit will suffer from disease due to pollution compared with the ONIL stove. The three-rock stove results in a higher likelihood of injury due to an unstable cooking surface, again straining the family unit's productive resources. At an even broader systemic level, with pollution eased and children free from the chore of gathering fuel, the productive capacity of the whole community is enhanced with the use of the new stove. Deep dialogue enabled O'Neal to distinguish between merely selling a stove and crafting a solution that was both labor-saving and health-enhancing. Multinational enterprises would do well to emulate the moral imagination and systems thinking that went into the design of O'Neal's food-preparation system. However, that is only part of the story. O'Neal also needed to be imaginative in thinking how to replace the badly engineered cooking methods of the Guatemalans while remaining acutely aware of what replacements would be appropriate and affordable in rural Guatemalan settings. He also had to be cautious of the political setting in which he, as an American, was working. O'Neal did a wonderful job partnering with the poor, but also he relied on one other partnership as well—with an NGO. Thus, O'Neal modeled moral imagination and systems thinking, pivotal components of successful profitable partnerships, as well as patience and deep dialogue with the Guatemalan village women.

In summary, moral imagination is required to overcome the mental models that impede the development of partnerships between private and public organizations. Not only is there carry-over from the regulator-regulated roles that historically governed the relationship between these two types of organizations, but essential differences between the two create negative impressions of "the other" that are difficult to overcome (Wymer & Samu, 2003). Nation-states, intergovernmental organizations and NGOs tend to see commercial organizations as prioritizing profit first and social responsibility second. This variant of the separation thesis that we described in Chapter 4 makes it appear that MNEs are unworthy partners in any poverty-alleviation effort. Similarly, the approach that private organizations take concerning scalability and transparency often makes it challenging to find a common ground with public organizations.

Public–Private Partnerships that Create Value

Despite differences in approaches there are many forms that public–private partnerships can take and have taken in successful poverty-alleviation efforts. While some defy categorization, there are several common trends.

Price Subsidies

Donald O'Neal sought an NGO partnership so he could drive down the price of his stove, which would then allow poor users to afford it. Multinational Proctor & Gamble (P&G) did the same to subsidize their water-purification products. Its PŪR division manufactures water-filter faucet mounts, pitchers, dispensers, coolers and filtration systems for refrigerators. The PŪR brand was developed along with related products by a Minneapolis-based company, Recovery Engineering, which P&G acquired in 1999. Initially, PŪR products were sold primarily in the United States and Europe. But P&G soon realized that there was a huge global demand for clean, safe water, especially in developing countries where water supplies are usually muddy and polluted. The problem, of course, was that most of the potential new customers had little money for any water-purifying product. Thus, PŪR products could help millions of people at the BoP who were without safe drinking water, if only the company could develop a product that was inexpensive and easy to use. With those parameters in mind, P&G developed a simple powder that it could produce in small packets. One packet, when mixed in almost any kind of water and let stand for 30 minutes, will settle mud and dirt at the bottom of the container and create safe drinking water.

P&G now provides PŪR at cost through its Children's Safe Drinking Water outreach program developed by its Health Science Institute, partnering with NGO Population Services International (PSI). PSI applies P&G's marketing skills to inform and to distribute PŪR to vulnerable local communities, and eventually all over the globe. Marketing was not without its challenges, however, since in some communities people are afraid of trying a new product and are used to the taste of their (usually polluted) water (Procter & Gamble Health Sciences Institute, 2007b). Again, as with the ONIL stove, deep dialogue with these communities was necessary first to understand why the product was not accepted, and, second, to help educate communities as to the importance of safe water, but in terms that are understood in each particular context.

P&G committed over US$5 million to this project, and the company and its NGO partner have pledged to provide over 100 million liters of safe drinking water to Africa. This is not a purely philanthropic venture, however, but one involving entrepreneurial moral vision. Local distributors of PŪR powder must make a profit when they sell the product, since P&G recognizes that even the very poor do not trust or value give-aways. P&G, too, stands to profit in the long term by this venture, building a positive brand image that will help it market other products to at least a billion potential new customers with a high-volume, low-margin business model (Procter & Gamble, 2007).

Market Intelligence

Often, an MNE lacks information about market realities at the BoP. In the case of PŪR in Africa, P&G lacked a clear sense of how various prospective customers might use their products and how to promote and market them (Peterson, 1988). PSI contributed to the partnership its knowledge of local conditions and its proven techniques of social marketing. PSI's approach to social marketing combines education, in order to motivate healthy behavior, with the distribution of PŪR and other health products to people at the BoP.

Direct Access to the Poor

Sometimes a CSP develops because a private venture has access to individuals at the BoP that a public organization wants to reach, or vice versa. MNE Vodafone sells phone services in the developing world. One product the company offers in South Africa is a service named "please call me" (or "PCM") asking the recipient to phone back the sender, even when the sender has run out of credit. The cost of running the service is covered by advertising that is included alongside the PCM message. NGOs pay for the ads, which deliver social-oriented messages (Vodafone, n.d.). For example, in a pilot message sponsored by Vodacom, SocialTxt partnered with two South African NGOs, South Africa National AIDS Helpline and HIV911, in order to share information on HIV counseling and services. SocialTxt is the first firm to make social (noncommercial) use of the marketing space in a PCM message (BBC, 2008; Praekelt Foundation, n.d.; Ramey, 2007).

Distribution Channels

Public organizations can also bring existing channels of distribution to the partnership. In Ghana, micro-finance has traditionally occurred through money-lenders known as "susus." For a small fee, susus have traditionally provided the means for those at the BoP to securely save and access their money, and to obtain small loans. Recognizable by their coats with many pockets, there are almost 1,000 members of the public organization known as the Ghanaian Susu Collector's Association. Recognizing that this pre-existing channel provided immediate access to the BoP micro-financing market, MNE Barclays Bank has partnered with the Association to offer an expanded set of financial products. For its part, Barclays offers the susu collectors training in delinquency management, financial credit and risk management. Moreover, Barclays uses the channel to provide end users with education in consumer finance and risk management, as well. In return, Barclays obtains access to the susu collectors' existing clients and also benefits from their goodwill and client knowledge (UN Development Programme, 2008).

Product Development

Sometimes, the contribution by the public entity involves assisting its private partner in developing the product to be offered to the poor. Tsinghua Tong-fang is a major computer company in Beijing. In 2005, it began a partnership with Beijing's municipal government to develop the Changfeng computer designed specifically for poor rural users. Packed with customized agricultural software based on jointly sponsored market research about the needs of farmers, the computer was developed through the CSP itself. As a result, the company was able to enjoy first-mover advantage in a market that originally was totally closed to it, and the government was able to meet its economic development goals (UN Development Programme, 2008).

Sustainable Supply of Raw Materials

The African country of Guinea is one of the largest suppliers of cashews in the world with fully 80% of its production coming from subsistence agriculture. After Guinea's independence, some of the plantations on which cashews had been growing were permitted to grow wild, reducing the crops significantly. However, recent research demonstrates that the aged trees could be some of the highest quality and yields in the world, if future production is managed effectively. In 2004, the US Agency for International Development (USAID) formed an alliance with MNE Kraft Foods to develop a sustainable supply of the cashew crop from Guinean farmers. As part of the alliance, USAID contributes US$500,000 and Kraft Foods, the large American-headquartered food company, contributes US$250,000 to provide training and to support a significant increase in the amount of land dedicated to cashew production. According to Brian Meinken, Senior Director, Commodity Procurement for Kraft, "through this alliance, we will be contributing to a sustainable future for farmers and their families, while helping to ensure a high quality supply of cashews for our consumers" (USAID, 2004).

The value to Kraft is clear: through the USAID partnership, Kraft has unprecedented access to local knowledge and agribusiness-development capacity which, in conjunction with its experience in market development, will generate "income for rural producers and a better product for our consumers" (USAID Guinea, 2004). As for partner USAID, consider what Frank Young, the deputy director of the agency's Africa Bureau, said: "Sustainable development is essential for countries such as Guinea to climb out of the depths of poverty. The alliance between Kraft and USAID creates a win-win situation for Kraft, USAID and, most importantly, for the farmers of Guinea" (USAID, 2004).

Market Penetration

MNEs often find that products and services intended for the BoP do not find their "early adopters" there. Instead, MNEs experience more initial market success among poor, but not destitute customers. That is certainly the case with mobile banking ("m-banking"). Banking through cellphones is now commonplace in the developed world; but the poverty-busting potential of m-banking may be to make basic financial services more accessible to those at the BoP who often do not live or work within any reasonable proximity to a secure financial institution. In 2006, the cellphone became the first communications technology to have more users in developing countries than in developed ones (Ivatury & Pickens, 2006). As cellphone usage continues to expand throughout this population, so may opportunities to extend m-banking services to the poor. WIZZIT is a start-up mobile-banking provider that offers a transaction banking account accessible via cellphone and debit card. Since its launch in December 2004, WIZZIT has grown to more than 50,000 customers in South Africa. WIZZIT is a "virtual bank" with no branches of its own. Customers can use their cellphones to make person-to-person payments, transfer money, purchase electricity and buy airtime for their phones; with WIZZIT, customers at the BoP no longer need to travel to distant bank branches to complete these routine transactions. Further, WIZZIT customers also receive a debit card with which they can make purchases and get cash back at retail outlets, and also withdraw money from ATMs. To appeal to poor customers, WIZZIT does not have a minimum balance requirement and does not charge fixed monthly fees. Instead it uses a per-transaction pricing model that facilitates adoption with only a modest sign-up fee (World Resources Institute, 2008; WIZZIT Bank, 2009).

WIZZIT uses an imaginative promotional strategy. Rather than using advertising to promote its service, it uses more than 2,000 "WIZZ Kids," typically young people drawn from the lower-income population. WIZZ Kids educate potential customers about WIZZIT and earn a commission for each new customer. All new users have to do to sign up is to key their national identification number into their cellphone. WIZZIT provides customer support that is available in the 11 official languages spoken in South Africa (World Resources Institute, 2008; WIZZIT Bank, 2009).

Cellphone MNE Vodafone has watched the success of WIZZIT with great interest. If WIZZIT can penetrate the BoP market to its lowest-income levels, Vodafone can enjoy a greatly expanded market. Moreover, the lessons learned by WIZZIT may apply to m-banking ventures in other developing countries. Accordingly, Vodafone entered an alliance with several poverty-fighting public organizations to discover how to extend m-banking services deeper into the BoP. With partners Consultative Group to Assist the Poor (CGAP) and the United Nations Foundation (UNF), Vodafone commissioned a study to identify barriers to WIZZIT adoption among the very poor in South Africa. They learned that the barriers included not only a preference for other modes of banking (branches, ATMs), but also a belief that WIZZIT was not a product of any use to the very poor. Armed with this information, Vodafone can now design consumer-education programs to point out the ease and efficiency of m-banking services using their product and in bundling their phones with m-banking services (Ivatury & Pickens, 2006).

Maintaining a Fair Price throughout the Supply Chain

Natura is a Brazilian MNE in the cosmetics business. In its Ekos line, Natura uses the raw material priprioca, a grass whose roots yield a rare, delicate fragrance. Priprioca is a plant only found in the heart of the Brazilian rainforest and it has been used by indigenous people for many centuries. To obtain priprioca, Natura finds itself at the end of a rather long supply chain since the root must be processed and reprocessed close to where it is extracted; and it has been vital to Natura that every entity on that chain receives a fair price. So, it cooperated with Brazilian communities and an NGO (the Brazilian Environment and Natural Resources Institute) to create a system by which all the parties agreed, transparently, to a reasonable profit margin: between 15 and 30%. Natura subsequently leveraged the program to differentiate its brand on the basis that it does not exploit indigenous populations (Boechat, n.d.).

The Messy Process of Forming CSPs

Not all private–public partnerships work out for the poor right away. Nonprofit organization Pésinet is an early-warning method for monitoring the health of children from BoP families in Senegal. Its concept is simple: a mother subscribes to Pésinet's service for a nominal fee and, in return, a local Pésinet representative weighs her child twice a week. Results are communicated through information and communications technologies to a local doctor, who reviews the weight chart and requests a follow-up exam if the child's weight is low.

Originally, Pésinet forged a partnership with Saint Louis Net, a for-profit business that offered a range of IT-based services such as job searches, classified ads, safety-related weather forecasts and marine information for the fishing community, and e-government services. However, Saint Louis Net's revenue was not sufficient to cover the costs of Pésinet, and the partnership failed because the CSP was unable to function as a sustainable enterprise.

One reason for the failure might have been the lack of synergy and mutuality between the two organizations. While Saint Louis Net's IT resources could be shared with Pésinet, Pésinet's success was not critically contingent on IT. Therefore, the collaboration was not balanced, as Saint Louis Net apparently received less than Pésinet (Cropper, 1996). Pésinet's subsequent commercial partners worked out much more effectively for, when Pésinet moved into Mali in 2007, it partnered with not one but two MNEs: Alcatel-Lucent (an IT/communications company) and Medex, a pharmaceutical wholesaler specializing in affordable drugs. Even though Pésinet's operation in Senegal was unsuccessful, the lessons it learned there, plus its new and more balanced and synergistic strategic partnerships, helped it to serve successfully hundreds of Malian children (Alcatel Lucent, 2007).

The Transformative Effect of Public–Private Partnerships

The moral imagination necessary to form profitable partnerships among public and private organizations transforms the relationship into something of a hybrid and, in the process, evolves each individual partner. As "working-level partnerships between MNEs and NGOs become more commonplace, there is growing evidence of a convergence of objectives between these two vastly different forms of organization" (Lodge & Wilson, 2004, p. 61). Or, as the head of an NGO that has worked with corporate partners put it: "Trust me, businesses and NGOs are getting closer, becoming more alike all the time" (Lodge & Wilson, 2004, p. 63). For example, the NGO Population Services International (PSI) has adopted many of the characteristics of a profit-making enterprise. PSI, Procter & Gamble's partner in the PŪR water program, promotes global health through marketing highly subsidized products and services that it sells, rather than gives away, in developing countries. According to its website,

> [t]o some, PSI is an enigma. It claims to be "social" in nature, but employs private sector terminology to describe itself: phrases from the world of business and advertising like "bottom line," "focus groups" and "entrepreneurship." It calls itself nonprofit but charges for many of its products and services. It has "population" in its name but also works in health areas that have little to do with population. Is this the result of an identity crisis, a lack of strategic planning or something else?
>
> Actually, PSI has a sure grasp of its identity and has very deliberately expanded the areas of its health impact. An amalgam of the worlds of commerce and charity, PSI borrows the best strategies from each and uses them to improve the health of the poor and vulnerable in a way that is tangible and measurable. It has turned its tool of social marketing, originally applied only to family planning, to other areas of health where social marketing could make a difference (Population Services International, 2008).

A similar transformation has occurred with the PŪR product line of Procter & Gamble. According to a UN report, even after efforts in vain to turn this innovation into a for-profit venture in various developing countries, P&G has given up the hope of selling it above cost and is now promoting it as a charitable initiative (UN Development Programme, 2008). By 2007 it had sold, at cost, 57 million water-purification packets to humanitarian organizations, with local entrepreneurs distributing them for profit. Clearly, PŪR brings P&G a strong public profile, and its experience with the product will help it sell products for profit at the BoP and other markets; so, PŪR is certainly not turning into a nonprofit enterprise. However, the transformative effect of CSPs has been noted by a number of organizational scholars. For example, O'Riain has observed that each party in a CSP "is *multiply embedded* within the others. Their boundaries cannot be clearly drawn, as each is intertwined with the others" (2000, p. 191).

Often start-up companies in less-developed countries need foundational support for capital formation. A 2008 start-up, the Indian company Husk Power Systems is one such company. This for-profit company, started by two MBA students with a small grant from the University of Virginia to develop their model, converts rice husks, a waste byproduct of rice harvesting, into micropower electrical energy in plants located in rural sections of India where rice is grown in abundance. This is an enormously morally imaginative project that, if successful, will provide electric power on a pay-for-service basis to over 2,500 villages at below-market rates. To date, Husk Power Systems has provided power for 12,000 people in five villages. To expand their technology to other villages, however, they need capital, and they have, to date, received a grant from the Shell Foundation, and are applying for funding from the Overseas Private Investment Corporation. Without this influx of capital from nonprofit foundations, this project would fail (Katz, 2008; Husk Power Systems, 2008).

Other Hybrid Models

Social Entrepreneurs and Social Entrepreneurship

Some of the organizations we have discussed in this and other chapters are called social entrepreneurships, and their founders, social entrepreneurs. A social entrepreneur is an individual or an organization whose primary mission is "to create and sustain social value (not just private value [for themselves or for shareholders])" (Dees, 1998). Social entrepreneurs are sometimes identified with NGOs. But let us examine that claim more carefully. The Grameen Bank of Bangladesh was started by a social entrepreneur Muhammad Yunus for the explicit purpose of reducing poverty among the rural poor through micro-lending. Husk Power System's mission is to create cheap electricity in villages in rural India where no electricity is available. The mission of PSI is to improve health in rural poor, underdeveloped communities that do not have access to health-care. Procter & Gamble's Health Science Institute's mission is to provide safe drinking water.

We list these missions explicitly to highlight two phenomena. All of these missions are socially valuable and, in fact, all of the organizations are making a difference in poverty reduction in ways that reflect their interest and expertise. But some are commercial for-profit entities, others are NGOs and most are hybrids. The Grameen Bank is a for-profit venture. It has never lost money and claims to be an exemplar of capitalism, with the aim to create economic value-added but, of course, economic value-added for more people than its owners and share-holders. Interestingly, as Benjamin Esty from the Harvard Business School has argued, investments made in banks other than a development bank such as Grameen would have produced more returns than investments in Grameen (Esty, 1995). Grameen, of course, argues that it has created economic value-added, but for four million women rather than for a few shareholders. A spin-off from the Bank is the Grameen Foundation, a US-based NGO that accepts donations (the Grameen Bank does not!) whose mission is to create and provide technology and financial resources for start-up micro-lending institutions (Dahle, 2005, p. 55).

Husk Power Systems is also a for-profit company, but will depend on financial support from NGOs with which to expand its power facilities, making it a hybrid organization. PSI sells its products to indigent communities, albeit at drastically reduced prices. P&G's Health Science Institute has created distributorships for PŪR that are profitable to the distributors.

Additionally, there are large micro-financing NGOs, such as Accion and Opportunity International, and a number of smaller organizations who work at funding entrepreneurial micro-lending projects worldwide. One of the biggest is Ashoka, which not only finances social innovation, but also serves as a net-working link to form global partnerships between social entrepreneurs and other businesses (Hammonds, 2005, pp. 60–64).

Our point is that social entrepreneurship defines a wide variety of individual projects and organizations, most of them hybrid organizations, whose defining characteristic is their mission to engage in social value-added and social change, broadly conceived. The magazine, *Fast Company*, calls these individuals and organizations "social capitalists." Social capitalists, according to the magazine, are individuals and organizations that do not merely have grandiose missions but are well-managed and, most importantly, actually "get stuff done" (Dahle, 2005, p. 47), i.e., execute much like profit-making enterprises. Some social capitalists are for-profit, some are NGOs and most are hybrid. All have the mission to improve "social" capital—the well-being of a community or social ecosystem.

In the next chapter, we will propose that MNEs, whether or not they have an explicit social mission driving their organizations, can create economic value-added in poor communities. Social entrepreneurs, particularly those who are "social capitalists," set the example and provide some of the fodder for thinking about this option in ways that are not antithetical to long-term profitability.

Community-Based Enterprises

One of the emerging models for poverty reduction in rural communities in less-developed countries is the phenomenon of community-based enterprises (CBEs). "CBEs are created by community members acting corporately.... [T]he community is completely endogenous to the enterprise and the entrepreneurial process ... [and] the community is simultaneously both the enterprise and the entrepreneur" (Peredo & Chrisman, 2006, p. 310). CBEs usually crop up in impoverished communities that have suffered setbacks due to job loss, environmental catastrophe or market collapse, or a failure of philanthropic or large development projects. These ventures are usually aimed specifically at community redevelopment through poverty reduction, disease control, or even, in some cases, basic security. In Peru, for example, during the heyday of guerrilla wars (1979 to 1982), a number of communities organized community patrols to prevent insurgency invasion and to protect their "investments" in sheep and land (Peredo, 2006).

Most CBEs are directed at "[community] sustainability, self-reliance, and improvement of life" (Peredo & Chrisman, 2006, p. 320) in projects that involve a whole community. One of the most successful CBEs is the Mondragon Corporation Cooperative (MCC), formed in the 1940s by the Basque community in Spain, both to protect the communities from persecution and to develop economic opportunities. It has become a highly successful commercial set of enterprises and today consists of 264 companies and entities active in various sectors, including agriculture and finance. It is still a cooperative run by its thousands of members; many of its member companies are highly profitable; and it is one of Spain's largest industrial companies (Greenwood, 1992; Cronan, 2007).

In the Peruvian Andes, the community of Llocllapampa has developed the Self-Managed Community Enterprise that organizes and oversees agriculture in that community. By working as a unit, the community has been able to improve its irrigation system and purchase heavy farm equipment to streamline and vastly improve productivity on its potato farms. It also depended on transferring the skills of community members who had previously worked in mining before that company left the area (Peredo, 2003).

Successful CBEs are models for other communities to emulate; but they depend on ingenuity and imagination by community leaders, a systems approach to community development and a sense of the importance of cooperation and solidarity in the community in order to be successful. They also depend on matching the talents and skills of community members not only with community needs, but with market demand as well. A systems approach coupled with moral imagination are particularly important. Community leaders will:

- assess the needs and desires of the community;
- link community projects to precipitating events such as the loss of jobs, security or other threats to the community;
- measure the proposed projects against the skills and potential training of community workers;
- create viable projects that will enhance positive change;
- manage dissidents and skeptics; be cheerleaders as well as visionaries.

In this process, leaders may find themselves reshaping certain mental models of community members, as well. The success of the Llocllapampa cooperative was the result of adaptable skills of the community, good agricultural practices and a demand for potatoes in Peru. The long-term success of the Mondragon cooperative was due to the hard-working determined Basque communities involved, a sense of solidarity among the Spanish and professional managerial skills.

What is to be learned from these examples is the importance of creating enterprises that are contextually viable, that are inspirational to the communities in which they are established, and that create value-added for both the enterprise and the community that they serve. CBEs offer MNEs important lessons for success when embarking in Profitable Partnerships.

CSP, Intra-Section Ideology and Moral Imagination

Some people conscientiously oppose cross-sector partnerships on ideological grounds. Free market devotees see alliances between businesses, governments and nonprofits as institutions that dilute the wisdom of the market. Progressives worry that commercial organizations engaging in such partnerships will ultimately succumb to greed, poisoning not only CSPs but also the poverty-alleviation projects that they are meant to support. While we are sympathetic to the power of ideology, extreme poverty is a matter of human rights; and it is difficult to maintain a stance based on ideology when the rights of the poor are at stake. Our position is not one based on pure pragmatism; rather, it is one that gives the poor and *their* ideology a preferential consideration. If their ideology makes them distrust businesses, NGOs or public organizations, then we would advocate an alliance involving a distrusted institution only if its poverty-fighting potential was incontrovertible.

We will end this chapter and transition to the next with a case history of a publicly traded US company that is entrepreneurial, that changed its mission and its vision for its products, that adapted an alliance model with public–private partnerships, and then became profitable in the developing world: the Female Health Company. The Female Health Company (FHC) was a start-up company formed by three former executives from G.D. Searle, a pharmaceutical company that was sold to Monsanto in 1985. FHC was originally a small pharmaceutical firm but, soon after its founding, the executives were able to purchase the patent for the female condom, which was then the only product of its kind on the market. The founders were ecstatic, thinking that because of the great success of the male condom in middle-class US markets, the female condom would be equally popular. Much to their dismay, however, the condom was a failure; American middle-class women simply would not buy or use it.

Almost in bankruptcy, the company then discovered that their product was being used in poor communities, particularly by women of color whose husbands refused to protect themselves, despite the HIV/AIDS epidemic that was threatening that particular population, among many others. So, the next step for FHC was to market its product to public-welfare agencies, although this activity, by itself, was not enough to make the company profitable.

Its next opportunity occurred when the Health Minister from Zimbabwe, a woman, approached FHC's COO, Mary Ann Leeper, with a proposition. The Health Minister delivered a petition signed by over 20,000 Zimbabwean women asking for help in protecting themselves against HIV/AIDS, which was now becoming a rampant pandemic in Zimbabwe. This was obviously a great opportunity for FHC and represented a growing customer base, what every company desires. There was only one problem: there was no money available—no funds from the health ministry and no funds from the women themselves. Zimbabwe was a poor country and most of the population was poor as well, too poor for a product such as a condom.

But this revelation turned out to be the defining moment for the FHC. It realized that, in order to market the female condom, it had to garner support from foundations and government agencies, such as USAID, the World Health Organization, UNAID and others. It had to partner with social-marketing organizations such as PSI; and it had to work with NGOs to market and to distribute

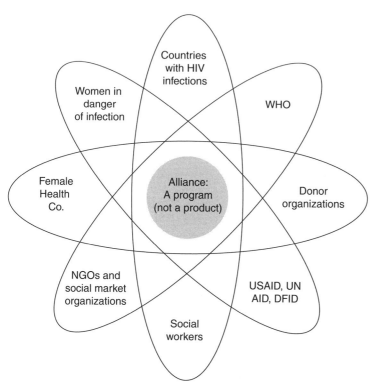

Figure 7.1 The Female Health Company's Alliance Model (source: model courtesy of Mary Ann Leeper, COO, Female Health Company. Used with permission).

the condom in disparate communities that did not understand the product nor its value in preventing HIV/AIDS. The FHC also had to change its marketing plan from marketing a *product* to marketing a *program*. Eventually, it began to rethink its mission, not merely as a commercial enterprise, but as a company focused on women's health, a company offering a program for HIV/AIDS prevention through alliances with various stakeholders, without whom the program would have failed (see Figure 7.1). Today, the FHC markets its product in over 90 developing countries, selling the product at cost plus 5%, or giving it away, and selling its product in 17 developed countries including the United States. Last year, for the first time since its founding in 1996, the company was profitable (Werhane, Posig, Gundry, Powell & Ofstein, 2007).

8

FUTURE PROSPECTS FOR PROFITABLE PARTNERSHIPS

Beginning in the late 1980s, Nike, Inc. gained a reputation for support-ing poor labor practices at the workplaces of its footwear and apparel suppliers in China, Vietnam, Thailand and Malaysia, among other loca-tions in Southeast Asia. As late as 1998, Phil Knight, Nike CEO and founder, stated that "Nike product has become synonymous with slave wages, forced overtime, and arbitrary abuse" (Levenson, 2008, p. 165). Initially, Nike did not perceive as an option contract termination with all manufacturers whose labor standards fell below Nike's own Code of Conduct. However, in response to extraordinary media and public outcry, the company began funding education and housing programs designed to improve the lives of its suppliers' workers and the com-munities in which Nike products are manufactured.

Consider the model established by Nike's activities in Vietnam. Nike has had a significant presence in Vietnam since 1995, where 31% of Nike's footwear is produced each year. Nike contractors and suppliers employ more than 160,000 people in 16 factories, making Nike the largest *indirect employer* in the country. These factories are owned pre-dominantly by Korean and Taiwanese manufacturing concerns. Nike also contracts for apparel manufacturing; yet, because these suppliers are shared with other corporations, Nike's influence is less with these operations than it is in their footwear-manufacturing facilities.

In 1997, Nike started a micro-enterprise loan program called the Microcredit (MC) program through the local Women's Union in Vietnam. The goals of the program are twofold. First, the MC program seeks to lend money to families or individuals with which they are able to run businesses. For example, in Cu Chi, a suburb of Ho Chi Minh City, where a Nike supplier maintains a plant, the MC program has loaned some 1 trillion VND (approximately US$57,000,000) and, according to the Women's Union, over 70% of the businesses funded with MC seed money have been successful. The second objective of the program is to ensure that ongoing support is available for borrowers so that they are most likely to be successful and sustainable.

The MC program requires that they submit a business plan and go through basic business training and health seminars before the plans and loans are approved. They also participate in loan groups to ensure that each of their individual payments are paid; if one of the members of these groups is unable to make a payment, other group members pay on her or his behalf and then help the member to make up the payment. It is a circle of reliance in which each group member helps to sustain the other and the process has created an environment where defaults are practically unheard of (Hartman, Arnold & Wokutch, 2003). Via the MC program, Nike has helped particular communities improve outside the factory itself.

In conjunction with its MC program, Nike also required that its suppliers fund and implement education programs for workers in factories that manufacture Nike-branded goods. These programs have been instrumental in staff retention, particularly in light of Vietnam's highly competitive skilled-labor market. Since its inception, employee-education programs have educated over 10,000 people, with an 85% completion rate; 1,500 have received the equivalence of a GED diploma. Control over these programs has been given to the factory owners themselves, who, in continuing these programs, recognize the importance of fostering an educated and skilled workforce.

In response to governmental concern about housing for factory workers, many of whom travel from the north, Nike's chief representative in Vietnam reached out to Habitat for Humanity to inquire about building dormitories with discretionary funds. As a result, Nike established a loan program, to be overseen by the Women's Union, that would contract with Habitat for Humanity either to build new housing facilities or to improve existing residential areas.

Today, Nike strives to require all of its over 800 contractors (and over 800,000 employees) to abide by its Code of Vendor Conduct, but this is a Herculean task to monitor, and Nike does not claim to have achieved its goal. Nike is most successful with its long-time footwear-manufacturing partners since it commands leverage with those suppliers, but it aspires for 100% compliance throughout its supply chain (Hartman et al., 2003; Levenson, 2008; Wolfe & Shepard, 2009, in press).

Nike's involvement in Vietnam is an example of profitable partnerships at their best. Nike found economic opportunity in that country; it used its own distinctive competencies as an organization; and it took a systemic approach to employment and manufacturing. As a result, Nike has enjoyed impressive financial returns while simultaneously helping to raise many Vietnamese out of poverty.

Throughout this volume, we have argued that well-run multinational enterprises (MNEs) can fulfill a vital role in alleviating poverty in developing nations. We have shown that the mental models that dominate our thinking cause us to assume dismissively that other institutions are in a better position to address global poverty. The caricature of greedy, cigar-smoking robber barons helping meek, bare-footed beggars is difficult to look beyond. Yet, this is certainly *not* the image that accurately represents narratives such as Nike's that have been featured in this volume. Repeatedly, we have urged MNEs to see the base of the pyramid (BoP) as a market opportunity for creating new suppliers, employees and customers in ways that enhance shareholder and other stakeholder value. We believe that MNE commercial engagement at the BoP will create a force in the campaign to alleviate poverty that will relieve suffering and will instill new hope among the bottom billion.

In this final chapter, we have three objectives. First, we review the three cornerstone ideas from this volume: moral imagination, systems thinking and deep dialogue. We do so again to strengthen our rationale for MNE entry into developing economies and so that you will look for them, as we do, in every success narrative involving the BoP. Second, we will propose two important provisos to our arguments in favor of profitable partnerships. We do so because we do not want our invitation to MNEs to result in some of the environmental and human-rights abuses that their involvement at the BoP has historically occasioned. Third, we situate our argument within the global economic downturn that has gripped the end of the first decade of the 21st century. MNE engagement at the BoP is even more critical in these economic circumstances, but fresh doubts about business as an institution may forestall the development of the partnerships that serve as a vital component of the answer to the problem. We end the chapter with a summary of the case in favor of MNEs tackling global poverty.

Moral Imagination, Systems Thinking and Deep Dialogue

The thesis of this book, that MNEs can alleviate poverty by seizing market opportunities at the BoP, rests on the implementation of three key processes: moral imagination, systems thinking and deep dialogue. We introduced each of these earlier, but it is fitting that we reiterate their importance now.

Moral Imagination

As we argued first in Chapter 3, our experiences are framed and ordered by a series of mental models, some of which create biases or blinders that skew our perceptions, our thinking and our decision making. In a pair of provocative articles, Max Bazerman and Dolly Chugh refer to these phenomena as "bounded awareness." Their thesis is, in brief, that no one can be aware of all that exists in their surroundings. Thus, we select and focus on what draws our attention or on what we imagine are salient phenomena for whatever purposes in which we are engaged (Bazerman & Chugh, 2006; Chugh & Bazerman, 2007). In our terminology, we create and perpetuate mental models that focus our attention, but they also serve sometimes to divert, or to cause us to ignore or miss other salient data important to our company, its projects or its key stakeholders. It is this kind of failure to notice that is most troubling and has perhaps the most significant impact. As Bazerman and Chugh warn, "[w]hat you fail to see can hurt you" (Chugh & Bazerman, 2007, p. 1). More importantly, we might add, it can hurt those among us who are most vulnerable.

In the preceding chapters we have intimated that the existence of extensive philanthropy, foundational funding and NGOs working in the poorest communities in the world have blinded our consideration of innovative approaches to poverty alleviation, even when many of these charitable efforts have failed (Easterly, 2006a). In parallel, MNEs, particularly Western-based MNEs, have often ignored or dismissed opportunities for commercial development in these same poor communities. Most of this lack of attention is not out of indifference or cruelty. To the contrary, many MNEs are in fact generous in their philanthropic support of international efforts at health, education, sanitation and the like. Rather, MNEs are often preoccupied with and develop commerce in communities with which they are already familiar, communities that are politically stable, that have a reliable customer base and economic and educational resources on which the MNE can depend. The pressure for short-term profitability mitigates risk taking in new areas where literacy rates are low, where there is political corruption, where transportation facilities are poor at best, and/or where there are health and security risks. Moreover, mental models that falsely characterize the abilities of the poor or separate producing profits and being ethical create blind spots in the array of strategic alternatives they consider.

In Chapter 5, we defined moral imagination as

a necessary ingredient of responsible moral judgment [that entails] ... the ability to discover, evaluate and act upon possibilities not merely determined by a particular circumstance, or limited by a set of operating mental models, or merely framed by a set of rules or rule-governed concerns (Werhane, 1999a, p. 93).

Engaging in morally imaginative decision making involves, first, disengaging from the present context and operative, often implicit, mindsets. The second step is to explore new alternatives that meet moral and economic standards. In this context, managers should question new alternatives in terms of viability, ease of entry, the values that are at stake and the long-term possibilities and downsides of the decision. Third, decision makers should delve into the consequences, second-guessing possible outcomes, the strength of developing relationships, questions of precedent and publicity, and the positive and negative effects.

Moral imagination is essential in uncovering specific market opportunities at the BoP. Indeed, in a changing global economic order, where developed economies are stagnating and where the rich are getting poorer, blinding "bounded awareness" or biased mental models must be discarded. The reasons for doing so are probably obvious, but they are also complex and interrelated. First, it is usually assumed that it is a "good thing" to be philanthropic and to help the poor. But that is rarely a good reason for an MNE to enter developing markets. Besides, as we have seen, philanthropy is not always successful in creating economic value-added in poor communities. Moreover, poor farmers did not want charity; they wanted their farm to be productive and commercially viable. Most of all, they wanted to be self-sufficient. This is the major take-away from micro-lending. When it is successful, it creates self-reliant, productive women and men, at the same time creating returns for the lenders.

Moral imagination is also important in unbinding our mental models about our core competencies. Entering new markets has little to do with charitable giving; in fact, there are few commercial enterprises that have charity as their core competency. Rather, profitable partnerships require leveraging corporate core competencies to develop productive capacities in new communities. The makers of PŪR know about what it takes to make clean water; by making their product available at the BoP, thousands are made more productive by being unburdened from disease and suffering. That is, P&G focused on one of its core competencies, water-cleansing products, created a distribution channel through its NGO, the Health Science Institute, and worked from their collective competencies. Second, as we argued in Chapter 7, profitable partnerships often require MNEs to form alliances with NGOs, foundations and governments in order to be successful in new markets. The market success of the Female Health Company was due, in no small part, not only to its foundational support, but also to its alliances with social workers and NGOs in marketing this product to disparate communities. But again, the FHC focused on its core competency: the ability to make a female condom that could improve female health. It did not and does not engage in other peripheral ventures that would not be within its know-how or capacity. Nike is successful in Vietnam because it leveraged its core competency, knowledge about sports-clothing manufacture, in partnering with other MNEs, with NGOs and with the Vietnamese government.

Systems Thinking

In Chapter 1, we introduced systems thinking as an approach to problem solving that is holistic and polycentered, where few things happen independently. Systems thinking is the habit of mind that considers any social entity to be a complex interaction of individual and institutional actors, each with conflicting interests and goals, and with a number of feedback loops (Wolf, 1999).

A systems approach presupposes that most of our thinking, experiencing, practices and institutions are interrelated and interconnected through a network of relationships. Each element in a particular set of relationships affects other components of that set as well as the entire system, as a whole. Systems thinking, therefore, requires that we conceive of stakeholder relationships as sets of interrelated and interconnected practices and forces, and that we recognize that almost no business phenomenon can be studied meaningfully in isolation from its networks and other relationships. The *interdependence thesis* illustrates this interconnectedness. This assumption of connectedness is nicely captured in the following description:

> The global corporation can be visualized as a *logical thread of relationships between a multitude of moving parts*—ideas, information, knowledge, capital, and physical products. These relationships define an organization and its extended network of collaborators, including suppliers and customers (Prahalad & Krishnan, 2008, p. 46).

Nike is an example of a large MNE engaging in a "thread of relationships," leveraging its core competencies in new markets and partnering with factory owners in Vietnam, despite the political and social risks of operating in what is still a communist country. It saw an opportunity, engaged in moral imagination to think through how to enter that market, and partnered with other MNEs, the Vietnamese government and NGOs in developing its presence there. Nike did not buy into the mental model of Vietnam as merely an "adversarial" communist country in which there was no opportunity to engage in commerce. Instead, it saw that, despite the political climate in that country, there were new business-development opportunities and resources. It then engaged in moral imagination by stepping out of the usual mindset that doing business in troublesome settings is too risky. It partnered with Korean and Taiwanese firms that were familiar with the Vietnamese cultural context, and set about establishing relationships in that country. Nike could have relied on simple, bilateral contracts to meet its manufacturing requirements and, similarly, could have ignored the behavior of its suppliers and their employees. Taking a more systemic approach, however, Nike has worked deliberately to build a system where it strives to hold suppliers accountable to its Code of Vendor Conduct (Hartman et al., 2003, pp. 145–190). Nike did not just mandate that code from corporate headquarters. Nike is "on the ground" in Vietnam, engaging in employment, safety, health and environmental audits of its contract factories, working with Habitat for Humanity to construct and

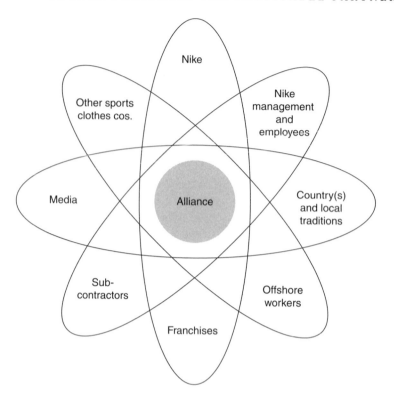

Figure 8.1 Nike's Alliance Model (source: model courtesy of Mary Ann Leeper, COO, Female Health Company, used with permission).

improve worker housing, and forming micro-lending partnerships modeled after the Grameen Bank. It has developed education programs, and has prohibited its partners from engaging in sweatshop activities such as excessive or unpaid overtime, despicable working conditions, child labor or unsafe working conditions (Levenson, 2008). Nike has taken a systems approach to its Vietnam operation, reflecting Prahalad and Krishnan's description of a global corporation. It sees itself not at the center of a web of relationships, but as part of a periphery of interdependent partnership alliances with its stakeholders much like that depicted in Figure 8.1.

Another fine example of systems thinking in practice is illustrated by the Swedish multinational food processing and packaging company, Tetra Pak. Ionescu-Somers and Steger describe Tetra Pak in their case study, "Fortifying the Business Model," as follows:

> Tetra Pak is a multi-million dollar global company that develops, manufactures and markets systems for processing, packaging and distributing food. It is the developer and world's leading supplier of aseptic carton packaging for milk, soup, fruit juices and other liquids. [Aseptic packaging is a special package-processing system that allows liquids to be stored at room temperature for up to a year without spoiling.] ... In the mid-1990s Tetra Pak set up partnerships with its Indonesian customers, the

U.S. Department of Agriculture and local NGOs to regularly supply milk in aseptic packages to government-funded school feeding programmes in Indonesia. The programme was a great success, with definable business, economic and developmental benefits; and it expanded rapidly. The benefits to children's health were significant; and it was also an exceptional opportunity for a global company to profile itself as an industry leader ... Tetra Pak found that it could enter the "hearts and minds" of rural people in an entirely different way to a traditional "sales and marketing"-focused business approach ... [by] adopting a "poor-centric" approach. Through the school feeding programmes, the company brand could be anchored at a lower cost, increasing knowledge of [new BoP] markets and improving rural reach.... Given the perceived added value of the Indonesian school feeding programmes,... the company decided to apply its years of expert knowledge to other developing-country environments (Ionescu-Somers & Steger, 2008, pp. 357–358).

Tetra Pak, like Nike, relied on systems thinking in entering a new market in Indonesia. It created partnerships with NGOs and with local government; it provided a much-needed product, milk, in spoil-resistant packages; it learned about rural culture in Indonesia; and it opened up new markets for its products. Moreover, it did not simply use its marketing-as-usual approach, which had proven very successful in richer communities. Instead, it saw its school-meal program as a learning opportunity. It developed a program that may be replicable in other BoP markets, and, as "first mover," it created enormous opportunities for its other products. Had it not relied on systems thinking, Tetra Pak might never have identified its intricate combination of elements that enabled it to prosper in the corruption-ridden country of Indonesia. Without thinking systematically about the rural Indonesian context and the background of its specific stakeholders, Tetra Pak might have approached marketing and product distribution from a Western industrial perspective, thus missing that market altogether.

Deep Dialogue

When we coined the phrase "profitable partnerships," we had two separate partnerships in mind: one with the poor and the other with not-for-profit and government entities. Communication with various stakeholders is an important activity for any business enterprise, but it is even more critical when one is involved at the BoP. As we described it in Chapter 7, deep dialogue is an engagement in various forms of communication and exchange where each actor or set of actors tries to grasp the mindset of the other and where each actor may benefit, albeit differently, from the communication or exchange in ways that increase trust between the involved parties (Hart, 2007, p. 196; Molm, Collett & Schaefer, 2007).

Again, mental models distance MNEs from their BoP stakeholders. "The poor are passive; they need to be taught how to care for themselves; their priorities are all wrong" are just some of the mental models that obstruct developing understanding about prospective customers. Or, "NGOs are inefficient; they think only in small numbers of people served; governments have no sense of urgency" are similar stereotypes that dominate MNE thinking about possible institutional partners. When combined with the obvious problems of language and culture, mental models like these are not overcome by more talk, better surveys, or even answers to probing questions.

Because engaging in deep dialogue strives for understanding but also requires both parties to inquire together about one another as equals, it both requires and produces trust on all sides. The result of deep dialogue is more than a set of shared purposes and projects. It is the development of a collective identity, where all parties accept each other's perspective, to the point of being able to act satisfactorily on one another's behalf without direction.

Throughout this volume, we have highlighted some of the visionary firms that have demonstrated their capacity to be morally imaginative risk takers by entering BoP markets effectively. In most cases, these firms engaged in deep dialogue with those communities in which they were trying to gain entry in order to craft a chameleon-like response to the BoP markets they served. For example, in developing washing products for the poorest customers in India, Hindustan Lever (HLL), a division of the multibillion-dollar European company, Unilever, required its employees, mostly middle-class Indians, to spend time living in rural villages all over India. This engagement with what were initially thought of as "fringe" customers enabled Hindustan Lever to capture almost 35% of the soap-powder market in these communities. These encounters also helped them to create Project Shakti to engage villagers as marketers and distributors of their products, thus providing jobs as well as products (Hart, 2007; Ahmad, Werhane & Gorman, 2004). In distributing PŪR in various communities, the Health Science Institute learned that different villages had varying views of what constituted "good" water, and their challenge was to customize their "sales pitch" to those communities who thought that the taste of their traditional but dangerously polluted water was best. The Female Health Company and its NGOs go village by village in every country where they have a presence, customizing their product and program to the mindset of that village. Deep dialogue enabled these pioneers to stake their claims not only as leaders in new markets of billions of new consumers, but also as partners in contributing to a sustainable future of some of the world's poor.

It is likely (although we did not directly observe it) that deep dialogue preceded Nike's decision to partner with Habitat for Humanity in providing housing for the Vietnamese workers who made Nike footwear, for, without an authentic understanding of their perspective, Nike's successful micro-lending system could not have been put in place. We know that the design of the ONIL stove resulted from deep dialogue; and we suspect that deep dialogue preceded the development of Cemex's novel home-construction program, especially since the company humbly and publicly declared its ignorance of these markets (Chapter 5).

Two Provisos to our Proposal

Enterprises have been attracted to the BoP before. During colonial times and afterward, commercial entities flooded into the developing world expecting sizeable shareholder returns. While their intent was not always prejudicially exploitative, manufacturing facilities frequently became sweatshops, and the natural environment in these countries was too often spoiled. Mining and drilling were primarily extractive industries, taking valuable resources out of a country without compensating with local economic development, or without doing so in a fair manner. Accordingly, while commercial investments at the BoP are an important step in poverty alleviation, it is our contention that they should be made only under two conditions.

Following a series of important and persuasive arguments by Aneel Karnani (2007b, c), we submit that, if companies are serious about long-term investments at the BoP, workers must be paid, and be paid a living wage. One reason is corporate economic sustainability. Prahalad (2005) suggests that we need to think of the poor as customers. This is fine, but it is not enough. In Karnani's words, "[w]e need to view the poor as producers, and emphasize buying from them, rather than [merely] selling to them" (Karnani, 2007c, p. 99). The value in these markets is in *employment*. As Adam Smith argued more than 235 years ago, if people have jobs with decent wages, they will become purchasers and, the more they earn, the greater will be the growth in markets. Thus, those at the BoP are not merely customers or consumers, they are workers who should also be thought of as partners in economic development where employees and entrepreneurs are creating value-added for themselves, as well as for MNEs. Otherwise, the temptation to exploit this needy labor force is always a possibility.

The other reason for demanding living wages is moral. Paying a living wage is fair and just. When sweatshops pay below a living wage (as defined in the country of payment, the "host" country), it is a form of human exploitation that simply exports productivity out of that country in order to provide cheaper goods for consumers in the developed world without creating any economic value-added for that community. Unfortunately, this is commonplace in the developing world. Too often, workers are paid less than a subsistence wage and are further cheated out of overtime and days off, as the data from sweatshop investigations demonstrate (National Labor Committee, 2009). For both economic and moral reasons, then, MNEs engaged in profitable partnerships should avoid sweatshop practices, or merely extracting value out of a community rather than building value within and with it. In some cases, this effort may require influencing the practices of business partners, as we saw in the case of Nike. In others, it necessitates violating local customs, or partnering with other organizations up and down the supply chain in order to bring exploitative practices to an end.

Our second proviso comes from the work of Stuart Hart (2007). MNEs need to develop and to use environmentally sustainable products and services in whatever venue they operate. This mandate is becoming obvious; on a planet that has become "hot, flat, and crowded" (T. Friedman, 2008), we can no longer outsource our landfills, our waste or our pollution, or we will all suffer as a result. The world is just too small to accommodate this continued practice. If we want to leave the Earth to future generations, the greening of industry and services is absolutely necessary. Moreover, as companies are learning, environmental sustainability is a value-added proposition. There are countless examples of companies that have reduced costs with green technology, such as Interface, a company that recycles all of its products and has thereby saved millions of dollars by not having to purchase new raw materials (Interface Flooring, 2009). So, the old arguments that being "green" imposes more costs than benefits are created from worn-out mental models that have failed to incorporate the inventive technology that is being used in forward-thinking, entrepreneurial companies. Indeed, environmental sustainability should be considered a necessary element in creating sustainable value-added for the MNE and its stakeholders. Cai and Wheale summarize this strategic advantage:

> [A] sustainable-value framework makes clear the nature and magnitude of the opportunities associated with [environmental] sustainability and connects them to dimensions of value creation for the firm, in particular, cost and risk reduction (for example, through the introduction of clean technologies), innovation (for example, the development of so-called alternative technologies), legitimacy and reputation (achieved for example, through product stewardship), and sustainable growth (for example, by identifying unmet needs and unexplored markets) (Cai & Wheale, 2004, p. 514).

This approach is sometimes referred to as "triple-bottom-line" thinking, and many companies now are trying to adopt quantitative valuations to measure their environmental impact, their social impact and their profitability (Elkington, 1994). We would expand the "social impact" aspect of the approach to argue that, in developing economies, companies need to measure the economic impact as well as the social impact of their entry on the community, as well as on their own bottom line.

But, as Hart intimates, technologies have to be transferred to initiatives at the BoP as well, and the results there are often mixed. The Indian division of Unilever, Hindustan Lever Ltd (HLL), has created a soap powder, *Wheel*, which is much less toxic than its competitor, Nirma. They also sell it in affordable single-use packets. Unfortunately, however, HLL has created a new environmental problem since the single-use packets are not biodegradable (Hart, 2007). Hart also cites a program by Daimler-Chrysler to use Brazilian coconut fibers found in the Amazon in its manufacture of Mercedes Benz seats and visors. Its alliance with these growers and processing plants has created about 4,000 Brazilian jobs and a biodegradable fabric for Daimler-Chrysler (Hart, 2007, pp. 153–154). Husk Power Systems, the start-up company we discussed in Chapter 7, also promises to create energy, jobs and waste reduction from rice husks, a triple-win situation for the company, the community and the environment. Whether this will be "clean" energy, however, remains to be determined.

There are a number of other clean-energy initiatives. For example, a Brazilian-based NGO called IDEAAS funds solar-energy systems in small rural communities. It rents (not gives away!) photovoltaic solar home systems for as little as US$10/month, approximately the same price that families pay monthly for nonrenewable fuels and candles. For families who cannot afford the US$10, IDEAAS has started a rural micro-lending project that lends money for small micro-enterprises that can be used for solar energy and business development (World Business Council for Sustainable Development, 2004; IDEAAS, 2009).

E+Co, another NGO, is setting a 21st-century standard for profitable partnerships that produce clean energy and provide new business venues in underdeveloped communities. E+Co has assisted in the formation of over 200 small, for-profit, clean-energy companies in Africa, Asia and South America over the last 15 years. E+Co lends money to these ventures at 8–12% interest and carefully monitors the enterprises, their projects, their processes and their financial success. These companies produce a variety of energy products including cook stoves, windmills, photovoltaic units and small hydroelectric plants. All these projects are aimed at producing clean carbon-reducing energy in small villages across these continents (Boss, 2008–2009). According to E+Co,

> [t]o calculate the return on investment, we measure our clean energy businesses across 34 social, environmental and financial indicators. E+Co collects data from each investee company biannually and then compiles the results into an organizational summary called an Impacts Table. Capturing the impact of the investments is critical to demonstrating the effectiveness of our approach.... The aim is, by 2020, to reach 80–100 million additional people with access to cleaner energy (E+Co, 2009).

Profitable Partnerships and the Economic Downturn

Since World War II, we have experienced the global expansion of market capitalism, albeit not always successfully, and certainly not uniformly. After the fall of the Berlin Wall and the disintegration of the Soviet Union, many in business and government, at least in the industrial nations, dismissed socialism and communism as defunct economic theories; and there seemed to be a universal embrace of market capitalism, often interpreted as unfettered laissez-faire, free enterprise. But in mid- to late 2008, Western economies experienced a collapse of markets, or at least of financial markets, particularly those functioning in comparatively unregulated environments.

The economic downturn understandably created considerable caution concerning new capital investments. On the face, this would seem to jeopardize MNE investment at the BoP. Yet, we contend that the growing paucity of attractive investment opportunities in the developed world ought to make projects at the BoP, more, not less, compelling. Indeed, one might even argue that now that MNEs have experienced their own economic crises, they can better imagine life without the luxuries that once spoiled them. In any event, in a new climate of sobriety, MNEs have no choice but to confront the reality of an ever-flattening global economy (T. Friedman, 2006). To do otherwise locks these companies out of potential markets and locks them into a parochial Western, stagnating economic order that has proven not to be impervious to failure.

This perspective is certainly not new. In his famous book *The Wealth of Nations* published in 1776, the well-known political economist Adam Smith argued that commerce will work, and work well, only under a rule of law and in an environment of trust, a respect for equal rights, fair play and a level playing field (Smith, 1776 [1976]; Werhane, 1999b). Smith recognized that abject poverty results in human-rights abuses and in poorly functioning markets. He also argued for what we would call a "living wage" today (Smith, 1776 [1976]: Book III); and he envisioned international economic expansion through free trade as the most effective means for economic development. Thus, while modern capitalism may be under fire, the thinker most responsible for its theoretical foundation would fully support profitable partnerships as a natural form of the political economic system he envisaged.

Smith would find incomprehensible the contemporary mental models that separate doing well and doing good. He would be baffled by a CEO's reluctance to report to shareholders that some of an MNE's profits came from doing business at the BoP. Smith would be confounded by a *New York Times* editorial that called attention to our both conscious and subconscious tendencies to applaud and honor low-paid NGO workers who enjoy modest localized results at poverty reduction while simultaneously castigating those handsomely paid business executives who transform entire industries in the developing world. By example, we laud the efforts of Mother Teresa (as we should), but we disparage the efforts of Howard Schultz, the CEO of Starbucks who revolutionized the coffee-growing and commercial practices of many hundreds of South American and African coffee growers, on the basis of his tremendous take-home pay (Kristof, 2008, p. 23). This is not to say that astronomical executive compensation should proceed unchecked, but simply that profits and concurrent profit-takers are not, merely by virtue of their existence, unethical per se. Smith would not have understood this gut-ready link between commercial affairs and greed that dominates contemporary mental models. For him, profit making, parsimony and fairness were inseparable. The juxtaposition of "profitable" and "partnerships" was as natural to Smith as it is perhaps unnatural to others today.

Obviously, Adam Smith did not imagine the pace and complexity of the modern international commercial system. His was a world of farmers and shopkeepers, not a global complex network of tightly woven economic interdependencies. However quaint Smith's world, it was one based on close psychological and social attachments. The industrial revolution had not yet separated work from craft, so employees could readily identify with the fruits of their labor. Organizations were small, providing a sense of community rare in contemporary bureaucracies. Business partners relied on transactions and trust rather than protracted negotiations and legal documents.

Of course, there is no going back to the allegedly halcyon days of Adam Smith's world (and we should be reminded of the abject poverty and illiteracy that existed in 18th-century Britain). But it is important to recognize that alleviating global poverty is not just another "flavor of the month" project. Smith saw the downsides of poverty a very long time ago, and it is good to be reminded of that. Sadly, the solution to poverty that occurred so naturally to him, job creation that creates economic growth, is no longer one that arises in normal discourse. As we have seen, the principal reason is that modern thinking about global poverty is based upon mental models that are *more modern than accurate*.

Even though the financial turmoil that began in 2008 may make the posture of some MNEs less strategic, those MNEs that position themselves today to capitalize on market opportunities at the BoP will be effectively positioned to be successful economically. We acknowledge the risks entailed by engagement in such projects, but propose that, in a flat world, non-engagement entails risks as well, both moral and economic.

Surviving in a global, but changing, economic context and creating economic growth are part of most aims of MNEs. Indeed, they are the implicit goals of any company, even though they are not always stated explicitly. If Prahalad (2005) is correct, the supersaturation of mature markets in the developed industrial countries means that companies not engaged in new markets will atrophy. But what makes these markets so promising? It is not merely that there are so many potential customers among the poor, but rather, as we argued earlier, that these markets create economic growth in that region. That can be done only if the economic well-being of the local communities is improved, thus creating new markets for goods and services. So, we suggest, opportunities at the base of the pyramid are vast, and MNEs should be engaged there if for no other reason than to be able to survive the market disruptions that began in 2008. Besides, since profitable partnerships hold the promise of adding to earnings, these can be reinvested with the idea that a larger scale will result in even higher returns. In Chapter 6 we discussed the partnership between insurance MNE Allianz and NGO CARE to offer micro-insurance in India. Even after the global risk-management industry turned down sharply in 2008, Werner Zedelius, member of the board of management of Allianz SE responsible for the company's growth markets, said:

> Traditionally, poor people cannot afford the premiums for insurance cover, but here we have developed a set of products the community can afford and actually wants to use. For us, microinsurance is a growing social business. We expect it to be profitable within the first year and plan to reinvest any profits into the project to enlarge it further (Allianz Group, 2008).

Investing in profitable partnerships ought not to be approached the same way as investments in charity. Profitable partnerships offer real growth opportunities!

There is one other factor that should encourage MNEs to look to the BoP in spite of the recent economic turbulence—profitable partnerships deeply engage a company's primary stakeholders. Not only are shareholders happy with their returns, but employees, suppliers, customers and other trading partners take pride in their association with a firm that is doing something about global poverty. Consider employees as one important stakeholder group. Attracting the brightest talent requires more than six-figure salaries today (Lockwood, 2007). Increasingly, gifted young people are after something deeper and more aligned with their values as global citizens and their involvement in community service (Konrad, 2006). Similarly, as MNEs struggle to capture knowledge and wisdom by retaining experienced workers, alleviating global poverty becomes a fresh source of engagement (Peterson & Stewart, 1996). Today's employees are looking for meaning, and corporate projects that address the world's most pressing needs offer them a sense of "vocation" and even a "calling" (Hall & Chandler, 2005). Other stakeholders are also likely to value their associations with MNEs that have poverty-alleviation projects. NGOs and other prospective partners seek alliances principally with organizations that have stellar reputations (e.g., Heller, 2008). In general, companies with positive reputations have higher market value, receive preferential treatment when raising equity and debt, and have more and happier customers (Fatemi, 2009; Vallens, 2008). Stakeholder engagement is strategically vital any time, but particularly during recessions when stakeholders are more prone to re-evaluating their relationships. When credit froze in late 2008, it was because stakeholders lost trust in their financial partners. It is hard *not* to trust an enterprise that is doing well by doing good.

Why should MNEs Enter BoP Markets?

MNEs, or at least some MNEs, have the capacity to alleviate poverty; and they should do so if only for their own interest. Entering markets at the BoP provides economic growth for themselves, and engaging in these markets is a means for enhancing their long-term survivability. If approached merely from a triple-bottom-line perspective, MNEs are best suited to achieve these ends. But there is another important reason to enter these markets. Let us not overlook what will happen to the poor without such investments. Poverty numbers will increase; global economic growth at the BoP will be undermined; and global environmental degradation will go unabated. In a flat world, all of us will suffer. As we have argued earlier, left to the institutions that have historically fought global poverty, the economic outlook for those at the BoP is anything but rosy. Thus, we are convinced by Prahalad's arguments (2005) that it is in the long-run interest of MNEs to do business at the BoP. But, we qualify his conclusion with the admonition that all organizations should operate within our two provisos. A number of small, medium and large commercial enterprises have already entered these markets. Some, like the Grameen Bank, Manila Water, Comparta-mos Bank and Anul, are locally owned companies or cooperatives. Some are small entrepreneurial ventures such as the Children's Development Bank and Husk Power Systems. Others are small, medium and large MNEs such as the Female Health Company, Cemex, P&G, Vodafone, Tetra Pak and Nike. Most have forged alliances with NGOs and local governments. Some had their origins as NGOs such as KickStart and E+Co. All serve as models for profitable partnerships at the base of the pyramid.

To conclude, we urge MNEs, entrepreneurs, NGOs and other organizations currently contemplating entry into new BoP markets (whether locally or as a foreign venture) to ask themselves the following questions:

- What factors have prevented us and others from entering BoP markets? Are these insurmountable barriers to entry, or can we find imaginative means to circumvent them?
- Is the market opportunity one in which there will be long-term gains for our shareholders? Will our involvement at the BoP satisfy our other primary stakeholders?
- Is this an opportunity that fits our core competencies?
- Is this an opportunity that can create economic value-added for local employees, customers and other stakeholders, or will our intentions be merely extractive?
- Have we entered or can we enter into deep dialogue with local communities, or are there barriers to communication and local understanding in this context?
- Is there a moral risk in overlooking this market opportunity? How does that compare to the risks of market entry?
- Is there an institutional infrastructure in place to support market solutions to this opportunity? If not, can we get around or work through these hardships?
- Is there a way for us to build the productive capacity in this community so that other new markets may develop in the future?

- Are our products and services environmentally sustainable?
- Can we have a market presence without treating any of our stakeholders in an unfair way? If we must disappoint any stakeholders, which ones are they, and what are the trade-offs, if any?

Conclusion

As business ethicists, the four of us writing this book are frequently asked to offer our opinions on various moral dilemmas that confront business profession-als. With some exceptions, we often find ourselves aligned with those who assert that good ethics and good business run hand in hand, that the business case for an action is rarely distinct from the ethics case. So it is with poverty alleviation. Throughout this volume, we have argued repeatedly that alleviating poverty is simply good business. The returns are self-evident, and alleviating poverty is an effective way to build an engaged community of stakeholders. Inevitably, when we are asked our opinions as ethicists, our posture is not to identify new con-straints or to specify higher standards. Rather, what we do as ethicists is reframe the question in order to illuminate a way of thinking that was overlooked in the initial problem formulation, to recalibrate our mental models. To put it very simply, our job as business ethicists is to awaken moral imagination.

If we have done our job in this book, you are aware that your previous per-spective on the role of business in addressing global poverty may have been incomplete. The narratives we have shared at the beginning of each chapter cannot help but tug at one's heart and plant a seed of hope where none seemed possible. Imagine playing a part in such a venture. Picture yourself waking every morning knowing that your labor will ease the suffering of those whose lives did not begin with the privileges you have enjoyed. MNEs tap into this reservoir of solidarity when they pursue projects at the BoP.

NOTES

2 FAILED STRATEGIES IN THE ALLEVIATION OF POVERTY

1. "A Day in the Life of Saroja" courtesy of Microplace, 2008. www.microplace.com/learn_more/globalpovertysaroja. Reprinted with permission.
2. www.imf.org/external/np/prsp/prsp.asp?view=ipr&sort=cty.

3 MENTAL MODELS AND CONTRIBUTING BIASES ON GLOBAL POVERTY

1. Selection from Chapter 3 reprinted from "Streetsment Bankers," by Meenakshi Sinha. Source: *The Times of India*. Copyright 2009, Bennett, Coleman & Co. Ltd. All Rights Reserved.

4 NARRATIVES OF MULTINATIONAL FOR-PROFIT ENTERPRISES AND CORPORATE SOCIAL RESPONSIBILITY

1. Readers might wonder why we have not appealed to Karl Weick's notion of sensemaking (Weick, 1979) rather than mental models. It is true that this concept would offer another way to approach our analysis. Weick appropriates a socially constructed assumption that all of our experiences are framed by mental models; and he calls the ways in which we frame our experiences "sensemaking." He writes, "[s]ensemaking involves the ongoing retrospective development of plausible images that rationalize what people [and organizations] are doing" (Weick & Sutcliffe, 2005, p. 401). "[S]ensemaking has to do with meaning construction and reconstruction by … involved parties as they attempt to develop a meaningful framework" (Gioia & Chittipeddi, 1991, p. 442). We would argue, however, that the term "mental model" does the same work without unduly depending on whether the mental models in question are retrospective (Weick, 1979) or reconstructive (Gioia & Chittipeddi, 1991).
2. Since this set of incidents in the 1900s, Shell has revamped its mission and code of conduct in an effort to prevent future events such as the Nigerian executions.
3. Parts of this section are derived from a previous publication by Patricia H. Werhane entitled "Corporate social responsibility/corporate moral responsibility: Is there a difference and the difference it makes," in Steve May, George Cheney and Juliet Roper (Eds.), *The debate over corporate social responsibility* (pp. 459–474), New York: Oxford University Press, 2007; and from "Corporate social responsibility, corporate moral responsibility, and systems thinking" in Gabriel Flynn (Ed.), *Corporate social responsibility: An Irish perspective* (pp. 269–289), Dordrecht: Springer Publisher, 2008. Reprinted by permission of the author and publishers.
4. Carroll has considerably expanded his thinking since this quoted definition. See, for example, Carroll (1993).
5. There has, of course, been a lively debate over whether corporations have moral responsibilities. For a sample, see French (1984), Smythe (1985), Werhane (1985) and Velasquez (1983, 2003).

5 GLOBAL POVERTY AND MORAL IMAGINATION

1. *Patrimonio Hoy* means, literally, "Patrimony Today" and refers to the tradition in Mexican society of creating something of value that can be passed down to future generations.
2. A problem that Edward Freeman (1994, p. 412) has defined as the Separation Fallacy:

It is useful to believe that sentences like, "x is a business decision" have no ethical content or any implicit ethical point of view. And, it is useful to believe that sentences like "x is an ethical decision, the best thing to do all things considered" have no content or implicit view about value creation and trade (business).

This way of thinking, suggests Freeman, fails to recognize that almost every business decision has some ethical content.

6 INSTITUTIONAL BARRIERS, MORAL RISK AND TRANSFORMATIVE BUSINESS VENTURES

1. In ethics, the distinction between killing and letting die is instructive. Asscher (2008) states,

   when an agent kills she takes responsibility, but when an agent lets die, she does not take responsibility. Therein lies the moral distinction between killing and letting die. The distinction, however, is defeated when an agent is already responsible for the surrounding situation (p. 280).

   Thus, if an MNE is partially responsible for the "surrounding situation" at the BoP, then it is as responsible if they had directly inflicted suffering there.
2. MNEs generally have the financial wherewithal to handle such challenges. For example, they can internally finance their venture and deal with inflation issues utilizing strategies such as arbitrage.
3. The Foreign Corrupt Practices Act (15 U.S.C. secs. 78dd-1, *et seq.*) is a United States statute which prohibits payments to a foreign official (bribes = cash or non-cash items) "for the purpose of influencing any act of that foreign official in violation of the duty of that official or to secure any improper advantage in order to obtain or retain business." It should be noted that the FCPA creates an exclusion for "facilitating payments," payments to a public official to expedite the performance of duties an official is already bound to do, as opposed to paying an official to engage in acts that she or he is not permitted to do.
4. Allen Hammond of the World Resources Institute, interviewed February 2, 2008.
5. Interestingly, Peace Corp volunteer Autumn Brown is currently attempting to build entrepreneurial motivation and skills in Cameroon. See her blog at http://autumnincameroon.blogspot.com/2008_02_01_archive.html.

7 PUBLIC–PRIVATE PARTNERSHIPS AND OTHER HYBRID MODELS FOR POVERTY ALLEVIATION

1. A development bank is a bank whose primary mission is to create economic or social value-added for blighted communities. Profitability for these banks is secondary to that primary mission. Nevertheless, the Grameen Bank has never lost money in more than 30 years of its existence.

REFERENCES AND FURTHER READING

Acemoglue, Daron, Johnson, Simon & Robinson, James. (2006). Understanding prosperity and poverty: Geography, institutions, and the reversal of fortune. In A. Banerjee, R. Bénabou & D. Mookherjee (Eds.), *Understanding poverty* (pp. 19–35). New York: Oxford University Press.

Acumen Fund. (2008). *Acumen Fund concept paper: The Best Available Charitable Option (BACO).* Retrieved March 11, 2008, from www.acumenfund.org/knowledge-center.html.

Adams, C. (2002). Internal organizational factors influencing corporate social and ethical reporting. *Accounting, Auditing Accountability Journal, 15,* 223–250.

Aghion, Philippe & Armendariz de Aghion, Beatriz. (2006). New growth approach to poverty alleviation. In A. Banerjee, R. Bénabou & D. Mookherjee (Eds.), *Understanding poverty* (pp. 73–83). New York: Oxford University Press.

Agle, B., Donaldson, T., Freeman, R. E., Jensen, M. C., Mitchell, R. K. & Wood, D. J. (2008, April). Dialogue: Toward superior stakeholder theory. *Business Ethics Quarterly, 18*(2), 153–190. Retrieved January 24, 2009, from www.ronaldmitchell.org/publications/BEQ07.pdf.

Ahmad, P., Mead, J., Werhane, P. H. & Gorman, M. E. (2004a). Hindustan Lever Limited and Project Sting. *Darden Case Study UVA-E-0268.* Charlottesville, VA: Darden Business School Publishing.

——. (2004b). Hindustan Lever Limited and Project Sting. *Darden Case Study UVA-E-0269.* Charlottesville, VA: Darden Business School Publishing.

Ahmad, P., Werhane, P. H. & M. E. Gorman. (2004). Hindustan Lever and marketing to the fourth tier. *International Journal of Entrepreneurship and Innovation Management, 4,* 495–511.

Airola, J. (2007). The use of remittance income in Mexico. *International Migration Review, 41,* 850–859.

Alcatel Lucent. (2007, July 4). *Alcatel-Lucent, the Orange Mali Foundation, Afrique Initiatives, Médicament Export and Kafo Yeredeme Ton provide preventative healthcare services in Bamako.* Retrieved January 5, 2009, from www.alcatel-lucent.com/wps/portal/newsreleases/detail?LMSG_CABINET=Docs_and_Resource_Ctr&LMSG_CONTENT_FILE=News_Releases_2007/News_Article_000402.xml&lu_lang_code=en.

Ali, A. M. (2001). Political instability, policy uncertainty, and economic growth: An empirical investigation. *Atlantic Economic Journal, 29,* 87–106.

Allianz Group. (2008). *Pioneering disaster insurance for some of India's poorest.* Retrieved January 23, 2009, from www.allianz.com/en/allianz_group/press_center/news/commitment_news/community/news_2008-03-11-2.html?hits=mutual+and+India.

Allianz Knowledge Partnersite. (2008). *Social entrepreneurship: The ultimate return on investment.* Retrieved August 21, 2008, from http://knowledge.allianz.com/en/globalissues/microfinance/microfinance_basics/socialentrepreneurs_study.html.

Amul. (2000). *Achievements of dairy cooperatives.* Retrieved August 21, 2008 from www.amul.com/achievementsdairycoop.html.

Anderson, Sara D. (2009). Husk power systems: Rice-fired electricity. *Fast Company, 131,* December/January.

Angell, Marcia. (2004). *The truth about the drug companies: How they deceive and exploit us, and what to do about it.* New York: Random House.

Annan, Kofi. (2000a). *We the peoples: The role of the United Nations in the 21st century.* Presented to the

United Nations General Assembly 55. Retrieved November 19, 2007, from www.un.org/millennium/sg/report/full.htm.

——. (2000b). *We the peoples: Fact sheet.* Presented to the United Nations General Assembly 55. Retrieved November 19, 2007, from www.un.org/millennium/sg/report/fact.htm.

Argandoña, Antonio. (1998). The stakeholder theory and the common good. *Journal of Business Ethics, 17,* 1093–1102.

Ashoka. (2007). *Albina Ruiz.* Retrieved January 2, 2007, from www.ashoka.org/node/3718.

Asscher, Joachim. (2008). The moral distinction between killing and letting die in medical cases. *Bioethics, 22*(5), 278–285.

Attanasio, Orazio P. & Frayne, Christine. (2005). *Do the poor pay more?* Retrieved January 25, 2009, from http://scid.stanford.edu/events/OrazioNov8,2005.pdf.

Austin, J. E. (2000). *The collaboration challenge: How nonprofits and businesses succeed through strategic alliances.* San Francisco: Jossey-Bass.

Balu, Rekha. (2001). Strategic innovation: Hindustan Lever Ltd. *Fast Company, 47,* 120.

Banerjee, Abhijit, Bénabou, Roland & Mookherjee, Dilip. (2006). Introduction and overview. In A. Banerjee, R. Bénabou & D. Mookherjee (Eds.), *Understanding poverty* (pp. 3–15). New York: Oxford University Press.

Batra, G., Kaufmann, D. & Stone, A. H. (2002a). *Voices of the firm 2000: Investment climate and governance findings of the world business environment survey.* New York: World Bank Group.

——. (2002b). *The firms speak: What the world business environment survey tells us about constraints on private sector development.* Retrieved August 19, 2008, from www.worldbank.org/wbi/governance/pdf/firmsspeak.pdf.

Bazerman, Max H. & Chugh, Dolly. (2006). Decisions without blinders. *Harvard Business Review, 84,* 88–97.

BBC. (2008, October 24). Texts tackle HIV in South Africa. Retrieved January 5, 2009, from http://news.bbc.co.uk/2/hi/technology/7688268.stm.

Beauchamp, T. L. & Bowie, N. E. (2001). The purpose of the corporation. In T. L. Beauchamp & N. E. Bowie (Eds.), *Ethical theory and business practice* (pp. 45–50). Upper Saddle River, NJ: Prentice-Hall, Inc.

Benhabib, S. (1992). *Situating the Self.* New York: Routledge.

Bennett, B. & Tomossy, G. (Eds.). (2006). *Globalization and health: Challenges for health law and bioethics.* New York: Springer.

Berry, Thomas. (1999). *The great work: Our way into the future.* New York: Bell Tower.

Beshouri, Christopher. (2006). A grassroots approach to emerging-market consumers. *McKinsey Quarterly, 4,* 60–71. Retrieved January 16, 2009, from www.mckinseyquarterly.com/article_page.aspx?ar=1866.

Bevan, David & Corvellec, Herve. (2007). The impossibility of corporate ethics: For a Levinasian approach to management ethics. *Business Ethics: A European Review, 16*(3), 208–219.

Bill & Melinda Gates Foundation. (2007). Retrieved November 21, 2007, from www.gatesfoundation.org/default.htm.

Bird, R., Hall, A., Momentè, F. & Reggiani, F. (2007). What corporate social responsibility activities are valued by the market? *Journal of Business Ethics, 76,* 189–206.

Boechat, Cláudio. (n.d.). *Ekos: Perfume essences produce sustainable development.* Retrieved January 5, 2009, from www.gim2008.ca/post-conference/pdfs/Claudio%20Boechat%20-%20Caso%20FDC_EKOS.PDF.

Bornstein, David. (2004). *How to change the world: Social entrepreneurs and the power of new ideas.* New York: Oxford University Press.

Bosco, David. (2007). The debt frenzy. *Foreign Policy,* July–August, 36–42.

Bose, G. (2004). Bureaucratic delays and bribe-taking. *Journal of Economic Behavior & Organization, 54,* 313–320.

Boss, Suzie. (2008–2009). Clean sweep: E+Co connects the dots between energy, poverty, and the environment. *Stanford Social Innovation Review.* Retrieved January 24, 2009, from www.ssireview.org/articles/entry/clean_sweep.

Bruno, M. & Easterly, W. (1998). Inflation crises and long-run growth. *Journal of Monetary Economics, 41,* 3–26.

Buber, Martin. (1996). *I and thou* (Walter Kaurmann, Trans.). New York: Simon & Schuster.

Burgis, Tom. (2008). Microfinance commercialization warning. *FT.com.* Retrieved January 24, 2009, from www.ft.com/cms/s/0/6f05707e-5cc5-11dd-8d38-000077b07658.html.

Busenitz, L. W., Gomez, C. & Spencer, J. W. (2000). Country entrepreneurial profiles: Unlocking entrepreneurial phenomena. *Academy of Management Journal, 43,* 994–1003.

BW Harris Poll. (2000). *Business Week/Harris Poll: How business rates: By the numbers.* Retrieved January 24, 2009, from www.businessweek.com/2000/00_37/b3698004.htm.

Cai, Zhuang & Wheale, Peter. (2004). Creating sustainable corporate value: A case study of stakeholder relationship management in China. *Business and Society Review, 109,* 507–547.

Caldwell, D. F. & Moberg, D. J. (2007). The effect of ethical cultures on the activation of moral imagination. *Journal of Business Ethics, 73*(2), 193–204.

Camerer, Colin & Lovallo, D. (1999). Overconfidence and excess entry: An experimental approach. *American Economic Review, 89,* 306–318.

Campbell, D., Craven, B. & Lawler, K. (2002). Social welfare, positivism and business ethics. *Business Ethics: A European Review, 11,* 268–281.

Campbell, J. L. (2007). Why would corporations behave in socially responsible ways? An institutional theory of corporate social responsibility. *Academy of Management Review, 32,* 946–967.

Carroll, A. B. (1979). A three-dimensional conceptual model of corporate social performance. *Academy of Management Review, 4,* 497–505.

——. (1993). *Business and society: Ethics and stakeholder management* (2nd ed.). Cincinnati, OH: South-Western Publishing.

Carroll, A. B. & Nasi, J. (1997). Understanding stakeholder thinking: Themes from a Finnish conference. *Business Ethics: A European Review, 6,* 46–51.

Carson, T. L. (1985). Bribery, extortion, and "The Foreign Corrupt Practices Act." *Philosophy and Public Affairs, 14,* 66–90.

Cemex. (2007). *Crece tu Patrimonio Hoy.* Retrieved June 18, 2007, from www.cemexmexico.com/se/se_ph.html.

Central Intelligence Agency. (2008). *The 2008 world factbook.* Washington, DC: CIA. Retrieved January 24, 2009, from www.cia.gov/library/publications/the-world-factbook/index.html.

Chambers, Robert. (1989). *Rural development: Putting the last first.* Harlow, UK: Longman Scientific & Technical.

Chandler, Sir Geoffrey. (2001). Introduction: Defining corporate social responsibility. *Ethical Performance Best Practices.* Quoted in Michael Stohl, Cynthia Stohl & Nikki C. Townsley. (2007). A new generation of global corporate social responsibility. In Steve May, George Cheney & Juliet Roper (Eds.), *The debate over corporate social responsibility* (p. 30). New York: Oxford University Press.

Chang, H. (2002). *Kicking away the ladder.* London: Anthem Press.

Changemakers. (2007). *Mosaic of innovative solutions: How to provide affordable housing.* Retrieved January 24, 2009, from www.changemakers.net/en-us/node/11805.

Chetwynd, Eric, Chetwynd, Frances & Spector, Bertram. (2003). *Corruption and poverty: A review of recent literature.* Washington, DC: Management Systems International.

Child, J. W. & Marcoux, A. M. (1999). Freeman and Evan: Stakeholder theory in the original position. *Business Ethics Quarterly, 9,* 207–223.

Chugh, Dolly & Bazerman, Max H. (2007). Bounded awareness: What you fail to see can hurt you. *Mind and Society, 6,* 1–18.

Cilliers, Paul. (1998). *Complexity and post-modernism: Understanding complex systems.* London: Routledge.

Citigroup. (2004). *Microfinance.* Retrieved January 24, 2009, from www.citigroup.com/citi/citizen/microfinance/index.htm.

CNN.com. (2004). Powell calls Sudan killings genocide. Retrieved January 24, 2009, from www.cnn.com/2004/WORLD/africa/09/09/sudan.powell/index.html.

Collier, J. (2006). The art of moral imagination. *Journal of Business Ethics, 66*(2/3), 307–317.

Collier, Paul. (2007). *The bottom billion: Why the poorest countries are failing and what can be done about it.* New York: Oxford University Press.

Collins, J. & Porras, J. (1994). *Built to last.* New York: HarperBusiness.

Combined Joint Task Force—Horn of Africa. (2007). Retrieved January 24, 2009, from www.globalsecurity.org/military/agency/dod/cjtf-hoa.htm.

Corbett, S. (2008, April 13). Can the cellphone help end global poverty? *New York Times Magazine.* Retrieved January 24, 2009, from www.nytimes.com/2008/04/13/magazine/13anthropology-t.html?pagewanted=all.

Coronado, Enrique, Krettecos, Christina & Lu, Yvonne. (2007). *What works: Mi Farmacita Nacional.* Washington, DC: World Resources Institute 2007. Retrieved January 24, 2009, from www.nextbillion.net/files/What%20Works-Mi%20Farmacita%20Nacional.pdf.

Cronan, Garry. (2007). *The Mondragon Corporation.* Retrieved January 2, 2009, from www.global300.coop/en/profiles/mcc.

Cropper, S. (1996). Collaborative working and the issue of sustainability. In C. Huxbaum (Ed.), *Creating competitive advantage* (pp. 80–100). London: Sage.

Crouch, C. & Streeck, W. (Eds.). (1997). *Political economy of modern capitalism.* Thousand Oaks, CA: Sage.

Cuffe, Jenny. (2006). Cameroon corruption hinders Aids fight. *BBC News.* Retrieved January 24, 2009, from http://news.bbc.co.uk/2/hi/africa/6198337.stm.

Dahle, Cheryl. (2005, January). The change masters. *Fast Company, 90,* 47–58.

Daily Star. (2007, September 5). Intel to give ICT education to students of Bangladesh. Retrieved January 24, 2009, from www.thedailystar.net/story.php?nid=2739.

D'Andrade, K. (1985). Bribery. *Journal of Business Ethics, 4,* 239.

Das, T. K. & Teng, B. S. (2001). Trust, control and risk in strategic alliances: An integrated framework. *Organization Studies, 22*(2), 251–283.

Davies, James B., Sandström, Susanna, Shorrocks, Anthony & Wolff, Edward N. (2008). *The world distribution of household wealth.* Retrieved January 24, 2009, from www.wider.unu.edu/publications/working-papers/discussion-papers/2008/en_GB/dp2008-03.

Davis, D. (Executive Producer), Malone, M. & Grove, R. (Series Producers). (2005). *The new heroes: The bottom line is lives* [Documentary]. Portland, OR: Oregon Public Prodcasting. Retrieved January 24, 2009, from www.pbs.org/opb/thenewheroes/meet/ruiz.html.

Davis, K. & Blomstom, R. (1975). *Business and society: Environment and responsibility.* New York: McGraw-Hill.

Deaton, Angus. (2006). Measuring poverty. In A. Banerjee, R. Bénabou & D. Mookherjee (Eds.), *Understanding poverty* (pp. 3–15). New York: Oxford University Press.

Dees, J. Gregory. (1998). The meaning of "social entrepreneurship." White Paper funded by the Kauffman Center for Entrepreneurial Leadership, Kansas City, MO.

De Haas, H. (2005). International migration, remittances and development: Myths and facts. *Third World Quarterly, 26,* 1269–1284.

De Soto, Hernando. (2000). *The mystery of capital: Why capitalism triumphs in the West and fails everywhere else.* New York: Basic Books.

Diamond, Jared. (2005). *Collapse: How societies choose to fail or succeed.* New York: Penguin.

DiMaggio, P. J. & Powell, W. W. (1983). The iron cage revisited: Institutional isomorphism and collective rationality in organizational fields. *American Sociological Review, 48,* 147–160.

Donaldson, Thomas & Dunfee, Thomas. (1994). Toward a unified conception of business ethics: Integrative social contracts theory. *Academy of Management Review, 19*(2), 252–284.

D'Orazio, Emilio. (2008). Le responsibilita degli stakeholder. Recenti svipuppi nella Business Ethics. *Politeia, xxiv*(89), 41–84.

Dugger, Cecilia. (2007, August 16). CARE turns down federal funds for food aid. *New York Times.* Retrieved January 24, 2009, from www.nytimes.com/2007/08/16/world/africa/16food.html.

Easterly, William. (2002). *The elusive quest for growth.* Cambridge, MA: MIT Press.

———. (2005a, March 13). A modest proposal. Review of *The End of Poverty* by Jeffrey Sachs.

washingtonpost.com. Retrieved January 24, 2009, from www.washingtonpost.com/wp-dyn/articles/A25562-2005Mar10.html.

——. (2005b). The utopian nightmare. *Foreign Policy*, Sept/Oct, 58–64.

——. (2006a). *The white man's burden: Why the West's efforts to aid the rest have done so much ill and so little good.* New York: Penguin Press.

——. (2006b). Interview by Paul Solman. In "Authors analyze, criticize foreign aid agencies in new books," *the Online NewsHour*, PBS, September 21, 2006. Retrieved January 24, 2009, from www.pbs.org/newshour/bb/social_issues/july-dec06/foreignaid_09-21.html.

——. (2007). The ideology of development. *Foreign Policy*, July/August, 31–35.

Easterly, W. & Fischer, S. (2000). *Inflation and the poor.* Policy Research Working Paper 2335. World Bank.

Eberlie, W., Führmann, B. & Falk, G. (2004). *Fighting poverty and corruption.* Eschborn: Deutsche Gesellschaft für Technische Zusammenarbeit, 28.

Elkington, John. (1994). Towards the sustainable corporation: Win-win-win business strategies for sustainable development. *California Management Review, 36*, 90–100.

Emanuel, Linda. (2000). Ethics and the structures of health care. *Cambridge Quarterly, 9*, 151–168.

EMBARQ & Center for Sustainable Transport in Mexico. (2006, October). *Sustainable mobility, 1*, 12–13. Retrieved August 21, 2008, from http://embarq.wri.org/en/index.aspx.

Esty, B. C. (1995). South Shore Bank: Is it the model of success for community development banks? *Journal of Marketing and Psychology, 12*(8), 789–819.

E+CO. (2009). *E+CO's impact.* Retrieved January 24, 2009, from www.eandco.net/SocialImpact.html.

Faranak, M. (2004). Public–private partnerships: The trojan horse of neoliberal development. *Journal of Planning Education and Research, 24*(1), 89–101.

Fatemi, Ali, Fooladi, I. & Wheeler, D. (in press). The relative valuation of socially responsible firms: An exploratory study. In *Finance for a Better World.* Hampshire, UK: Palgrave Macmillan Publishers.

First enquiry into the bribery propensity of leading exporting nations. (1997). Retrieved January 24, 2009, from www.icgg.org/downloads/contribution01_lambsdorff.pdf.

Fisher, Martin. (2007). *How a $33 investment helped one family out of poverty.* Retrieved January 24, 2009, from http://kickstart.org/documents/HipPump.pdf.

Fleming, John E. (1992). Alternative approaches and assumptions: Comments on Manuel Velasquez. *Business Ethics Quarterly, 2*(1), 41–43.

Foreign Policy. (2007). The failed states index 2007. *Foreign Policy*, July/August, 54–63.

Forge, P. G. (2004). Cultivating moral imagination through meditation. *Journal of Business Ethics, 51*(1), 15–29.

Fowler, A. (1990). Doing it better? Where and how NGOs have a comparative advantage in facilitating development. *AERDD Bulletin, 28*, 11.

Freeman, E. R. & McVea, J. (2005). Stakeholder theory: A names and faces approach, how focusing on stakeholders as individuals can bring ethics and entrepreneurial strategy together. *Journal of Management Inquiry, 14*, 57–69.

Freeman, R. E. (1984). *Strategic management: A stakeholder approach.* Boston, MA: Pitman Publishing.

——. (1994). The politics of stakeholder theory: Some future directions. *Business Ethics Quarterly, 4*, 409–421.

——. (1999). Divergent stakeholder theory. *Academy of Management Review, 24*, 233–236.

——. (2002). Stakeholder theory of the modern corporation. In T. Donaldson, P. Werhane & M. Cording (Eds.), *Ethical issues in business* (7th ed., pp. 38–49). Upper Saddle River, NJ: Prentice Hall.

——. (2004). A stakeholder theory of the modern corporation. In T. Beauchamp and Norman Bowie (Eds.), *Ethical theory and business practice* (7th ed., pp. 55–64). Upper Saddle River, NJ: Prentice Hall.

——. (2006). *Company stakeholder responsibility: A new approach to CSR.* Business Roundtable Institute for Corporate Ethics Bridge Paper. Retrieved January 24, 2009, from www.corporate-ethics.org/pdf/csr.pdf.

French, P. A. (1984). *Corporate responsibility and corporate personhood.* New York: Columbia University Press.

Freud, Sigmund. (1961). *Civilization and its discontents.* New York: Norton.

——. 1989. *The future of an illusion.* New York: Norton.

Friedman, Michael A., den Besten, Henk & Attaran, Amir. (2003). Out-licensing: A practical approach for improvement of access to medicines in poor countries. *The Lancet, 361,* 341–344.

Friedman, Milton. (1970, September). The social responsibility of business is to increase its profits. *New York Times Magazine, 13,* 32–33, 122, 124, 126.

——. (2002). *Capitalism and freedom.* Chicago, IL: University of Chicago Press.

Friedman, Milton & Friedman, Rose D. (1981). *Free to choose: A personal statement Milton & Rose Friedman.* New York: Avon.

Friedman, Thomas L. (2006). *The world is flat: A brief history of the twentieth century.* New York: Farrar, Straus and Giroux.

——. (2008). *Hot, flat, and crowded.* New York: Farrar, Straus and Giroux.

Frontline. (2004). *Ghosts of Rwanda.* Retrieved January 24, 2009, from www.pbs.org/wgbh/pages/frontline/shows/ghosts.

Frontline World. (2005). *Sudan: The quick and the terrible.* Retrieved January 24, 2009, from www.pbs.org/frontlineworld/stories/sudan/thestory.html.

Fyvie, C. & Ager, A. (1999). NGOs and innovation: Organizational characteristics and constraints in development assistance work in the Gambia. *World Dev, 8,* 1383–1395.

Gates, W. (2007). *Harvard University commencement address.* Retrieved January 24, 2009, from www.news.harvard.edu/gazette/2007/06.14/99-gates.html.

——. (2008, January 24). *A new approach to capitalism in the 21st century.* Given at World Economic Forum, Davos, Switzerland. Retrieved January 24, 2009, from www.microsoft.com/Presspass/exec/billg/speeches/2008/01-24WEFDavos.mspx.

Gaur, A. S. & Lu, J. W. (2007). Ownership strategies and survival of foreign subsidiaries: Impacts of institutional distance and experience. *Journal of Management, 33,* 84–110.

Gentner, D. & Whitley, E. W. (1997). Mental models of population growth: A preliminary investigation. In M. Bazerman, D. M. Messick, A. E. Tenbrunsel & K. Wade-Benzoni (Eds.), *Environment, ethics, and behavior: The psychology of environmental valuation and degradation* (pp. 209–233). San Francisco, CA: New Lexington Press.

Gioia, Dennis & Chittipeddi, Kumar. (1991). Sensemaking and sensegiving in strategic change initiation. *Strategic Management Journal, 12,* 443–448.

Gioia, Dennis & Thomas, J. B. (1996). Identity, image, and issue interpretation: Sensemaking during strategic change in academia. *Administrative Science Quarterly, 41,* 370–403.

Global Exchange. (2007, October 28). *Top reasons to oppose the WTO.* Retrieved January 24, 2009, from www.globalexchange.org/campaigns/wto/OpposeWTO.html.

Gnyawali, D. R. & Fogel, D. S. (1994). Environments for entrepreneurship development: Key dimensions and research implications. *Entrepreneurship Theory and Practice, 18,* 43–62.

Goheer, Ali. (2007). *Airwaves of progress: Tuning in to Projet Radio.* Retrieved January 24, 2009, from www.bopnetwork.org/node/183.

Goodpaster, K. E. (1991). Business ethics and stakeholder analysis. *Business Ethics Quarterly, 1,* 53–73.

Gore, Al. (2006). *An inconvenient truth: The planetary emergency of global warming and what we can do about it.* New York: Melcher Media.

Gorman, Michael. (1992). *Simulating science: Heuristics, mental models and technoscientific thinking.* Bloomington, IN: Indiana University Press.

Grameen Foundation. (2007). *Fighting poverty with microfinance.* Retrieved January 24, 2009, from www.grameenfoundation.org.

Grameenphone. (2006). *Annual report 2006.* Retrieved January 24, 2009, from www.grameenphone.com/assets/annual_reports/pdf/Grameenphone_Annual_Report_06.pdf.

——. (2007). Retrieved January 24, 2009, from www.grameenphone.com/index.php?id=63.

Gray, B. (1989). *Collaborating: Finding common ground for multiparty problems*. San Francisco, CA: Jossey-Bass.

Greenwood, D. J. (1992). Labor-managed systems and industrial redevelopment: Lessons from the Fagor Cooperative Group of Mondragon. In F. A. Rothstein & M. L. Blim (Eds.), *Anthropology and the global factory: Studies of the new industrialization in the late twentieth century*. New York: Bergin and Garvey, 177–190.

Greenwood, R. & Hinings, C. R. (1996). Understanding radical organizational change: Bringing together the old and the new institutionalism. *Academy of Management Review, 21*, 1022–1054.

Guyon, J. (1997, August 4). Why is the world's most profitable company turning itself inside out? *Fortune*, 120–125.

Hall, Andy, Clark, Norman & Naik, Guru. (2007). *Technology supply chain or innovation capacity? Contrasting experiences of promoting small scale irrigation technology in South Asia*. United Nations University—MERIT Working Paper series #2007-014. Retrieved January 24, 2009, from www.merit.unu.edu/publications/wppdf/2007/wp2007-014.pdf.

Hall, D. T. & Chandler, D. (2005). Psychological success: When the career is a calling. *Journal of Organizational Behavior, 26*(2), 155–176.

Hammond, Al. (2008). Interview, February 5 at Santa Clara University.

Hammond, A., Kramer, W. J., Tran, J., Katz, R. & Walker, C. (2007). *The next 4 billion*. Washington, DC: World Resources Institute.

Hammonds, Keith H. (2005, January). A Lever long enough to move the world. *Fast Company, 90*, 60–63.

Harford, Tim. (2006, March). Why poor countries are poor: The clues lie on a bumpy road leading to the world's worst library. *Reason Online*. Retrieved January 24, 2009, from www.reason.com/news/show/33258.html.

Hargrave, T. J. & Van de Ven, A. (2004). Social, technical, and institutional change: A literature review and synthesis. In M. S. Poule & A. H. Van de Ven (Eds.), *Handbook of organizational change* (pp. 259–303). New York: Oxford University Press.

Harjula, L. (2007). Tensions between venture capitalists' and business-social entrepreneurs' goals. *Greener Management International, 51*, 79–87.

Hart, Stuart. (2007). *Capitalism at the Crossroads: The unlimited business opportunities in solving the world's most difficult problems* (2nd ed.). New Jersey: Wharton School Publishing.

Hart, S. L. & Milstein, M. B. (2003). Creating sustainable value. *Academy of Management Executive, 17*(2), 56–67.

Hartman, L. P., Arnold, D. G. & Wokutch, R. (Eds.). (2003). *Rising above sweatshops: Innovative management approaches to global labor practices* New York: Praeger Books.

Hartman, L., Kelley, S. & Werhane, P. (2009). Profit, partnerships and the global common good. In H. C. Bettignies & F. Lépineux (Eds.), *Business, globalization and the common good* (pp. 251–276). Oxford: Peter Lang Academic Publishers.

Hartman, L. P., Werhane, P. & Moberg, D. (2008, March 24). Hey Bill, What were you waiting for? *Ethisphere*. Retrieved January 7, 2009, from http://ethisphere.com/hey-bill-what-were-you-waiting-for.

Hauerwas, Stanley. (1974). *Vision and virtue: Essays in Christian ethical reflection*. Notre Dame, IN: Fides Press.

Heller, N. A. (2008). The influence of reputation and sector on perceptions of brand alliances of nonprofit organizations. *Journal of Nonprofit and Public Sector Marketing, 20*(1), 19–36.

Helps International. (2004). *The Onil Stove*. Retrieved May 11, 2009, from http://www.helpsintl.org/programs/stove.php.

Hendry, J. (2001). Economic contracts versus social relationships as a foundation for normative stakeholder theory. *Business Ethics: A European Review, 10*, 223–232.

Herbst, Kris. (2002). *Enabling the poor to build housing: Cemex combines profit & social development*. Arlington, VA: Ashoka. Retrieved January 24, 2009, from http://proxied.changemakers.net/journal/02september/herbst.cfm.

Hezel, Francis X., S. J. (1995). *Strangers in their own land: A century of colonial rule in the Caroline and Marshall Islands*. Honolulu, HI: University of Hawaii Press.

146

Hindustan Lever Limited. (2004). *Project Shakti.* Retrieved January 24, 2009, from www.hllshakti. com/sbcms/temp15.asp.

Hobbes, Thomas. (1660; 1958). Chapter XIII: Of the natural condition of mankind as concerning their felicity and misery. *The Leviathan.* New York: Bobbs-Merrill Company, Inc.

Hofstede, G. H. (1980). *Culture's consequences: International differences in work-related values.* London: Sage.

Hollenbach, D., S. J. (2002). *The common good and Christian ethics.* New York: Cambridge University Press.

Horney, K. (1950). *Neurosis and human growth.* New York: W. W. Norton.

Hudson Institute. (2006). *Index of global philanthropy.* Retrieved January 24, 2009. from http://gpr. hudson.org/files/publications/GlobalPhilanthropy.pdf.

Husk Power Systems. (2008). Retrieved January 24, 2009, from http://huskpowersystems.com.

IBM. (2008). *IBM's corporate service corps heading to six emerging countries to spark socio-economic growth while developing global leaders.* Retrieved January 24, 2009, from www-03.ibm.com/press/us/en/ pressrelease/23743.wss.

IDE India—The color red. (2008). YouTube. Retrieved January 25, 2009, from www.youtube.com/ watch?v=SGIUmKuJQ7g.

IDEAAS. (2009). *Instituto para o Desenvolvimento de Energias Alternativas e da Auto Sustentabilidade* [Institute for the Development of Natural Energy and Sustainability]. Retrieved January 25, 2009, from www.ideaas.org.br/index_eng.htm.

Ilesanmi, Simeon O. (2004). Leave no poor behind: Globalization and the imperative of socio-economic and development rights from an African perspective. *Journal of Religious Ethics, 32*(1), 71–92.

India Knowledge@Wharton. (2006, October 31). *Indian NGOs: Learning to walk the line between social responsibility and commercial success.* Retrieved January 24, 2009, from http://knowledge.wharton. upenn.edu/india/article.cfm?articleid=4112.

Institute of Integrated Rural Development (IIRD). (n.d.). *IIRD development terminology (& target family classification).* Retrieved January 24, 2009, from www.iird.interconnection.org.

Interface Flooring. (2009). Retrieved January 24, 2009, from www.interfaceflooring.com/prod-ucts/sustainability.

International Monetary Fund. (2008). *Poverty reduction strategy papers.* Retrieved January 24, 2009, from www.imf.org/external/np/prsp/prsp.asp?view=ipr&sort=cty.

Ionescu-Somers, Aileen & Steger, Ulrich. (2008). Fortifying the business model. In Prabhu Kanda-char & Minna Halme (Eds.), *Sustainability challenges and solutions at the base of the pyramid* (pp. 357–368). Sheffield, UK: Greenleaf Publishing Limited.

Ivatury, G. & Pickens, M. (2006). Mobile phone banking and low-income customers: Evidence from South Africa. In *Economic Empowerment through Mobile: The Vodafone CR Dialogues.* Retrieved January 24, 2009, from www.vodafone.com/start/responsibility/cr_dialogues/dialogue_3_-_eco-nomic.html.

Iyer, E. (2003). Theory of alliances: Partnership and partner characteristics. *Journal of Nonprofit and Public Sector Marketing, 11*(1), 41–57.

Jensen, M. (2001). Value maximisation, stakeholder theory, and the corporate objective function. *European Financial Management, 7,* 297–317.

Jensen, R. (2007, August). The digital divide: Information (technology), market performance, and welfare in the Southern Indian fisheries sector. *The Quarterly Journal of Economics, 122*(3), 879–924.

Jeurissen, R. (2004). Institutional conditions for corporate citizenship. *Journal of Business Ethics, 53,* 87–96.

Johnson and Johnson. (2009). *Our credo values.* Retrieved January 24, 2009, from www.jnj.com/ connect/about-jnj/jnj-credo/?flash=true.

Johnson, Kay & Nhon, Xa. (2005, April 17). Selling to the poor. *Time Magazine.* Retrieved January 24, 2009, from www.time.com/time/magazine/article/0,9171,1050276,00.html.

Johnson, Mark. (1993). *Moral imagination: Implications of cognitive science for ethics.* Chicago, IL: University of Chicago Press.

Kahneman, D. & Lovallo, D. (1993). Timid choices and bold forecasts: A cognitive perspective on risk taking. *Management Science, 39*(1), 17–31.

Kanter, Rosabeth Moss. (2008). Transforming giants: What kind of company makes it its business to make the world a better place? *Harvard Business Review,* January, 43–52.

Karnani, Aneel. (2006). *Fortune at the bottom of the pyramid: A Mirage.* Ross School of Business Paper No. 1035. Retrieved January 24, 2009, from http://ssrn.com/abstract=914518.

——. (2007a). The mirage of marketing to the bottom of the pyramid. *California Management Review, 49,* 90–111.

——. (2007b). Microfinance misses its mark. *Stanford Social Innovation Review,* Summer, 34–40.

——. (2007c). Misfortune at the bottom of the pyramid. *Greener Management International, 51,* 99–110.

Katz, Rob. (2008, October 26). Pop!Tech: Rice power to the people with Husk Power Systems. *NextBillion.net.* Retrieved January 5, 2009, from www.nextbillion.net/blogs/2008/10/26/pop-tech-rice-power-to-the-people-with-husk-power-systems.

Kelley, John. (2000). *Freedom in the Church: A documented history of the principle of subsidiary function.* Dayton, OH: Peter Li, Inc., p. 13.

Kelley, Scott. (2008). Subsidiarity and global poverty: Development from below upwards. In M. Tavanti & C. Mousin (Eds.), *What would Vincent do? Vincentian higher education & poverty reduction, Vincentian Heritage Journal, 28*(2).

Kelley, Scott, Hartman, Laura P. & Werhane, Patricia H. (2008a). The end of foreign aid as we know it: The profitable alleviation of poverty in a globalized economy. In Charles Wankel (Ed.), *Alleviating poverty through business strategy* (pp. 5–33). London: Palgrave Macmillan.

Kent, George. (2005). *Freedom from want: The human right to adequate food.* Washington, DC: Georgetown University Press.

Kets de Vries, Manfred F. R. (1980; 1994). *Organizational paradoxes: Clinical approaches to management.* London: Tavistock Publications.

Khor, M. (2006). *NGOs criticize outcome of IMF—World Bank meeting.* Third World Network Info on Finance and Development. Retrieved January 24, 2009, from www.twnside.org.sg/title2/finance/twninfofinance007.htm.

KickStart. (2007). *Micro-irrigation technologies.* Retrieved January 24, 2009, from http://kickstart.org/tech/technologies/micro-irrigation.html.

King, Dr. Martin Luther. (1963). *Letter from Birmingham Jail.* Retrieved January 24, 2009, from www.africa.upenn.edu/Articles_Gen/Letter_Birmingham.html.

Kinzer, Stephen. (2006). *Overthrow: America's century of regime change From Hawaii to Iraq.* New York: Times Books.

Kirby, Alex. (1998). Sci/Tech: Brent Spar's long saga. *BBC Online Network.* November 25. Retrieved July 6, 2008, from http://news.bbc.co.uk/1/hi/sci/tech/218527.stm.

Konrad, Allison. (2006). Engaging employees through high involvement work practices. *Ivey Business Journal Online,* March–April, 1–6. Retrieved January 19, 2009, from www.iveybusinessjournal.com.

Kovesi, Julius. (1967). *Moral notions.* New York: Humanities Press.

Kramer, D. A. (1983). Post-formal operations? A need for further conceptualization. *Human Development, 26,* 91–105.

Kristof, Nicholas. (2008, December 24). The sin in doing good deeds. *New York Times,* 23.

Kurer, O. (2005). Corruption: An alternative approach to its definition and measurement. *Political Studies, 53,* 222–239.

Landler, Mark. (2007, December 15). Britain overtakes U.S. as top World Bank donor. *New York Times.* Retrieved January 24, 2009, from www.nytimes.com/2007/12/15/world/15worldbank.html.

Langewiesche, William. (2000). The shipbreakers. *Atlantic Monthly, 48,* 31–49.

Laszlo, Alexander, and Krippner, Stanley. (1998). Systems theories: Their origins, foundations and development. In J. Scott Jordan (Ed.), *Systems theories and a priori aspects of perception* (pp. 47–74). Amsterdam: Elsevier.

Leisinger, Klaus. (2005). The right to health: A duty for whom? *Global Compact Quarterly, 2.*

Retrieved January 25, 2009, from www.enewsbuilder.net/globalcompact/e_article000375786.cfm?x=b11,0,w.

——. (2007a). Corporate philanthropy: The "top of the pyramid." *Business and Society Review, 112*(3), 315–342.

——. (2007b). Capitalism with a human face: The UN global compact. *The Journal of Corporate Citizenship, 28.* Retrieved January 25, 2009, from *http://unglobalcompact.net/NewsAndEvents/articles_and_papers/Capitalism_with_a_Human_Face_JCC.pdf.*

——. (n.d.). *Globalization,* minima moralia, *and the responsibilities of multinational companies.* Retrieved January 25, 2009, from www.unglobalcompact.org/docs/news_events/9.5/leisinger.pdf.

Lerrick, A. & Meltzer, A. (2001, August 1). The World Bank is wrong to oppose grants. *AEI Online.* Retrieved January 25, 2009, from www.aei.org/publications/pubID.14847/pub_detail.asp.

Letelier, M. F., Flores, F. & Spinosa, C. (2003). Creating and developing productive customers in emerging markets. *California Management Review, 54*(4) (Fall), 77–103.

Letelier, Maria & Spinosa, Charles. (2002). *The for-profit development business: Good business, good policy, good to foster.* Retrieved June 25, 2009, from http://74.125.95.132/search?q=cache:5LYZg5_Dbh8J:www.yearofmicrocredit.org/docs/For-Profit_Development.doc+The+For-Profit+Development+Business:+Good+Business,+Good+Policy,+Good+to+Foster&hl=en&ct=clnk&cd=1&gl=us&client=safari.

Levenson, Eugenia. (2008, November 24). Citizen Nike. *Fortune,* 165–170.

Levinas, Emmanuel. (1981). *Otherwise than being.* Pittsburgh, PA: Duquesne University Press.

——. (1999). *Alterity and transcendence.* London: Athlone Press.

Lockwood, Nancy. (2007). Leveraging employee engagement for competitive advantage. *HR Magazine, 52*(3), 1–11.

Lodge, George & Wilson, Craig. (2004). *A corporate solution to global poverty.* Princeton, NJ: Princeton University Press.

London, Ted. (2007). *A base-of-the-pyramid perspective on poverty alleviation.* Working Paper, University of Michigan, William Davidson Institute. Retrieved January 25, 2009, from www.erb.umich.edu/News-and-Events/colloquium_papers/BoP_Perspective_on_Poverty_Alleviation_London%20(UNDP).pdf.

London, T. & Hart, S. L. (2004). Reinventing strategies for emerging markets: Beyond the transnational model. *Journal of International Business Studies, 35*(5), 350–370.

Lonergan, Bernard J. F. (1958). *Insight: A study of human understanding.* New York: Longmans, Green & Co.

——. (1971). *Method in theology.* Toronto: University of Toronto Press.

——. (1975). *A second collection* (Edited by William F. J. Ryan & Bernard J. Tyrrell). Philadelphia, PA: Westminster Press, 73–75.

Maitland, A. (2005, February 3). From a handout to a hand up. *Financial Times.* Retrieved January 25, 2009, from www.ft.com/cms/s/c13c209e-7589-11d9-9608-00000e2511c8.html.

Malkin, Elisabeth. (2008, April 5). Microfinance's success sets off a debate in Mexico. *New York Times.* Retrieved January 7, 2009, from www.nytimes.com/2008/04/05/business/worldbusiness/05micro.html?_r=1.

Manila Water Company Inc. (2007). *Annual report.* Retrieved January 16, 2009, from www.manila-water.com/files/MWC_AR2007.pdf.

Marcoux, A. M. 2003. A fiduciary argument against stakeholder theory. *Business Ethics Quarterly, 13,* 1–24.

Marquardt, Niels. (2006). *Business action against corruption in Cameroon: Joint government-private sector strategies.* Remarks given on November 7, 2006. Retrieved August 19, 2008, from http://yaounde.usembassy.gov/ambassador_corruption_business.html.

McDonough, William & Baungart, Michael. (2002). *Cradle to cradle.* New York: North Point Press.

McKinsey Quarterly. (2006). *Global survey of business executives.* Retrieved January 25, 2009, from www.mckinseyquarterly.com/The_McKinsey_Global_Survey_of_Business_Executives__Business_and_Society_1741.

McLean, Bethany & Elkind, Peter. (2004). *The smartest guys in the room: The amazing rise and scandalous fall of Enron.* New York: Portfolio (Penguin Group).

McVea, John & Freeman, R. E. (2005). A names-and-faces approach to stakeholder management. *Journal of Management Inquiry, 14,* 57–69.

Mead, E., Hartman, L. & Werhane, P. (2008). BHP Billiton and Mozal. UVA-E-316-7. Charlottesville, VA: Darden Publishing, University of Virginia Darden School Foundation.

MicroPlace. (2008). *A day in the life of Saroja.* Retrieved January 25, 2009, from www.microplace. com/learn_more/globalpovertysaroja.

Miles, Morgan P. & Covin, J. G. (2000). Environmental marketing: A source of reputational, competitive and financial advantage. *Journal of Business Ethics, 23,* 299–311.

Milne, G. R., Iyer, E. S. & Gooding-Williams, S. (1996). Environmental organization alliance relationships within and across nonprofit, business, and government sectors. *Journal of Public Policy and Marketing, 15*(2), 203–215.

Mitroff, I. & Linstone, H. (1993). *The unbounded mind.* New York: Oxford University Press.

Moberg, D. J. (2001). Diagnosing system states. *Emergence, 3*(2), 19–36.

——. (2006). Ethics blind spots in organizations: How systematic errors in person perception undermine moral agency. *Organizational Studies, 27*(3), 413–428.

Moberg, D. J. & Seabright, M. (2000). The development of moral imagination. *Business Ethics Quarterly, 10,* 845–884.

Molm, Linda D., Collett, Jessica L. & Schaefer, David R. (2007). Building solidarity through generalized exchange: A theory of reciprocity. *American Journal of Sociology, 113,* 205–242.

Moreno Barcelo, I. (2008, October). Patrimonio Hoy: Low-income housing that improves quality of life. *Development Outreach,* The World Bank Institute. Retrieved January 7, 2009, from http://www1.worldbank.org/devoutreach/article.asp?id=492.

Murali, D. & Padmanaban, G. (2008, March 26). A tightening jobs market is a hugely powerful engine for poverty reduction. *The Hindu.* Retrieved January 25, 2009, from www.thehindu.com/holnus/002200803261862.htm.

Murdoch, Jonathan. (2006). Microinsurance: The next revolution? In A. Banerjee, R. Bénabou & D. Mookherjee (Eds.), *Understanding poverty* (pp. 337–355). New York: Oxford University Press.

Nahser, Byron. (2008). *Journeys to Oxford.* New York: Global Scholarly Productions.

National Labor Committee. (2000). *The hidden face of globalization: What the corporations don't want us to know.* Video documentary.

——. (2009). *Welcome to NLC.* Retrieved January 24, 2009, from www.nlcnet.org/index.php.

Neufeldt, Victoria. (Ed.). (1997). *Webster's new world dictionary.* New York: Simon & Schuster, 313.

Newburry, W. E. & Gladwin, T. N. (1997; 2002). Shell and Nigerian oil. In T. Donaldson and P. Werhane (Eds.), *Ethical issues in business* (7th ed., pp. 522–541). Upper Saddle River, NJ: Prentice Hall.

Niebuhr, H. Richard. (1999). *The responsible self: An essay in Christian moral philosophy.* Louisville, KY: Westminster John Knox.

North, D. C. (1990). *Institutions, institutional change, and economic performance.* New York: Cambridge University Press.

OECD. (2007). *African economic outlook 2007.* Retrieved January 25, 2009, from www.oecd.org/document/22/0,3343,en_2649_15162846_38561046_1_1_1_1,00.html.

OneWorld.net. (2008, July 26). *"Phantom aid" accounts for $20bn a year.* Retrieved January 25, 2009, from http://uk.oneworld.net/article/view/135857/1.

One World Trust. (2006a). *Global accountability report.* Retrieved December 18, 2008, from www.oneworldtrust.org/index.php?option=com_content&view=article&id=76&Itemid=65.

——. (2006b). *Global accountability report briefing.* Retrieved January 5, 2009, from www.oneworldtrust.org/index.php?option=com_docman&task=search_result&Itemid=55.

Onil Stove. (2007). Health Benefits. Retrieved November 17, 2007 from http://www.onilstove.com/benefits.htm.

O'Riain, S. (2000). States and markets in an era of globalization. *Annual Review of Sociology, 26,* 187–213.

Oxfam America. (2008). *History of fair trade*. Retrieved January 25, 2009, from www.oxfamamerica. org/whatwedo/campaigns/coffee/background/ft_history.

Painter-Morland, Mollie. (2007). Defining accountability in a network society. *Business Ethics Quarterly, 17*, 515–534.

———. (2008). *Business ethics as practice: The everyday business of business*. Cambridge: Cambridge University Press.

Parker, Emily. (2008, March 1). Muhammad Yunus: Subprime lender. *The Wall Street Journal*. Retrieved April 6, 2009, from http://online.wsj.com/article/SB120432950873204335. html?mod=googlenews_wsj.

Peredo, Ana Maria. (2003). Emerging strategies against poverty: The road less traveled. *Journal of Management Inquiry, 12*, 155–166.

Peredo, Ana Maria & Chrisman, James J. (2006). Toward a theory of community-based enterprise. *Academy of Management Review, 31*, 309–338.

Perkins, John. (2004). *Confessions of an economic hitman*. San Francisco, CA: Berrett-Koehler Publishers.

Perrault, W. D., Jr. & McCarthy, E. J. (2002). *Basic marketing: A global-managerial approach*. Burr Ridge, IL: McGraw-Hill.

Peterson, B. E. & Stewart, A. J. (1996). Antecedents and contexts of generativity motivation at midlife. *Psychology and Aging, 11*, 21–33.

Peterson, R. (1988). Understanding and encouraging entrepreneurship internationally. *Journal of Small Business Management, 26*(2), 1–8.

Pfeffer, J. & Fong, C. T. (2005). Building organization theory from first principles: The self-enhancement motive and understanding power and influence. *Organization Science, 16*(4), 372–388.

Phillips, R. (2003). Stakeholder legitimacy. *Business Ethics Quarterly, 13*, 25–41.

Pless, N. & Maak, T. (in press). Developing responsible leaders as agents of world benefit: Learnings from Project Ulysses. In P. Werhane & L. Hartman (Eds.), *Ethical and Effective Practices of Global Corporations*. London: Routledge.

Plsek, P. (2001). Redesigning health care with insights from the science of complex adaptive systems. In *Crossing the quality chasm: A new health system for the 21st century* (pp. 310–333). Washington, DC: National Academy Press.

Polak, Paul. (2008). *Out of poverty: What works when traditional approaches fail*. San Francisco, CA: BK Publishers.

Politeia. (2007). Proceedings of the Fourth Annual Forum on Business Ethics and Corporate Social Responsibility in a Global Economy, Milan, September 13–14. Retrieved April 9, 2009, from www.politeia-centrostudi.org/forum.

Politeia. (2008). Proceedings of the Fifth Annual Forum on Business Ethics and Corporate Social Responsibility in a Global Economy, Milan, May 22–23. Retrieved April 9, 2009, from www. politeia-centrostudi.org/forum.

Polzer, J. T., Kramer, R. M. & Neale, M. A. (1997). Positive illusions about oneself and one's group. *Small Group Research, 28*(2), 243–266.

Population Services International (PSI). (2008). Retrieved January 25, 2009, from www.psi.org/ about_us/explained.html.

Porter, M. E. & Kramer, M. R. (2006). Strategy and society: The link between competitive advantage and corporate social responsibility. *Harvard Business Review, 84*(12), 78–92.

Post, J., Preston, L. & Sachs, S. (2002). Managing the extended enterprise: The new stakeholder view. *California Management Review, 45*, 6–28.

Power, Samantha. (2003). *A problem from hell: America and the age of genocide*. New York: Harper Collins.

Praekelt Foundation. (n.d.). *Social txt*. Retrieved January 5, 2009, from www.praekeltfoundation. org/products-and-services/socialtxt.

Prahalad, C. K. (2005). *The fortune at the bottom of the pyramid: Eradicating poverty through profits*. New Jersey: Wharton School Publishing.

Prahalad, C. K. & Brugmann, Jeb. (2007, February). Cocreating business's new social compact. *Harvard Business Review, 85*(2), 80–90, 156.

Prahalad, C. K. & Hammond, Allen. (2002). What works: Serving the world's poor, profitably. *Harvard Business Review.* [Original publication, 2002: Washington, DC: Markle Foundation and World Resources Institute.]

Prahalad, C. K. & Hart, Stuart. (2002). The fortune at the bottom of the pyramid. *Strategy + Business, 26,* 54–67.

Prahalad, C. K. & Krishnan, M. S. (2008). *The new age of innovation.* New York: McGraw-Hill.

Procter & Gamble. (2007). Home page. Retrieved January 5, 2009, from www.pg.com.

Procter & Gamble Health Sciences Institute. (2007a). *Safe drinking water.* Retrieved January 25, 2009, from http://pghsi.com/safewater.

——. (2007b). *Social marketing of PŪR purifier of water by PSI.* Retrieved January 25, 2009, from www.pghsi.com/pghsi/safewater/video_library.html.

Rakfeldt, J., Rybash, J. M. & Roodin, P. A. (1996). Affirmative coping: A marker of success in adult therapeutic intervention. In M. I. Commons & J. Demick (Eds.), *Clinical approaches to development* (pp. 295–310). New York: Oxford.

Ramey, Corinne. (2007, December 15). Please Call Me messages with HIV info: Mobile social marketing in South Africa. *MobileActive.org.* Retrieved January 5, 2009, from http://mobileactive.org/please-call-me-messages-hiv-info-mobile-social-marketing-south-africa.

Rangan, Kasturi V., Wheeler, David & Comeault, Jane. (2007). Manila Water Company. *Harvard Business Review,* 9-508-004.

Reck, Jennifer & Wood, Brad. (2003). *What works: Vodacom's community services phone shops.* Washington, DC: World Resources Institute Digital Dividend. Retrieved January 25, 2009, from www.digitaldividend.org/pdf/vodacom.pdf.

Rice, Susan E. (2006). The threat of global poverty. *The National Interest,* Spring, 76–82. Retrieved January 25, 2009, from www.brookings.edu/articles/2006/spring_globaleconomics_rice.aspx.

Rivoli, Pietra. (2005). *The travels of a t-shirt in the global economy: An economist examines the markets, power, and politics of world trade.* Hoboken, NJ: John Wiley & Sons, Inc.

Robins, Nick. (2006). *The corporation that changed the world: How the East India Company shaped the modern multinational.* New York: Pluto.

Rutherford, M. (1994). *Institutions in economics: The old and the new institutionalism.* Cambridge: Cambridge University Press.

Sachs, Jeffrey D. (2005a). *The end of poverty: Economic possibilities for our time.* New York: Penguin Press.

——. (2005b, March 27). Letters. *washingtonpost.com.* Retrieved January 25, 2009, from www.washingtonpost.com/wp-dyn/articles/A64541-2005Mar24.html.

——. 2008. *Common wealth: Economics for a crowded planet.* New York: Penguin Press.

Save Darfur. (2007). *Learn.* Retrieved January 25, 2009, from www.savedarfur.org/content.

Schuck, Michael J. (1991). *That they be one: The social teaching of the papal encyclicals 1740–1989.* Washington, DC: Georgetown University Press.

Schulz, William F. (2001). *In our own best interest: How defending rights benefits us all.* Boston, MA: Beacon Press.

Schumpeter, Joseph A. (1950). *Capitalism, socialism, and democracy* (3rd ed., chapter VII). New York: Harper and Brothers.

Scott, W. R. (2001). *Institutions and organizations* (2nd ed.). Thousand Oaks, CA: Sage.

Selsky, J. W. & Parker, B. (2005). Cross-sector partnerships to address social issues: Challenges to theory and practice. *Journal of Management, 31*(6), 849–873.

Sen, Amartya. (1999). *Development as freedom.* New York: Anchor Books.

Senge, Peter. (1990). *The fifth discipline.* New York: Doubleday.

Senge, P. M., Kleiner, A., Roberts, C., Ross, R. B. & Smith, B. J. (1994). *The fifth discipline fieldbook: Strategies and tools for building a learning organization.* New York: Doubleday.

Shleifer, A. & Vishney, R. W. (1993). Corruption. *Quarterly Journal of Economics, 108,* 519–617.

Shah, Anup. (n.d.) *US and foreign aid assistance.* Retrieved January 24, 2009, from www.globalissues.org/TradeRelated/Debt/USAid.asp#GovernmentsCuttingBackonPromisedResponsibilities.

Shue, Henry. (1980). *Basic rights*. Princeton, NJ: Princeton University Press.

Silverthorne, Sean. (2007, February 5). Business and the global poor. *Working Knowledge*. Retrieved January 7, 2009, from http://hbswk.hbs.edu/item/5529.html.

Simanis, Erik & Hart, Stuart. (2008). *The base of the pyramid protocol: Toward next generation strategy*. Ithaca, NY: Center for Sustainable Development.

Singer, Peter. (1972). Famine, affluence, and morality. *Philosophy and Public Affairs, 1*(1) (Spring), 229–243 [revised edition].

——. (1999, September 5). Peter Singer's solution to world poverty. *New York Times Sunday Magazine*. Retrieved January 25, 2009, from http://people.brandeis.edu/~teuber/singermag.html.

——. (2003, October 29). *One world*. Speech delivered at The Carnegie Council, New York. Retrieved May 21, 2009, from http://www.utilitarian.net/singer/by/2031029.htm.

——. (2006, December 17). What should a billionaire give—And what should you? *New York Times Magazine*.

——. (2007a, March 18). Can you be too rich? *Los Angeles Times Op-Ed*. Retrieved January 25, 2009, from http://articles.latimes.com/2007/mar/18/opinion/op-toorich18.

——. (2007b, June 9). Why we all should give away 25% of our pay. *Brisbane Times*. Retrieved January 25, 2009, from www.brisbanetimes.com.au/news/world/why-we-all-should-give-away-25-of-our-pay/2007/06/08/1181089326370.html.

Sinha, Meenakshi. (2008, March 2). Streetsmart Bankers. *The Times of India*. Retrieved January 25, 2009, from http://timesofindia.indiatimes.com/Special_Report/Streetsmart_bankers/articleshow/2829924.cms.

Smith, Adam. (1759; 1976). *The theory of moral sentiments* (Edited by A. L. Macfie & D. D. Raphael). Oxford: Oxford University Press.

——. (1776; 1976). *The wealth of nations*. New York: Oxford University Press.

Smythe, T. W. (1985). Problems about corporate moral personhood. *Journal of Value Inquiry, 19*, 327–333.

Spencer, J. W. & Gomez, C. (2004). The relationship among national institutional structures, economic factors, and domestic entrepreneurial activity: A multicountry study. *Journal of Business Research, 57*, 1098–1107.

Stiglitz, Joseph E. (2003). *Globalization and its discontents*. New York: W. W. Norton.

Sustainable Tree Crop Program (STCP). (2008). *About STCP*. Retrieved January 25, 2009, from www.treecrops.org/aboutstcp/aboutstcp.asp.

Terry, D. & Watson, G. (2006). *Sending money home: Leveraging the development impact of remittances*. Washington, DC: Inter-American Development Bank.

Tharoor, Shashi. (2007). *The elephant, the tiger, and the cell phone: Reflections on India the emerging 21st-century power*. New York: Arcade Publishing.

The Economist. (2004, March 11). Global economic inequality: More or less equal?, pp. 84–87.

——. (2007, January 11). Pyramid power.

——. (2007, July 7). Are we nearly there yet?, pp. 12–13.

——. (2007, July 7). The eight commandments, pp. 25–28.

——. (2007, July 7). More money than sense, p. 60.

——. (2008a, January 17). Just good business. Retrieved January 18, 2008, from www.economist.com/specialreports/displaystory.cfm?story_id=10491077.

——. (2008b, May 22). Has "a dollar a day" had its day? Retrieved July 8, 2008, from www.economist.com/finance/displaystory.cfm?story_id=11409401.

——. (2008c, June 26). The meaning of Bill Gates. Retrieved January 2, 2009, from www.economist.com/opinion/displaystory.cfm?story_id=11622119.

——. (2008d, January 17). Going global. Retrieved January 2, 2009, from www.economist.com/surveys/displaystory.cfm?story_id=10491136.

Thurman, E. (2006). Performance philanthropy: Bringing accountability to charitable giving. *Harvard Educational Review*, 18–20.

Times of India. (2007, October 19). Finding profit in servicing the poor. Retrieved January 25,

2009, from http://timesofindia.indiatimes.com/Business/India_Business/Finding_profit_in_servicing_the_poor/articleshow/2471922.cms.

Topova, P. (2008, March). India: Is the rising tide lifting all boats? IMF Working Paper WP/08/54.

Transparency International. (2007). *Report on the Transparency International global corruption barometer 2007.* Retrieved January 25, 2009, from www.transparency.org/policy_research/surveys_indices/gcb/2007.

——. (2008). *Corruption perceptions index 2008.* Retrieved January 25, 2009, from www.transparency.org/policy_research/surveys_indices/cpi/2007.

Unerman, J. & Bennett, M. (2004). Increased stakeholder dialogue and the Internet: Towards greater corporate accountability or reinforcing capitalist hegemony. *Accounting Organization and Society, 29*(7), 685–707.

United Nations. (2000). *Resolution 55/2: United Nations Millennium Declaration.* Retrieved January 25, 2009, from www.un.org/millennium/declaration/ares552e.htm.

——. (2007). *United Nations Millennium Development Goals.* Retrieved January 25, 2009, from www.un.org/millenniumgoals.

——. (2008). *Questions and answers about the universal declaration of human rights.* Retrieved January 25, 2009, from www.unac.org/rights/question.html.

United Nations Development Programme. (2006). *Malawi data sheet.* Retrieved January 25, 2009, from www.undp.org.mw/index.php?option=com_content&view=article&id=46&Itemid=41&58930effcf1f629ed28c9ca6846cfdcd=29dc1231781c6ed6b805131f18f7628b.

——. (2007). *About the MDGs: Basics.* Retrieved January 25, 2009, from www.undp.org/mdg/basics.shtml.

——. (2008). *Creating value for all: Strategies for doing business with the poor.* New York: UNDP.

United Nations Global Compact. (2007). Retrieved January 25, 2009, from www.unglobalcompact.org/AboutTheGC/index.html.

United Nations Millennium Campaign. (2007). Retrieved January 25, 2009, from www.endpoverty2015.org.

United Nations Millennium Project. (2005). *Halving hunger: It can be done.* Retrieved January 25, 2009, from www.unmillenniumproject.org/documents/HTF-SumVers_FINAL.pdf.

——. (2007). Retrieved January 25, 2009, from www.unmillenniumproject.org/index.htm.

Ureta, H., Charvel, R. & Moreno, I. (2007). *Patrimonio Hoy: A perspective on its evolution.* Concurrent session given at "Business with Four Billion: Creating Mutual Value at the Base of the Pyramid" (September 9–11, Ann Arbor, MI). Retrieved January 7, 2009, from www.wdi.umich.edu/files/Conferences/2007/BoP/Speaker%20Presentations/PDF/CEMEX.pdf.

USAID. (2004, August 5). *USAID announces partnership with Kraft Foods Inc.* Press release. Retrieved January 5, 2009, from www.usaid.gov/press/releases/2004/pr040805.html.

USAID Guinea. (2004, December 22). *USAID, Kraft Foods work together to help Guinean cashew sector.* Retrieved January 5, 2009, from www.usaid.gov/gn/gn_new/news/2004/041220_kraft_gda/index.htm.

Vachani, S. & Smith, C. (2004). Socially responsible pricing: Lessons from the pricing of AIDS drugs in developing countries. *California Management Review, 47*(1), 117–144.

Vallens, Ansi. (2008). The importance of reputation. *Risk Management, 55*(4), 36–43.

Velasquez, Manuel. (1983). Why corporations are not morally responsible for anything they do. *Business and Professional Ethics Journal, 2,* 3–11.

——. (1992). International business, morality and the common good. *Business Ethics Quarterly, 2*(1), 27–40.

——. (2003). Debunking corporate moral responsibility. *Business Ethics Quarterly, 13,* 531–562.

Velasquez, Manuel, Andre, Claire, Shanks, Thomas, S. J. & Meyer, Michael J. (1992b). The common good. *Issues in Ethics, 5*(2) (Spring). Retrieved January 25, 2009, from www.scu.edu/ethics/practicing/decision/commongood.html.

Vodafone. (n.d.). *Access to communications in emerging markets.* Retrieved January 5, 2009, from www.vodafone.com/start/responsibility/our_social_economic/access_to_communications/new_business_models.html.

Vogel, D. (2006). *The market for virtue: The potential and limits of corporate social responsibility.* Washington, DC: Brookings Institution Press.

Volvo Cars of North America. (2006). Volvo for life awards heroes: Donald O'Neal. Retrieved November 17, 2007, from http://www.volvoforlifeawards.com/cgi-bin/iowa/english/heros/hero2004/8881.html [subsequently removed by Volvo; *for similar information, see* Helps International. (2008, May 22). *YouTube video.* Retrieved May 11, 2009, from http://www.youtube.com/watch?v=ZmBw6EC8New].

Wall, B. (2006, September 12). Facing global challenges while turning a profit. *International Herald Tribune.* Retrieved January 25, 2009, from www.iht.com/articles/2006/07/07/yourmoney/mthreat.php.

Walzer, M. (1973). Political action: the problem of dirty hands. *Philosophy and Public Affairs, 2*(2), 160–180.

——. (1983). *Spheres of justice.* New York: Basic Books.

Weick, Karl. (1969; 1979). *The social psychology of organizing.* Reading, MA: Addison-Wesley.

Weick, Karl & Sutcliffe, Kathleen. (2005). Organizing and the process of sensemaking. *Organization Science, 16,* 401–421.

Weisbrod, B. A. (1997). The future of the nonprofit sector: Its entwining with private enterprise and government. *Journal of Policy Analysis and Management, 16*(4), 541–555.

Werhane, Patricia H. (1985). *Persons, rights, and corporations.* Englewood Cliffs, NJ: Prentice Hall.

——. (1994). The normative/descriptive distinction in methodologies of business ethics. *Business Ethics Quarterly, 4,* 175–180.

——. (1999a). *Moral imagination and management decision-making.* New York: Oxford University Press.

——. (1999b). *Adam Smith and his legacy for modern capitalism.* New York: Oxford University Press.

——. (2002). Moral imagination and systems thinking. *Journal of Business Ethics, 38,* 33–42.

——. (2007). Corporate social responsibility/corporate moral responsibility: Is there a difference and the difference it makes. In Steve May, George Cheney & Juliet Roper (Eds.), *The debate over corporate social responsibility* (pp. 459–474). New York: Oxford University Press.

——. (2008a). Mental models, moral imagination and systems thinking in the age of globalization. *Journal of Business Ethics, 78,* 463–474.

——. (2008b). Corporate social responsibility, corporate moral responsibility, and systems thinking. In Gabriel Flynn (Ed.), *Corporate social responsibility: An Irish perspective* (pp. 269–289). Dordrecht: Springer Publisher.

Werhane, Patricia H. & Gorman, Michael. (2005). Intellectual property rights, moral imagination, and access to life-enhancing drugs. *Business Ethics Quarterly, 15,* 595–613.

Werhane, Patricia, Posig, Margaret, Gundry, Lisa, Powell, Elizabeth & Ofstein, Laurel. (2007). *Women in business: The changing face of leadership.* New York: Praeger.

Werhane, Patricia H., Velamuri, Rama & Boyd, D. Eric. (2006). Corruption and moral risk in business settings. In Kirk Hanson (Ed.), *The responsible corporation* (pp. 235–258). New York: Greenwood Publishers.

Williams, Edward J. (1995). *The maquiladora industry and environmental degradation in the United States—Mexican borderlands.* Presented at the annual meeting of the Latin American Studies Association, Washington, DC, September 1995, Retrieved January 25, 2009, from http://beatl.barnard.columbia.edu/urbs3525/2007/OtherCities/MexicoCity/maquil-stats.htm.

Williamson, O. E. (1975). *Markets and hierarchies: Analysis and anti-trust implications.* New York: Free Press.

——. (1985). *The economic institutions of capitalism.* New York: Free Press.

WIZZIT Bank. (2009). Home page. Retrieved January 25, 2009, from www.wizzit.co.za.

Wolf, Susan. (1999). Toward a systemic theory of informed consent in managed care. *Houston Law Review, 35,* 1631–1681.

Wolfe, Regina & Shepard, Nathan. (in press). *Nike in Vietnam.* UVA-E-0376. Charlottesville, VA: University of Virginia Darden Publishing.

World Bank. (2006). *Population 2006.* Retrieved January 24, 2008, from http://web.worldbank.

155

org/WBSITE/EXTERNAL/DATASTATISTICS/0,,contentMDK:20399244~menuPK:1504474~p agePK:64133175~theSitePK:239419,00.html.

World Bank Group. (2008). Doing business 2008 Cameroon. *Doing Business Project*. Retrieved August 19, 2008, from www.doingbusiness.org/Documents/CountryProfiles/CMR.pdf.

World Business Council for Sustainable Development. (2004). *Distributed solar energy in Brazil: Fabio Rosa's approach to social entrepreneurship*. Retrieved January 24, 2009, from www.wbcsd.org/ plugins/docsearch/details.asp?txtDocTitle=Brazil%20Fabio%20Rosa&DocTypeId=24&CharVal List=24;&ObjectId=NjUzMg&URLBack=result%2Easp%3FtxtDocTitle%3DBrazil+Fabio+Rosa% 26DocTypeId%3D24%26CharValList%3D24%3B%26SortOrder%3D%26CurPage%3D1.

World Cocoa Foundation. (2006). *GDA report 2006*. Retrieved January 25, 2009, from www.world-cocoafoundation.org/for-the-media/pdf/GDA_Report_Jan2006_Part2a.pdf.

World Health Organization. (n.d.). *Children's environmental health*. Retrieved April 3, 2009, from www.who.int/ceh/risks/otherisks/en/index2.html.

World Resources Institute. (2006, October). *Sustainable mobility: A publication of EMBARQ and the Center for Sustainable Transport in Mexico*. Retrieved January 25, 2009, from www.embarq.wri.org/ en/index.aspx.

——. (2007). *The next 4 billion: Market size and business strategy at the base of the pyramid*. Retrieved January 25, 2009, from www.wri.org/publication/the-next-4-billion.

——. (2008). WIZZIT—Bringing cellphone banking to the unbanked. *Activity Database*. Retrieved January 8, 2009, from www.nextbillion.net/activitycapsule/wizzit.

Wright, Robert. (2005). *Reading between the lines: The incredible shrinking planet. What liberals can learn from Thomas Friedman's new book*. Retrieved January 25, 2009, from www.slate.com/id/2116899.

Wymer, W. W. & Samu, S. (2003). Dimensions of business and nonprofit collaborative relation-ships. *Journal of Nonprofit and Public Sector Marketing, 11*(1), 3–22.

Yager, Paul. (2008). *A point-of-care diagnostic system for the developing world*. Paul Yager Research Group. Retrieved January 25, 2009, from http://faculty.washington.edu/yagerp/pyresearchcur-rent.html#Gates.

Yunus, Muhammad. (2003, March 11). *Halving poverty by 2015: We can actually make it happen*. Com-monwealth Lecture delivered at the Commonwealth Institute, London. Retrieved January 25, 2009, from www.grameen-info.org/index.php?option=com_content&task=view&id=220&Itemid =172.

——. (2007). *Creating a world without poverty: Social business and the future of capitalism*. New York: Public Affairs.

Yunus, Muhammad with Jolis, Alan. (2003). *Banker to the poor: Micro-lending and the battle against world poverty*. New York: Public Affairs.

Zakiuddin, Almas. (2008). *Corruption in Bangladesh: An analytical and sociological study*. Retrieved January 25, 2009. from www.ti-bangladesh.org/docs/research/CorBang1.htm.

Zellere, Tom, Jr. (2005, October 24). Yahoo in China: Rising tide of anger. *International Herald Tribune*. Retrieved January 25, 2009, from www.iht.com/articles/2005/10/24/business/yahoo. php.

Zobel de Ayala, Fernando. (2006, September 23). *The CFO challenge to sustainable CSR*. Speech at CSR Expo, Manila, Philippines. Retrieved January 25, 2009, from www.ayalafoundation.org/ news.asp?id=109.

INDEX

eBooks – at www.eBookstore.tandf.co.uk

A library at your fingertips!

eBooks are electronic versions of printed books. You can store them on your PC/laptop or browse them online.

They have advantages for anyone needing rapid access to a wide variety of published, copyright information.

eBooks can help your research by enabling you to bookmark chapters, annotate text and use instant searches to find specific words or phrases. Several eBook files would fit on even a small laptop or PDA.

NEW: Save money by eSubscribing: cheap, online access to any eBook for as long as you need it.

Annual subscription packages

We now offer special low-cost bulk subscriptions to packages of eBooks in certain subject areas. These are available to libraries or to individuals.

For more information please contact webmaster.ebooks@tandf.co.uk

We're continually developing the eBook concept, so keep up to date by visiting the website.

www.eBookstore.tandf.co.uk